Geies

General Studies
Issues and Discussions

EDITED BY NEIL DENBY

CONTRIBUTORS:
MIKE HEMMINGS • SHAUN McCARTHY
• KEVIN WALSH

Hodder & Stoughton
A MEMBER OF THE HODDER HEADLINE GROUP

Note about the Internet links in the book: The user should be aware that URLs or web addresses change regularly. Every effort has been made to ensure the accuracy of the URLs provided in this book on going to press. It is inevitable, however, that some will change. It is sometimes possible to find a relocated web page, by just typing in the address of the home page for a website in the URL window of your browser.

Orders: please contact Bookpoint Ltd, 130 Milton Park, Abingdon, Oxon OX14 4SB. Telephone: (44) 01235 827720, Fax: (44) 01235 400454. Lines are open from 9.00–6.00 pm, Monday to Saturday, with a 24-hour message answering service. You can also order through our website at www.hodderheadline.co.uk

British Library Cataloguing in Publication Data
A catalogue record for this title is available from The British Library

ISBN 0 340 80483 1

First published 2002

Impression number 10 9 8 7 6 5 4 3 2 1
Year   2006 2005 2004 2003 2002

Copyright © 2002 Neil Denby, Shaun McCarthy, Mike Hemmings, and Kevin Walsh

Front cover images: *Girl with a Pearl Earring* by Vermeer (top left); © Howard Davies/Corbis (top right); © Galen Rowell/Corbis (bottom left); Photodisc (bottom right)

Produced by Gray Publishing, Tunbridge Wells, Kent.
Printed in Great Britain for Hodder & Stoughton Educational, a division of Hodder Headline Ltd, 338 Euston Road, London NW1 3BH by J.W. Arrowsmith, Bristol.

Contents

AREA 3 SOCIETY, POLITICS AND THE ECONOMY 147

GENERAL STUDIES

Introduction

The purpose of this book is to provide a starting point for issues, discussions and questions on a number of subjects. It includes topical issues (but ones which are likely to have a lasting resonance) and provides background, information and views on these issues. Topics are presented as prose, narrative or argument, at a word length that is designed to be short enough to be taken in at one go yet long enough to provide necessary detail and argument. Topics are written to be suitable for students studying at AS level or at A2 level; they are divided into the three key areas studied under the General Studies banner, namely:

- Culture, Morality, Arts and Humanities

- Science and Technology

- Society, Politics and the Economy.

Each topic starts with a short preview, which flags up the issues in the topic area to be discussed. The main topic may then be written as prose, script, interview or other stimulus material such as collections of letters. After the topic there are questions both for discussion and for written answer. The questions for discussion can form the basis for debate within a classroom. The questions for written answer usually have at least a couple of questions which are based on actual A-level questions that have been set. These are marked according to a 'levels of response' marking scheme as follows:

Level 0: No response of any relevance.
Level 1: Inadequate attempt to deal with the question.
- Knowledge, understanding and appreciation: limited.
- Justification or illustration: limited.
- Expression: weak.
- Overall grasp or coherence: non-existent.
Level 2: Weak response to the demands of the question.
- Knowledge, understanding and appreciation: basic but uncertain.
- Justification or illustration: sparse or vague.
- Expression: some weakness.
- Overall grasp or coherence: poor.
Level 3: Competent attempt at answering the question
- Knowledge, understanding and appreciation: some but limited.
- Justification or illustration: some shown.
- Expression: reasonably accurate.
- Overall grasp or coherence: attempted conclusion, some coherence.
Level 4: Good response to the demands of the question.
- Knowledge, understanding and appreciation: sound.
- Justification or illustration: a fair range.
- Expression: accurate.

- Overall grasp or coherence: reasonable conclusions and coherent structure.

Level 5:   Commanding treatment of the question.
- Knowledge, understanding and appreciation: comprehensive and clear.
- Justification or illustration : an extensive range.
- Expression: accurate and fluent.
- Overall grasp or coherence: effective conclusions, overall command and excellent structure.

Further details of the criteria for each level are published by the examination boards.

Each topic then has one or more activities, on which a General Studies lesson may be based, tips for further research and web links. Margin notes provide further food for thought, information or activities as do short quizzes or sets of multiple-choice questions.

How to use this resource

Each topic may be taken on its own to form a single General Studies lesson or to form the basis for a series of lessons by using the extended exercises and tips for further research. In class, discussions and arguments should be engendered by the deliberately controversial nature of some of the pieces. Activities generally involve whole class or small group work, with groups reporting findings or opinions back for further discussion. The book may also be used by individual students. Students may read through a passage which interests them and attempt the written parts of the exercises or activities.

A précis of each topic is included below, along with an indication of the focus of the topic within a particular area of study.

Area 1: Culture, Morality, Arts and Humanities

1. Goodness gracious me! Does everyone want to be Asian?
(Nature and importance of culture)

An Asian comedy becomes popular among all parts of society. Some mixing of style and popular culture of 'mainstream' British culture and British-Asian ideas takes place at street level. But is this apparent swapping of styles between two usually quite separate cultures just window dressing? Are young British-Asians and their white counterparts still largely living different lives in the same country?

2. Shakespeare as script: the Globe Theatre
(Aesthetic evaluation/appreciation of performance)

A-level examiners for English Literature have repeatedly commented that students fail to take into account one crucial thing in their study of Shakespeare and their examination answers: the plays are first and foremost scripts. They are undoubtedly some of the greatest literary texts in the world, but they were written for actors to perform before a live, often very lively audience.

3. Is television 'dumbing down'?
(Aesthetic evaluation/nature and importance of culture)

This topic offers a fictional extract from a letter to underpin a discussion on the quality of television broadcasting. Try to identify the background themes that underlie the discussion: for example, does television, as an entertainment resource available literally out there in the air, have to have a duty or role to educate as well as amuse?

4. The Dalai Lama and cultural tourism
(Beliefs, values and moral reasoning)

People from all over the world travel to Dharamsala to gain audience with the Dalai Lama, exiled spiritual leader of Tibetan Buddhists. But is this just cultural tourism? Can you go round the world to join a religion that was until recently the exclusive preserve of an isolated mountain people? Can someone from a Western society ever really be part of such a religion? Is it just a fashionable thing to do? If it is, does it matter?

5. The Celtic tiger – social and economic changes in Ireland
(Nature and importance of culture)

In this fictional script, an older Irish man returns to his family in a small, more traditional village in the country after spending a few days in the 'new Dublin'. Such discussions could happen in any country that has rapidly shrugged off its old image and economy for a new global one.

6. Crowds and silence: the Vermeer exhibition as cultural event
(Nature and importance of culture/aesthetic evaluation)

Today Vermeer's works are rare, and hugely valuable. About 35 or 36 paintings are now generally attributed to him and most are on display as 'prize works' in major world-class art galleries. All his works are admired for the sensitivity with which he rendered effects of light and colour and for the poetic quality of his images. An exhibition of Vermeer's paintings drew huge and appreciative audiences despite art critics complaining that the public were flocking to the paintings for the 'wrong reasons': that they were attracted by the fuss the media had drummed up, by the event rather than the pictures.

7. Why do we put people in prison? (Beliefs, values and moral reasoning)

Every country in the world operates some sort of penal system, whereby people who break the law are punished for their crimes, usually by being put in prison. Being incarcerated is not just a removal of liberty: it has been argued at various times that prison is supposed to deter, reform, to punish in some degree or other, and remove a wrong-doer from the rest of law abiding society. But do we take the idea of sending wrong-doers to jail for granted? How exactly is it justified? Does it work? And what are our reasons for locking people away?

8. The man who was Private Widdle (Nature and importance of culture/aesthetic evaluation)

This is the eye-catching title of a newspaper review of a book published in the autumn of 2001, a biography of Charles Hawtrey. Hawtrey was an actor who was one of the longest serving members of the cast who played in nearly 30 Carry On films. Were they funny? Was he?

What makes us say something is funny? Why does so much old humour get recycled? As a nation, are we predisposed to a certain sort of humour? Or do we laugh at what we are given?

9. The 'creative industries' – a career choice? (Nature and importance of culture)

The image of hundreds of men streaming out of a big factory at the end of the shift, now almost belongs to history in this country. Once, Britain was the most industrialized nation on earth, Now it is de-industrialized, with a reducing manufacturing base, and few career opportunities in traditional industries. Britain at the start of the twenty-first century has a thriving post-industrial economy based heavily on creative and service industries.

10. Reputations: 'Das Boot' (Aesthetic evaluation)

A recent television series of this name set out each week to 're-appraise' the careers of public figures. Usually the subjects chosen have enjoyed general public acclaim. If not heroes, they have been well regarded. Some are important historical figures who contributed to world-shaping politics or military events. Others were film stars, or even 'celebrity' intellectuals. All had their reputations examined.

Is this constant re-appraising of the reputations of public figures a good thing? It keeps our perspective on history alive and stops us just accepting the word of other people. On the other hand, re-appraisal was one of the elements of Stalin's terrible purges in Soviet Russia, where 'heroes' were suddenly revealed to be subversives and sent off to exile, or executed.

11. Are there only so many good stories? (Nature and importance of culture/aesthetic evaluation)

Why do so many writers rework stories from other earlier writers or from myths and legend? Are they being lazy or are there only so many basic good stories, and they've all been done at least once? A playwright discusses his reworking of the Dr Faustus legend with an interviewer.

12. Harry Potter and the Hollywood giants (Nature and importance of culture)

The Harry Potter books for children have, like their author, become the stuff of myths. Not the sort of myths that Harry might come across in world of Hogwart's school and its magical characters; but the sort of media, public relations and marketing legends that have been created around the enormous success of the books.

But can JK Rowling's vision of the curious, gentle world of Harry Potter, and the imaginations of the millions of children who create the world of Hogwart's in their minds through the words alone, survive this onslaught of media hype, film development and merchandising?

Area 2: Science and Technology

13. The times they are a changing (Scientific progress)

The main difference between the ideas of Isaac Newton and those of Albert Einstein is the way they dealt with the idea of time and space. Everyone has had some kind of idea about time gleaned from science fiction, television or even science fact! It is just a matter of drawing the line between ideas based on scientific research and the step into imagination that fiction writers have taken. Newton gave us the physics that we use and are familiar with. Einstein opened the door to the universe, and his ideas on time were a key factor in this.

14. Common sense and nonsense (Objective data and its limitations)

We are bombarded with views and opinions and all of them claim to be right. How can you sort out good ideas from bad, is it enough to 'stick to the facts'? Is commonsense a good guide? Three hundred years ago Descartes (1596–1650) became well known for his statement that he was certain of only one thing: 'Cogito ergo sum' which means 'I think therefore I am'. What is scientific truth or fact?

15. Does unlocking DNA mean perfection or problems?
(Moral responsibility: social and ethical considerations)

On 12 February 2001 the *New York Times* published the news that two competing groups had mapped the human genome. There was a world-wide reaction to the news and wonderful claims were made for the importance of this 'book of the entire human genetic code'. It was hailed as being a bigger scientific breakthrough than the discovery of antibiotics and comparable to the landing on the moon. We were told that its impact on all of us would be rapid and dramatic because cancer, ageing and congenital disease would all soon disappear. But surely a breakthrough such as this can't be without problems – or a moral dimension?

16. Genetically modified crops and the nature of progress
(Nature of scientific objectivity and the question of progress)

Is the reaction to GM crops comparable to the reaction to the loom? In the Midlands and Yorkshire around 1811 a group of workers went round smashing up machinery – they were known as Luddites (after their captain, Ned Ludd) or as Shatterers. They were objecting to the new machinery that was being introduced in the textile industry. They were trying to halt progress and, inevitably, they lost. The jobs they had and the way of life they were used to all changed with the introduction of the new technology. Recently people have been burning GM crops as they say they are a threat. The argument is that GM crops are part of the same unstoppable force – progress.

17. An experience that changes your life...?
(Relationships between science, culture and ideology)

The internet appears to be the most significant area of technological innovation in centuries. The internet allows us to communicate by e-mail and also carries the World Wide Web, a vast network of websites. The web is new technology – created at a particle physics laboratory in Geneva in 1991, it first appeared on the internet only in 1993. In the ensuing few years, it has come to dominate telecommunications and has changed the habits of both individuals and businesses. It has the potential to significantly affect the way we live – but will it?

18. Darwin: right or wrong?
(Nature of scientific objectivity and the question of progress)

Evolution is a concept with which we are all familiar – but do we realize that it is still a theory? And that some people still do not believe in it? Scriptures, in all religions, have other ways of explaining how mankind came about and what its purpose is here on Earth. If we believe in Darwin's theory of evolution (not

GENERAL STUDIES

supported by any major religion) rather than creation by a divine force or being, does this mean that we can't possibly believe in God?

19. Pollution: a consequence or a threat? (Evaluation of evidence)

Sometimes predicted disasters actually do happen – with dire consequences for those who ignored the predictions. Sometimes, however, they don't happen (the supposedly devastating effect of the 'millennium bug' on computers being one of them). The threat of global warming and the consequences of a melting ice cap have been put forward as inevitable 'facts' that are about to ruin the planet. But is the Earth really in danger from pollution or is this just another scare story.

20. Technological determinism (Relationships between technology, science and culture)

Does technology shape society or vice versa? The 'nature' or 'nurture' debate looks at whether human behaviour is more or most affected by the genetic history of the individual or by the environmental factors that impact on him or her. Believers in the 'nurture' theory of Rousseau would claim that major changes to society are driven by technological change. If this is the case, how will current changes in technology affect society?

21. Quantum theory (Relationships between science, culture and ideology)

Pure chance or a plan we cannot yet understand? Quantum theory has implications for science as if it is accepted in full then it appears to deny the existence of God or even the possibility of an ordered universe ruled by logical laws. The full implication of quantum theory would mean there is only uncertainty – chaos. The study of divine beings led to the study of the stars. This, in turn, led to the study of time. This eventually led to quantum theory. However, quantum theory would deny the existence of the very divine being that led to its discovery ....

22. The next 10 years

Famous physics professor and motor-neurone sufferer Stephen Hawking has said that, 'the eventual goal of science is to provide a single theory that describes the whole universe'. Einstein himself searched for this 'unified theory' but without success. An enormous amount of research has gone into the pursuit of this 'grand theory for everything' to find a way of combining quantum theory and relativity. It is thought that one way to do this is to find out how our universe began. This would explain how atoms were formed and how energy keeps them together. In the next 10 years this may be discovered.

23. Dolly: a longer life or an end to humanity?
(Scientific objectivity, ideology and culture)

Cloning and morality. A clone is a living thing which has exactly the same genetic make-up as the parent. Cloning had been developing on a small scale – individual cells and then groups of cells, for a while when on 23 February 1997 it was announced that scientists had cloned a sheep and now had a six-month-old lamb called 'Dolly'. Dolly was proof that cloning is possible for large mammals. It also meant that before long it will be possible to clone people.

24. Looking into the crystal ball
(Nature of scientific progress)

For a scientist the best way to shoot yourself in the foot is to make a prediction about the future. The history of science is littered with important scientists making predictions that turn out to be totally wrong, often quite soon after they were made. Predictions about the impossibility of powered flight and space travel are some of the better known examples of leading scientists being wrong. It has been said that the science fiction written as entertainment is better at predicting the future than scientists are. Here are some scientific predictions to consider.

Area 3: Society, Politics and the Economy

25. Europe: are we becoming too European?
(Political processes and goals)

The UK has never existed in isolation, nor can it. But what form should its relationships with its global partners take? Already a member of the European Union (EU), should the UK integrate its future more into the EU by abandoning the pound sterling and adopting the euro, or should it stay outside the euro zone? The UK has a unique position in the world – should it try to maximize that, or do closer ties to Europe mean saying goodbye to traditional friends?

26. Is the NHS terminally ill?
(Social and economic trends and constraints)

The National Health Service has shown itself to be having difficulties at the end of the twentieth century and at the beginning of the twenty-first. Indeed some would say the NHS is in crisis. This has been demonstrated by sensational newspaper stories of patients dying on trolleys in overcrowded hospitals after waiting for treatment over many hours, cancer victims being diagnosed in time but not being treated in time and allegedly dying as a result, and many other horror stories. As a result, the NHS has been labelled by many as a third world health service from a first world country.

27. The mobile revolution
(Explanation and evaluation of human behaviour)

The mobile phone has had a huge, and perhaps unexpected, impact on all our lives. There are 45 million mobiles in use in the UK for a population of 60 million, and that includes babies and toddlers. Most adults and teenagers therefore have their own phones, some on monthly contract, many pay as you go. It is not just the UK – far from it, it is a world-wide trend. This article looks briefly at the history of this phenomenon, and tries to give some suggestions as to what the future might hold. The chances are though, that the future of this industry will hold many surprises!

28. The landfill tax: what is it and is it working?
(Relationship between law and ethics)

In the early to mid-1990s, it became clear that Britain has a major problem with waste, much more so than many of our neighbours. This waste is produced industrially (e.g. scrap materials from production plants), commercially (e.g. waste documents from office blocks) and privately (our ordinary dustbin contents). Most of the waste goes to landfill sites, that is, filling holes in the ground, or creating hills!

The problem is that, as a very crowded island, Britain is running out of space, especially in the highly densely populated areas such as, but not only, the south-east of England. This waste is polluting the environment, and as more waste has to be transported further, so the costs of disposal rise, as does pollution from the lorries carrying it. In addition we are using more landfill per head of population than many of our European neighbours.
Something had to happen, and it did – the landfill tax. But have the barons of the waste management industry managed to hijack the landfill tax and turn it to their own advantage?

29. Are we lunatic with our asylum policy?
(Relationship between law, culture and ethics)

Finally, a court case may close the refugee facility situated less than a mile from the French end of the Channel tunnel. However, asylum seekers are still killed or injured trying to ride trains into the country, or found suffocated in the back of long distance haulage wagons. But what are we supposed to do about it? Are these genuine asylum seekers or 'economic migrants'? A bigoted view which includes the way in which racist connotations are mixed up with the 'real' issues is presented.

30. The impossible dream
(Political processes and goals: economic trends and constraints)

Governments set themselves series of economic targets, which they hope to achieve by manipulating the economy through various tools and measures. But are these government targets ever reachable; is a managed economy ever possible? Should tinkering at the edges with taxation, government investment, interest rates, the money supply and all the rest be abandoned in favour of the might of the market? Surely, if the price system was allowed to take over completely, there would be no need for chancellors.

31. Who's free trade for anyway?
(Examination and appreciation of ideologies and values in society)

Rich world, poor world. The 'north/south' global split, why it has happened and what we should do about it (if anything).What is the nature of the global divisions and how is the freeing of trade meant to close the gap? Reasons for and against free trade are discussed.

What is the World Trade Organization (WTO) and what are the conflicting arguments for and against its operation? Why has it attracted quite so much vehement opposition in the form of protests and disruption when it was set up to help all the world's trading nations?

32. Electoral systems
(Political processes and goals)

The good, the bad and the indifferent. There are numerous different electoral systems in use, including several within the UK itself. Which of these appears to be the most fair and unbiased? Are there systems which give particular bias to a ruling party, or which give an excessive proportion of power to a smaller party? Which system best reflects the wishes of the voters?

33. 'My Dad says ...'
(Examination and appreciation of ideologies and values in society)

The opinions in the common room or the coffee bar are often found to reflect those that young people have heard in the saloon bar or the barbers chair. In many cases, however much young people try to deny it, or stop it from happening, they are parroting the opinions of parents or other adults.
They may vehemently reject a viewpoint or ideology that a parent espouses only to argue it as their own in a peer group. John and Kate discuss making Britain more equal; equal opportunities legislation, its effects and its effectiveness.

34. 11 September
(Examination and appreciation of ideologies and values in society)

The events of 11 September are looked at in their political and social context. What actually happened, why did it happen, and how could anyone condone it? What are the factors that make people into 'terrorists' in certain eyes and 'freedom fighters' in others? This final piece puts the horror of 11 September into a global context and explains some of the history and some of the thinking behind the actions.

Acknowledgements

The publisher would like to thank the following for permission to reproduce the following copyright illustrations in this book:

AKG London pages 33, 36; Associated Press, AP: © Eric Draper page 186, © Robert F. Bukaty page 199, © Suzanne Plunkett page 209, © Stringer page 211; Associated Press, Department of Defense: © Shane T. McCoy page 42; Ward Batham page 124; © BBC Picture Archives page 15; BBC TWO page 4; BFI Stills, Posters and Designs page 64 (below); Donald Cooper © Photostage pages 64 (above), 11 (below); Corbis: © Galen Rowell page 21, © Hulton-Deutsch Collection page 31 (below), © Bill Gentile page 84, © Clay Perry page 88, © Michael T. Sedam page 105, © Bettmann page 106, © Dennis di Cicco page 130, © Martin Rogers page 192; Ecoscene/Ray Roberts page 166; Eyewire page 159 (below); Simon Fraser/Science Photo Library page 156; Ronald Grant Archive pages 40, 45, 47 (left), 47 (right), 57, 67, 98, 140; Guildhall Library page 11 (above); Hodder page 195; Illustrated London News page 75; Imperial War Museum page 59; Herbie Knott page 112; Emma Lee/Life File pages 159 (above), 162; New Line Cinema page 69; Stuart Norgrove page 135; Ruth Nossek page 202; PA Photos: © Owen Humphreys page 5, © Louis Hollingsbee page 23, © Chris Bacon page 31 (above), © John Stillwell page 86, 173, 182; Popperfoto page 80; Redferns page 51; Andrew Ward/Life File pages 151, 203;

Every effort has been made to trace and acknowledge the ownership of copyright. The publisher will be glad to make any suitable arrangement with copyright holders whom it has not been possible to contact.

GENERAL STUDIES

Area 1

CULTURE, MORALITY, ARTS AND HUMANITIES

01 Goodness Gracious Me — does everyone want to be Asian?

Preview

It could be argued that one of the most innocent, and therefore honest, indications that Britain at the start of the twenty-first century is becoming a multicultural society has been the success of the television comedy *Goodness Gracious Me*. Suddenly, white kids were endlessly repeating catch-phrases from this British–Asian series that, a few months ago, would have only been know to some young British Asians. It was cool to be white and like Asian things. Some mixing of style and popular culture between 'mainstream' British culture and British–Asian ideas did take place at street level. But is this apparent swapping of ideas between two usually quite separate cultures just window dressing? Are young British Asians and their white counterparts still largely living different lives in the same country?

Degrees of prejudice

The skinhead era permeated London and several other major British cities by the late 1960s; it also spread to a number of European cities. Although comparatively harmless compared to the British National Party's involvement in the race riots in northern British cities in the summer of 2001, the skinhead culture of white supremacy and street violence was still shocking in those perhaps more innocent times.

Skinheads were white working class: anti-immigration, racist. But it was a style movement as much as a 'political' one. Shave your head, wear boots and braces. Every element of dress, down to the number of lace holes in your Doc Marten's boots, was encoded. So was the music that went with this rigorous dress code: it had to be ska, blue beat or rock steady, the then obscure precursors of reggae. Skinheads danced to the music of Jamaican dance halls, the music of the black Jamaican working class. It didn't fit.

When asked about their attitude to black and Asian British people, one skinhead said that although he wouldn't have them as friends, Afro-Caribbeans were OK, not just for the music, but because 'They're like us, you know, but just black'. There were skinhead attacks on black youths, but their real venom was reserved for Asians.

'Paki bashing' and business success

To white racists of those days, anyone of Asian origin was a 'Paki' (from Pakistan). White racists hated them for what they saw as several 'good reasons'. Most Afro-Caribbean immigration had occurred through the 1950s, whereas Asian immigration was going on in the 1960s and 1970s, often in waves generated by political events such as the dictator Idi Amin throwing the Asian professional class out of Uganda in the early 1970s.

Afro-Caribbeans spoke English; Asians spoke Urdu, Hindi or other languages. They were Hindu or Muslim, and tended to be very family orientated. This created a close community that separated itself from white society. Not surprisingly, they tended to gather in certain areas where they felt safer 'among their own' in the face of racism. Most Asians who came to Britain had a burning drive to get on and do well. Extended families would work together to set up small businesses, especially retail ones where long hours had to be worked. In the space of a few years, most local shops in the country changed from quiet places carrying limited stock, open from nine to five and run by a traditional 'white', often white-coated, shop-keeper, to mini bazaars crammed with stock, with often (to the local community) exotic goods beside the usual ranges, and open up to 24 hours a day.

Nothing upsets a racist more than to see an immigrant community work hard and achieve success. 'Pakis' couldn't win: if they didn't struggle to make their small businesses work they were thought of as scroungers who had 'come here' to live off the dole. If they did well, they were taking away jobs and businesses from white people. The signs for future integration were not good.

Back to the future

Thirty years on and some of the most successful business people in the UK are of Asian descent. Curry has replaced fish and chips as the nation's favourite take-away. Hindu, Sikh and Muslim festivals are celebrated in cities around the country, and the white community is often invited to share the experience. The British–Asian community is also sufficiently established to be able to laugh at itself.

The success of *Goodness Gracious Me* is the unrelenting way 'typical' Asian characters are observed and mocked. The title comes from a fake-Indian novelty song sung by Peter Sellers in a 1960 film of the same name. In those days it was quite acceptable for the white Sellers to black up, put on an accent and play an Indian.

'Mr Everything is Indian'

Goodness Gracious Me began life as three short series of radio comedy programmes, with the cutting working title 'Peter Sellers is Dead'. However, in keeping with a show that has never compromised its position or its Asian credentials yet also never apparently given offence to white audiences, the title was dropped for the less contentious one. It was always intended to transfer the idea to television if it worked on radio. After the three radio series (1996–1998) with a total of 14 episodes, the first of 19 television programmes appeared in 1998. They became hugely successful; cult viewing for young people especially.

Despite a 'cross-over' agenda, the programme has clung exclusively to its Indian origins. Understanding the comedy requires non-Asian audiences to be 'educated' by the programme into the truth behind some of the stock characters. Like 'Mr Everything is Indian' who claims the Mona Lisa's smile 'is not enigmatic – that is Indian lady saying "You like this painting – how much

Look in your food storage areas at home and make a list of all the foods that have been imported from other cultures (you could start with tea – an Indian drink). In your next lesson, discuss what effect you think this has had on 'British' culture.

Still from BBC television series
Goodness Gracious Me

you pay me for it?" ' This carries a double twist, not only is the speaker typical of the sort of person who idolizes the country they have left behind, but the idea of the woman keen for a business opportunity is also a well-known image in a society that has had to develop its own economic independence to survive.

That process of education – turning the tables might be a better description – has continued with sketches such as the English recruit to a Bombay company. At his welcome party no one can pronounce his 'difficult' name: John Smith. He is told he will not get on unless he learns new ways and drops the silly name, so he invents a 15-syllable Indian tongue twister and is instantly made at home. How many Asian people in Britain have been told in the past that their names were 'unpronounceable' by people who couldn't be bothered to try?

Hearing white youths quoting catch-phrases from the show suggests a society where two sectors often too easily divided are finally integrating with one another. Those same white youths probably have 'cross-over' music – from the likes of Talvin Singh, Nitin Sawnhey (winner of the Mercury Music Award with his dance and traditional Indian music fusions) and Bhangra-influenced Black Star Liner – on their Walkmans.

WEB LINKS
Search the web using 'goodness gracious me' and you will find a huge number of sites. A few 'official' sites such as the BBC-run ones give detailed profiles of the series. Others are less useful sites set up by fans.

Race riots

Local issues (housing, schooling) and lack of employment may have been the root cause of the race riots that sprang up through northern British cities in the early summer of 2001. The right-wing British National Party, which has enjoyed

In spring 2001 hundreds of Asians gathered in Bradford as tensions flared over a National Front demonstration in the city

a small but worrying increase in support in 2000–2001, dived in to escalate what started as purely local incidents between white communities and long-established British–Asian ones. Both sectors have suffered economic downturn and local community leaders were quick to blame boredom and lack of opportunity for young people as the real cause of the tension that erupted into riot. Having been the victims for so long, Asian young men have a new-found 'confidence' in their ability to defend their own communities.

TIPS FOR FURTHER RESEARCH

Devise an (anonymous) questionnaire to canvas opinions on racism in your school or college. Do not ask direct questions about racism: think about issues and details within the issue of relations between different ethnic groups.

Comedy versus terrorism?

But perhaps the biggest threat to a popular culture-led merging of communities in Britain into a truly multicultural society comes from the likely backlash to Islamic-inspired terrorism. The differences, and indeed tensions, between a British–Asian Hindu with family living back in India near the Pakistan border, and a Muslim extremist using the UK's liberal laws of freedom of speech and human rights in Britain to create a platform for his/her views, are at least as great as those between that same Muslim extremist and any 'white westerner'. Yet already two Sikhs in Britain have been attacked for being 'the sort of people that support terrorists'. It is too easy, when one is frightened, to see anyone even remotely resembling the ethnic group from which the terrorists were recruited, as the enemy.

A comedy show that pokes fun at its own cultural stereotypes and is eagerly taken up by the rest of the community in the UK may be a small stand against the possible narrowing of liberal views that the World Trade Center attacks could unleash. On the other hand, white British youths falling about laughing at young British–Asian actors pretending to be Bombay lads out on a Friday night bender, going to the local Harvester-type English restaurant, insulting the waiter and daring each other to have the blandest food possible, mocking the laddish British attitude to the 'Friday-after-pub curry', might just show that we are finally becoming a truly tolerant multicultural society. Or at least a bit more aware of our own failings.

Questions for discussion

1. Apart from music and television comedy, in what other ways has Asian culture and style influenced life in the UK? (Think about the shops and businesses in your nearest big town.)

2. Can you think of examples of other television shows that have used racial or cultural stereotypes to create humour or the stories of the programme?

3. Should we learn more about the cultures and languages of immigrant communities in this country? To what extent should we encourage them to retain the culture of the countries they have left behind by understanding it ourselves? To what extent should we expect them to adapt to our ways?

Questions for written answer

1. Eventually elements of all immigrant cultures will become part of the basic fabric of the new, multi-racial community that is British society. Many people think this will be a good thing, encouraging diversity and excitement in our society. Do you? Give reasons for your ideas.

2. Imagine you were writing the pilot for a comedy show in India that was going to be a British version of *Goodness Gracious Me*. What would it be called? What stock British characters could you develop into comedy figures? What traits of British life would you exaggerate to use as the basis for humour?

3. Many works of art are specifically created in order to put forward a political, social or moral viewpoint. Discuss the possibility that *Goodness, Gracious Me* has a particular agenda.

Examiners will look for the following in your written answer:

- Evidence that you have understood the source material and can make appropriate use of it.
- You need to be able to make value judgements based on it and support these with evidence or interpretation.
- You need to have something of your own to say and to be able to state it clearly.
- You need to show you can relate this work to other relevant areas of study.

ACTIVITY 1

Work in small groups. List the names of all the people in your class plus other people (neighbours, friends) that you know. Next to each name, write down what you think the derivation of the name is – for example, some may be Saxon, some Norman-French, others of more recent vintage or cultures. Some are simple (Jones is a shortened 'Johns' son'), others more difficult to pin down. Report your suppositions back to the larger group. What conclusions can you draw from this mini-investigation?

ACTIVITY 2

Search the internet for sites which reflect the diversity and energy of Asian life and culture in the UK. What key words would you use? Build a list of sites. Beside each say what it primarily deals with. At the end of your list write a paragraph giving your impression of British–Asian life based on what you have found in your search. Conclude by saying if you believe British–Asian society excludes 'outsiders', or if the sites encourage people to take an interest in what is going on in Britain.

02 Shakespeare as script and The Globe Theatre

Preview

A-level examiners for English Literature have repeatedly commented that students fail to take into account one crucial thing in their study of Shakespeare and their examination answers: the plays are first and foremost scripts. They are undoubtedly some of the greatest literary texts in the world, but they were written for actors to perform before a live, often very lively, audience.

Shakespeare acted in many of his own plays and spent most of his life in the theatre: rehearsing, directing, cutting and getting the plays we regard as masterpieces today ready to go on before an audience. It is essential to remember this if one is to understand the true dramatic dynamics of the plays. A performance at The Globe in London gives us a unique insight into what Shakespeare intended his audience to see, and how his scripts translated into action on stage.

Shakespeare's genius and difficulty

Almost every school student in the country has had to study at least one Shakespeare play. He is the only playwright who appears in every single public examination board's English literature syllabus at both GCSE and A level.

Not bad for a writer of scripts who wrote his last play nearly 400 years ago, in a style that is so different from our contemporary way of speaking and writing as to be almost a foreign language. But the difficulty of first reading Shakespeare, especially for a class of 14 year olds who might not be interested in theatre, means that very often his plays have been regarded, and taught, very much like a foreign language: one that has to be carefully studied line by line to be properly decoded.

Go with the flow

Teachers may urge students just to go with the flow – pick up on the drama of scenes and not worry about the allusions, references and difficult vocabulary – but unfortunately students have to demonstrate some degree of close reading and understanding in exams, and that means back to unpicking exact meaning line by line.

Why can Shakespeare appear so difficult at first acquaintance? Here are some reasons:

- As was just said, he wrote his plays 400 years ago, and even ordinary people spoke and wrote differently then.
- All the plays are written in verse. This does not often happen in theatre today. They are mostly written in the same basic form known as blank verse.

(Lines are 10 syllables long with five stresses or beats on alternate syllables making the rhythm. There are generally only rhymes at the end of the last two lines at the end of some scenes.)

- He was very, very clever! He packed more double meanings, erudite references and subtleties of language into his lines of verse than anyone before him. This is why studying a Shakespeare play in depth can take a very long time, with new levels of meaning revealing themselves in even apparently simple scenes.
- He has been revered, too much so to some people's minds, by critics for centuries. There have been whole libraries of books of criticism written on every aspect of Shakespeare's work. This makes assessing the plays difficult as there is always some opinion or commentary in the background.

Many students see at least one production of the play they are studying. But the theatres in which the plays are generally performed, and the style of design, direction and acting, are completely different from anything that Shakespeare could have imagined. Nothing like the modern proscenium arch theatre (a raked or angled auditorium of seats facing a stage with wings and a curtain) existed in Shakespeare's time.

Wanamaker's vision

In the late 1940s Sam Wanamaker, the American film-maker and actor, visited London. He expected to find a living monument to Shakespeare in the form of a working Elizabethan theatre, which of course there wasn't. Instead there was just a little plaque on a wall in a drab industrial area beside the murky Thames, marking the site of the original Globe, which burned down when a cannon fired during a performance set fire to the thatched roof.

Wanamaker was no simple tourist visiting the quaint, if war-battered, old country. He admired Shakespeare's work enormously and vowed that one day there would be a proper recognition of the English language's greatest playwright: a reconstruction of his theatre on the site of the original. From this vision came the new Globe Theatre – a vision which Sam Wanamaker and his daughter Zoe followed through research, planning and execution almost to completion. Sadly, Sam Wanamaker died before his dream was completed.

Why performances at The Globe are so important

The new Globe Theatre opened its doors in London in 1996: an accurate reconstruction of an Elizabethan wooden theatre. The importance of The Globe performances, especially to school and college students, is enormous. It is much more than just going to see a sort of harmless historical mock-up of how the plays were performed in the days before 'proper' (i.e. modern) theatres.

TIPS FOR FURTHER RESEARCH

It is suggested that you do some research into The Globe, the design of theatres, especially of Elizabethan theatres, and the way plays were performed in them. Some advanced study notes on Shakespeare's plays carry a standard section on the way wooden theatres were built and operated.

The new Globe tries to recreate the experience of an Elizabethan theatre as faithfully as possible, but there are limits! In Shakespeare's time the south bank of the Thames, where the Globe now stands between the Tate Modern art gallery and some rather good pubs and wine bars, was an area of stews: slums and brothels. Nearby were bear- and bull-baiting pits. The cries of dying animals would have carried into the theatre during the daytime performances.

The Elizabethan audience did not have one or two long intervals where they could nip to the bar and enjoy a cool gin and tonic. Rather there was usually a short break between each act of a play (so four in the longer plays such as *Hamlet* and *Romeo and Juliet*). People could exchange views about what was happening on stage and buy drinks and snacks from vendors who toured the pit. Up to 2000 people would cram into The Globe, mostly standing up in the pit, so the atmosphere in Shakespeare's time must have been closer, on occasion, to a modern football terrace than a hushed theatre.

Disreputable and sleazy

Although Elizabethan nobles and the gentry went to see Shakespeare's plays (and several were premiered at court before Elizabeth I), the playhouse 400 years ago was considered a rather disreputable and sleazy place. Actors were thought of as vagabonds because companies travelled round the country, like the gypsies that Elizabethan society so despised, touring their plays to inns and the occasional hall of a great country house.

Many people thought plays were immoral, their writers dangerous purveyors of lies and slanders; and the church practically thought anyone who paid a penny to stand in the pit of the original Globe was committing a sin. Nonetheless, plays were hugely popular with ordinary working people. There was none of the potential snobbery about visiting the Elizabethan theatre that there can be about a theatre visit for some people today.

A performance at the original Globe Theatre in Shakespeare's day was a much more rough-and-ready affair than an outing to plush modern theatre, where the audience often dresses up for the occasion. Theatre is still thought of by many people as a special event, unlike say cinema. It can also be expensive. One of the great things about The Globe is that compared to the West End theatres just across the river, where a top seat can cost over £50, the best place in The Globe, standing up in the pit as a groundling, costs only £5. It is the best place to be not only because you are closest to the stage, and can even lean on it, but because all the more expensive seats in the galleries have only a partial view of the action. Shakespeare can in this sense really be said to be a playwright for the common man: those who pay least get the best view!

WEB LINKS

For further information on The Globe check some of the many websites about it: search under 'Globe'. Sites maintained by the theatre itself (www.shakespeares-globe.org/) and The Globe site of Reading University's Department of English (www.rdg.ac.uk/globe/) are especially recommended.

There is an interesting unattributed anecdote about how modern audiences learned to react to plays at The Globe. With little scenery, no lighting and no technology or special effects, seeing a play on an stage where the actors can see you just as clearly as you can see them is a novel experience. Before The Globe opened Mark Rylance, the theatre's director, wondered how audiences would

A view of part of a map of London showing
the old Globe theatre

The new Globe theatre

react. And in the first season (the summer of 1996) they began by standing or sitting as quietly and reverently as if they were in the expensive seats of a normal theatre. Then a school party of less than well-behaved children arrived. They booed the villains as they hatched their plots and cheered the heroes when they drove home their revenging swords. While this sort of pantomime response is obviously not suitable for all the plays all of the time, the school party bought some of the exuberance and engagement of an Elizabethan audience into the theatre. Rumours spread about how it might be acceptable to react to the plays at The Globe. Mark Rylance saw such audience reaction and interaction as a vital part of the authenticity of The Globe. (Although he didn't take authenticity as far as having boys play all the women's parts!)

For many young people, a visit to The Globe helps them make sense of Shakespeare. The theatre has pulled off a very difficult trick. It has created a unique and living theatrical experience based on showing Shakespeare's plays in as close a setting to their Elizabethan original as possible. It could have turned out a rather shallow tourist experience, a sort of lifeless historical reconstruction that is spectacular but ultimately unbelievable. Luckily for us, it didn't.

Questions for discussion

1. Why does the fact there is so much criticism written about a writer like Shakespeare make it hard for you to form your opinion of his work?

2. What would you imagine to be the differences between a performance in the Globe and a 'command' performance at a royal palace in Shakespeare's time?

3. Brainstorm a list of as many general differences as you can think of between a performance of a play in The Globe and the same play in a modern auditorium.

4. Do you think The Globe is a serious attempt to show how Elizabethan plays were performed, or a novel tourist attraction? Make a few notes to argue the case either way. Does it matter if the theatre is both these things at the same time?

5. Who was Sam Wanamaker? Why was it unrealistic for him to expect to find a working theatre in 1940s London that dated from Shakespeare's time?

Questions for written answer

1. How do you think seeing a Shakespeare play (or any play) being performed on stage is different from reading the words on the page? (Think about direction, design, the pace at which the story unfolds.)

2. Having a clear picture of how a Shakespeare play was performed when it was a new work is essential to understanding the words on the page. Do you agree? Explain why you think this is so, or say why you think the plays can be read just as texts in a book.

3. 'Everything's so much more interesting now everything's a museum'. A contemporary poet wrote this about Britain's heritage industry. Do you think a reconstructed Elizabethan theatre in the middle of one of the world's greatest modern cities at the start of the new millennium can offer a genuine artistic experience, or is it just a spectacle for tourists? How could you judge?

? Quiz

1. What is blank verse?
2. What is Shakespeare's favoured verse form called?
3. What sort of area was London's South Bank in Elizabethan times?
4. What other forms of entertainment competed with plays?
5. Why did boys play the girl's parts?
6. How many people could the original Globe hold?
7. Why were actors looked down on by polite Elizabethan society?
8. Who were the groundlings?

Examiners will look for the following in your written answer:

- Evidence that you have understood the source material and can make appropriate use of it.
- You need to be able to make value judgements based on it and support these with evidence or interpretation.
- You need to have something of your own to say and to be able to state it clearly.
- You need to show you can relate this work to other relevant areas of study.

ACTIVITY

This activity is designed so that you can 'feel' the difference between the page and the performance. You will need a group of six people.

1. First read the scenario below and discuss what might happen, and how it might develop.

The scene is a street, the action as follows.

- Chris and Jo enter; they boast about how good they are and the sort of things they will do to any United supporters they meet.
- Les and Pat enter.
- Chris and Jo tease Les and Pat who respond in kind.
- A fight ensues, Jamie arrives and tries to break it up.
- Nicky arrives and, thinking Jamie is fighting, challenges him.

---

2. Then rehearse and act out the scene. You should do this in isolation from the other groups and then present your piece to them. The characters are:
   - Chris and Jo; year-10 City supporters
   - Les and Pat; year-10 United supporters
   - Jamie; year-11 City supporter
   - Nicky; year-11 United supporter

3. Discuss your live performances developed. What are the benefits/drawbacks of the live performance?

4. Now read Act 1 Scene i of *Romeo and Juliet*, up to the entry of the officer and citizens.

5. Choose parts and act out this opening scene. Again, what are the benefits/drawbacks of the live performance?

Preview

The phrase 'dumbing down' is much used in the on-going 'free to air' debate about the quality and content of the five terrestrial, publicly available (without sign-up or subscription) television channels available in the UK. No-one has absolutely defined the term, and the debate has reached no real conclusions, but the general feeling among most contributors to the discussion is that 'dumbing down' means a reduction in quality of what is broadcast, and that this is occurring (compared to say 20 or 30 years ago) on every channel.

Does television, as an entertainment resource available literally out there in the air, have a duty or role to educate as well as amuse? This unit uses a fictional extract from a letter to underline one of its premises.

Dumbing down: a media analyst writes

'Dumbing down' is generally taken to mean not only a general decline in the overall quality of what is broadcast, but a lowering of standards of taste and intellectual content. Dumbing down can be seen to operate in several ways:

- The choice of subject matter for individual programmes – less serious documentaries, more soap operas and garden make-over shows.
- The televisual quality of individual programmes – some critics believe that, generally, peoples' attention spans are declining and programmes are made in a way that panders to this.
- The intellectual content of programmes – it is claimed that not just documentaries, but drama output is less intellectually challenging or engaging than it used to be.
- The scheduling of output – 'serious' programmes are pushed out to early or late slots, leaving the peak viewing hours for soaps, police dramas, fly-on-the-wall documentaries, etc.
- The suspicion of deliberate lowering of standards of taste and 'decency' in certain late-night slots.

For most people, the issue of dumbing down is mostly about the first and last entries in this list.

First, is it true to say that the 'serious' subject matter of programmes has completely vanished? At first glance there seem to be numerous programmes on decorating and gardening, along with situation comedies, game shows and compilations of 'funny' TV moments from television's past. (Yes, television now has a history!) However, a closer examination also reveals that some of the 'lightweight' programmes are tackling serious issues. *EastEnders* and *Coronation*

TIPS FOR FURTHER RESEARCH

Look at archive copies of the *Radio Times* (BBC) or *TV Times* (ITV) to see what the 'quality' of programmes was in the past. Has anything really changed?

WEB LINKS

www.radiotimes.beeb.com/film/
contains film reviews, as does
www.film.com/

Street have tackled violence, crime, homosexuality and homophobia, drugs, dealing with bereavement and post-natal depression – amongst other things. Even the American cartoon series *The Simpsons* may be said to address serious issues – even if it does do it through humour. Casting a wider net in one typical week will find serious programmes on the situation in Palestine and Israel, mental illness, the plight of single mothers, coping with trauma and so on. Not to mention slots on archaeology, history and the natural world. This is on top of the 'heavyweight' news and news review programmes.

Secondly, are late-night slots deliberately reserved for 'adult' movies and programmes? Certainly there would be a legitimate complaint if such programmes were shown during the early evening, but should they be shown at all?

Some channels might be accused of trying to build their late-night 'after-pub' audience with programmes designed to do little more than titillate. These include studio-based chat shows that revel in bad language (and bad jokes) and 'erotic' programmes disguised as documentaries. Some programmes even save a 'raunchier' version for later showing, as opposed to the one they show at prime time. There is no harm in this (as people are not forced to watch any of these offerings), but can it be argued that such scheduling contributes to 'dumbing down'?

Are You Being Served – a 1970s sitcom. Has television comedy really dumbed down since then?

Has the invention of broadcasting itself led to an intellectual downturn in society? Research what the Victorians did for entertainment. Comment on how you think such entertainment would be received in the twenty-first century.

The little yellow triangle – why it might have been dropped

In the early days of its late-night broadcasting one channel displayed a little yellow triangle in the corner of the screen throughout any film with content thought likely to offend. Often these were films made for the intellectual art-house cinema circuit. Although this letter is fictional, a version of it was actually sent into a radio discussion on the broadcasting of sexually explicit material on television.

Dear Sir,

The little yellow triangle – what a great idea!

Now when me and me mates come back from the boozer on Friday nights we can bang on the old telly and check if the triangle is there.

If it is we know there's going to be plenty of rude bits, so 'corse then we stay tuned. No more sitting there watching and hoping for a glimpse of flesh only to be left disappointed.

Well done, you've done us blokes a great service. Keep it up, as they say ...

Yours ...

A Friday Night Watcher

The BBC is a public corporation, set up by Act of Parliament and owned by the government on behalf of the people. This means licence fees and no advertising. It also means some control/interference – for example, there is still a requirement for a certain amount of religious broadcasting.

A writer complains

In the 1960s and 1970s the BBC reserved several peak evening viewing slots for new, original one-off dramas: *The Sunday Play*, *Play for Today*, *The Wednesday Play*. Of course not everything commissioned and broadcast turned out to be a classic piece of drama, but the overall idea was a good one: to create, as nearly as possible, a theatre experience for viewers at home. One BBC executive in the mid-1960s declared rather grandly, but with some justification, 'We are the national theatre'. He meant that more people than could ever attend the actual National Theatre on London's South Bank were experiencing, through BBC drama broadcasting, quality plays of a sort that they might see in a theatre.

The BBC recruited writers mainly through looking at who was writing good new plays for theatres. Willy Russell, one of the country's most successful playwrights on stage, got his first breaks on television because the BBC saw the work he was doing in theatres in Liverpool. Looking back on the late 1960s and the 1970s, the list of writers who produced dramas for the BBC reads like a list of writers who were also exciting theatre audiences with their plays.

The crucial thing was that the BBC were prepared to broadcast dramas that were complete events. Like a play for stage, it took place in one evening. They were also prepared to show work that challenged viewers, that addressed current and often contentious issues. Some of the plays were definitely radical in their content. Plays like *Cathy Come Home* set new standards for social comment and caused long-running debates in the media.

Today, television drama is all about creating characters for a series. Broadcasters want to get viewers and hold them, not for one night, but for a six- or eight-part series or whatever. There is a very different approach to working out a story that can run for several episodes than for writing a conventional play that focuses on telling a story in a single two-hour intense dramatic event. Many current highly popular television 'dramas' are really only soap operas with high production values. The similarities are obvious: a large cast of characters, some of whom are only tenuously connected to one another, and an ongoing series of individual story lines which overlap, never allowing the whole programme to reach a single, all-involving climax (as is required in a play for stage or screen).

Adaptations of classical novels may appear to start from a more artistically valid base, but in fact cutting and filleting a long Victorian novel for a four-part Sunday night drama is now a formulaic process. Only the same three or four writers are ever employed by the television companies to do this work and their style permeates every adaptation. In every case it could be argued that dumbing down is an inevitable part of the adaptation. Classic novels usually feature large casts, with readers following the dramatic journeys of several figures towards the climax. Critics of the various classic adaptations for television have all noted that the first thing an adaptor seems to do is decide which character from the original will be the main focus, the one they want viewers to care about, then they cut down the scope and breadth of the book until this character clearly becomes the focus. This, it might be argued, is a necessary part of compressing a big text into handy bite-sized television slots, but you might also suggest that the adaptor is pandering to lazy viewers who want to watch a costume epic that's easy on the brain on a Sunday evening.

Is it all dumbed down? – a few observations on today's television

It's quite easy to get hold of tapes of past 'great' television. Some of the sitcoms make you weep! They are so hackneyed, so wooden, so corny. Today's imported American comedies are so much more slick and original. If the best has been preserved, what rubbish has been hidden by the passing of time?

Television now trains and employs dramatists who want to write specifically for the small screen. They are no longer poached from theatre. Writing for actors on a stage is a whole different skill to writing drama for television where modern equipment means that the story can be shot on diverse locations. No one would sensibly argue that writers such as Jimmy McGovern (*Cracker*) don't use all the opportunities that television provides for creating great drama.

And if the intellectual or educative content of television is declining why did Channel 4 recently show a three-hour documentary over two consecutive nights on the sinking of the Second World War battleships *Hood* and *Bismarck*? Not only did they screen these highly detailed accounts of naval history, they part funded the expedition that went and searched for the battleships' wrecks.

News bulletins – particularly at regional level – often feel that they must end with a 'human interest' story (the rescued dog, the 100th birthday, the primary school success). This has been institutionalized as the 'and finally' slot. Why do you think news editors feel the need for this item?

Questions for discussion

1. Should television, which is available to anyone in their homes at the flick of a switch, be more careful about not offending 'taste and decency' than work in the cinema or theatre where people make a decision to go and see whatever is being shown?

2. If television is dumbing down, does it matter?

3. Should all television stations devote at least some of their broadcasting to educating people, via documentaries, political discussion shows, etc.?

4. Do you think some television is 'dumb'? Do some sorts of programmes strike you as crass and silly (as opposed to just being programmes that you don't like)? Give examples and say why the examples you have chosen are objectively 'dumb'.

5. Should the role of television be primarily to inform or to entertain? Can it do both successfully?

Questions for written answer

1. The five terrestrial channels have to compete with cable and satellite broadcasting. Some critics think they will, or even should, do anything to keep viewers. What do you think? What effect do you think the proliferation of available channels might have on broadcasting standards generally? Should the five free channels have a different focus and set of responsibilities to the cable and digital ones which people choose to buy and receive?

2. The BBC is funded by the licence fee. If you own a television you have to have a licence, and therefore have to contribute to the BBC's budget. How much say should the public have over how the BBC spends the licence fees its receives? As the national television station with a world reputation for seriousness and quality, how much should the BBC define its own policy for what it makes and shows?

3. Is it possible to actually say that television today is 'dumber' than it was say 20 years ago? Society has changed, and this has affected what it is possible to show on television, what people want to see and how they react to it. Think about the possible cultural connections between broadcasting and society and say whether you think the role of television has changed, and maybe become 'dumber', or whether television has just changed along with society.

4. Discuss to what extent you think that certain groups (young people, for example) need protecting against certain broadcast material (in the way that the yellow triangle tried to provide a warning)? Is there ever a case for censorship?

❓ Quiz

1. What is meant by a 'free-to-air' channel?

2. What are the five ways in which 'dumbing down' is seen to operate?

3. What was Channel 4's original broadcasting remit?

4. What was the purpose of the 'little yellow triangle'?

5. Which writer got his first breaks on television after writing for the Liverpool theatre?

6. Who wrote *Cracker*?

7. Give one major difference between a television series and a one-off play (apart from the length).

ACTIVITY 1

In small groups look at a copy of a television guide. Take a typical weekday and categorize the programmes for the terrestrial channels into information, education and entertainment. (Satellite channels are already categorized by subject matter, e.g. MTV, Sky News, Discovery.) You will need to devise your own sub-categories for some programmes – for example an early-morning quiz show may be 'entertainment' but so might a late-night crime thriller. Rate the programmes on a scale of 1 to 10 from 'really dumb' to 'very intelligent'. Work out the percentages for each category. Which channel is 'dumbest' according to your figures? Compare them with other groups. Can you agree on classifications or is it a matter of opinion?

Now do the same exercise for a Saturday and compare this with a weekday. What differences can you detect? Why do you think this is so?

ACTIVITY 2

Watch a whole mid-week evening's television. Choose programmes from any or even all channels. Keep a log of what you watched.

In small groups share your logs. Can you come to group decisions about what was quality broadcasting and what might be described as dumb? Justify your selections for both quality and dumb categories.

04 The Dalai Lama and cultural tourism

Preview

The religious and temporal leader of the Tibetan people, the Dalai Lama, fled to Northern India in 1959, to avoid persecution from the Chinese who had invaded Tibet. Over 80,000 Tibetans also made the dangerous journey over the mountains to be with him in exile. Tibet's unique culture was being systematically wiped out by China.

The Dalai Lama became the centre for a Tibetan capital in exile in the northern Indian hill town of Dharamsala. With help from the Indian government and the United Nations, the exiled Tibetans have worked hard on practical plans to create a new home, setting up housing schemes, hospitals, Tibetan schools and Tibetan Buddhist monasteries and nunneries (nearly 200 of them).

Now people from all over the world flock to Dharamsala. Some want to contribute to the practical work being done to help the exiled. Many more however just want to gain a place in one of the public audiences given by the Dalai Lama. Their interests are apparently spiritual not practical. The most committed claim to convert to Tibetan Buddhism.

But is this just cultural tourism? Can you go round the world to join a religion that was until recently the exclusive preserve of an isolated mountain people? Can someone from a Western society ever really be part of such a religion? Is it just a fashionable thing to do? If it is, does it matter?

Dalai Lama

Tensin Gyatso (1935–) the present Dalai Lama (which means 'ocean-like guru') is the fourteenth incarnation (Lamas are seen as reincarnations of a previous leader and must be recognized as such while still children). He was designated as the Dalai Lama at the age of two and took over government when he was 15. In 1989 he won the Nobel Prize for Peace for his commitment to the non-violent liberation of Tibet.

The Panchen Lama (1938–1989), tenth reincarnation of the Buddha Amitabha, and second only to the Dalai Lama, was taken under the 'protection' of China in his childhood. This led Tibetans to dispute his status, claiming he had been 'kidnapped'.

Gurus

Before people started visiting the Tibetans in remote Dharamsala, there had been many other cultural tourists travelling to India in search of enlightenment. If the numbers trekking to the Dalai Lama increased when Hollywood stars such as Richard Gere went there and professed themselves converted to Tibetan Buddhism, this is only a more recent version of the flood of hippies who went to seek enlightenment from gurus in India in the 1960s and 1970s after the Beatles were seen meditating with the Maharishi Mahesh Yogi.

Of course, it is impossible in either case to say what percentage of travellers in search of a new faith are genuine, how many would have been there whether or not some popular public figure had not already made the trip. If a 'short written test' of more than the absolute basics of Tibetan Buddhism were given to returning 'pilgrims', how many would pass? But does this matter?

Inherited beliefs

Generally speaking, throughout history people tended to hold the belief system they were born into, unless they made a public and often life-changing conversion. You were born into a Catholic family, so you grew up Catholic. You attended mass and continued a family and social tradition that was part of your immediate heritage. You married another Catholic and, when you had children, they were brought into the church. If you gave up going to church you were considered 'lapsed'. If you actively converted to another version of Christianity you were seen to be severing serious social and spiritual ties, and you might find yourself regarded as a traitor to your abandoned faith, as well as an outsider who had to prove themself to the new host belief.

Such rigid belonging to a religion or a belief system might be thought of as tribal. It offers the comfort of belonging. But it also leads to distrust between religions, to a 'my country right or wrong' attitude among many devote believers. Throughout history millions have died in Europe as Catholics fought Protestants. Then there were wars between Christianity and Islam, and persecutions by Christians of Jews and other smaller religions.

Today, far fewer people in the West are committed to Christianity of any form, though fighting between Catholic and Protestant communities continues sporadically in Northern Ireland. The majority of people in the UK do not attend church. Many people go further and claim no need for any belief system to define a spiritual dimension in their lives. They are happy to live in a world free from any religious elements. This sort of world makes perfect sense for them. They might be materialists (not just in the sense of wanting to acquire material goods!) or humanists, who believe any spirituality that exists is created by and exists solely within the realms of the human. They might be atheists or agnostics. They may simply be staunch communists, whose social, economic and political view of the ideal world system has no place for religion of any form.

Looking for something new

But many people who have rejected an inherited belief system, or grown up in a family or community that does not particularly have one, appear to want to go out to find one. People in Western countries convert to Islam in small but significant numbers, attracted perhaps by the rigorous frame it places on their lives, controlling their relationships with the opposite sex, how they dress, how they behave and so on. What might seem like unacceptable restrictions to many liberal thinkers are embraced as personal support structures by others.

Some people travel in search of new beliefs. Some go to remote places like Dharamsala. It might be that many of these travellers are attracted mainly to the trappings of comparatively obscure religions like Tibetan Buddhism. Real converts will change their name, and have to alter their entire lifestyle when they return to Europe, if they are to remain committed Tibetan Buddhists. Of course, it is impossible to really know if someone is genuinely moved and convinced by the spiritual depth of Tibetan Buddhism, or whether they liked the adventure of going to see its spiritual leader. What is certain is that in an increasingly material world where science is removing all the mysteries that

Some of the thousands of Hare Krishna devotees who gathered in central London for their annual Rathayatra Chariot Festival

religions once used to try to explain by holy stories (e.g. Big Bang and evolution theories replacing the Bible's version of how it all began), many people want to find some new spiritual depth, some mystery, and they look increasingly further afield. In Europe in particular, they look away from the established religion, Christianity, that historically is their birthright. After centuries in which Europeans went out and converted (often by force) whole continents that were up to then quite happy with their own belief systems, it is ironic that some Europeans are rejecting Christianity in search of other, more esoteric, religions.

What China did to Tibet

The Dalai Lama is a superstar in this world of new religious figures. In the company of most young people, and liberals of any age, it is heresy not to condemn China for its appalling military and cultural invasion of Tibet. And quite rightly. China has made no bones about its aim to destroy Tibet's unique cultural identity, founded entirely on its religion, and absorb the country into a sort of socialist 'greater China'; and the The Dalai Lama and his monks are clearly such calm and placid figures with so much to teach the West.

But we might play devil's advocate for a moment, and argue that it is not a simple case of good people thrown out of their own country by bad. Liberal thinkers have traditionally deplored the intervention of the church into the political life of Western countries. Throughout the twentieth century the removal of church influence from governments was the necessary precursor to increases in democratic and personal freedoms. Wars, such as the Spanish Civil War, were in part fought over this issue. In Europe, we came to see religious (i.e. Christian) influences as generally repressive influences on public life.

But Tibet was a theocracy, that is, a country where civil rule was in the hands of the church. Religious authority and practical government were indivisible, sadly to the detriment of the latter. Tibet is a small, sparsely populated mountainous country. When it was still independent, it lacked basic infrastructure such as roads, and medical facilities were very poor. But there were 6259 monasteries when the Chinese invaders poured in. Living conditions for ordinary people were appalling.

An Indian correspondent who once travelled from China, through Tibet and back to India, found himself amazed at the end of the journey when he wrote that ultimately he would support China's way of running public life over the Tibetan one (and even over his own country's shaky, but enduring democracy), for the simple reason that China (and China in Tibet) had ensured that no one actually starved. The monks of 6259 monasteries had not done this.

WEB LINKS
A CNN special on the Dalai Lama can be found at www.cnn.com/specials/ 2001/dalai.lama/. Also try the Dalai Lama's own website at www.dalailama.com

Robes and chanting

Somehow, if a religion has exotic trappings, it is more appealing to many people, especially young people who have grown up in a European culture where religion is generally not central to life. If it imposes strict patterns of prayer and requires the wearing of certain clothes, so much the better. But ask yourself, if all these apparently appealing things were provided by a version of Christianity, or some other belief system that was part of their 'home' culture, would so many people rush to adopt it?

Adopting religions from other parts of the world may be seen as part of a process of multiculturalism that in other areas of life we would wholeheartedly encourage. Almost everyone thinks a society made up of different races creating a culture that both recognizes roots and encourages innovation is a good thing. Living in harmony is a good thing. Learning about and sharing other cultures is a good thing. These tenets are basic to most people's thinking if they have any liberal feelings at all. So adopting a religion or a belief system from another culture must also be a good thing.

But are religions a special case? Of course, a convert can become the most perfect devotee of a religion. Yet the sight of Western people in the orange robes of Buddhist monks seems odd, rather affected and false. Perhaps the problem is the fact that, in the bigger picture, all religions have much more in common than they have differences, and that many people who affect to become devotees of a religious system from another culture are exactly those people who would avoid contact with the established religions in their home countries.

TIPS FOR FURTHER RESEARCH

Look up the meaning of the following words. Why are they important to Buddhism?
- Mahayana
- Bodhisattva
- Nirvana.

Questions for discussion

1. Does one country have the right to invade another if the invader can clearly offer people a better standard of living? Or should powerful countries always stand back and respect the sovereignty of other states, even if it appears that some governments are failing or abusing their people?

2. Are there elements of public life and laws in Britain in which you can see the influence of the church, or at least the spirit of what you might identify as Christian thinking? Discuss and make a list of things that have changed (laws and trends in public life generally) as the influence of the church has declined.

3. Should we always respect the view that religious belief is a purely personal thing? Or should anyone who professes religious feelings be expected to defend their beliefs, especially if they have gone out and converted to a religion from a different culture?

4. China sought to destroy Tibet's culture by force. The USA has sought to dramatically influence the economic, political and daily life of many countries by supporting political parties that would allow US companies to build factories to exploit cheap labour, establish American businesses and export huge quantities of American goods to the country. What's the difference? Discuss your ideas.

Questions for written answer

1. Is it right to choose our religion like we choose anything else in our life? How will we know when we have found the 'right' belief system? What might there be in religious belief that sets it apart from all other beliefs we may hold?

2. Imagine a remote and relatively poor area of northern India accepting 8000 exiles to set up home. Then these exiles appear to attract thousands of tourists. Discuss the possible good and bad effects of this on all the population of Dharamsala.

3. Cultural tourism has been a phenomenon of the late 1990s. People travel to understand the cultures of other countries, not just look at ruins or laze on the beach. Is this always a good thing? Could cultural tourism be invasive? What guidelines would you draft for someone wanting to understand and experience, for example, the religious beliefs of another country?

4. Travellers to Tibet may claim that 'travel broadens the mind'. Choose any one place that you have visited (either at home or abroad) and discuss what you found out about its cultural, artistic and social heritage. Discuss whether you think that this experience has 'broadened your mind'.

5. Some people think that what China has done is 'right', some that it is 'wrong'. What factors do you think contribute to our understanding of 'right' and 'wrong'? Discuss whether it is possible to accept another person's viewpoint even though you think it is 'wrong'.

? Multiple-choice questions

1. Dalai Lama means:
   a) sea-like figure
   b) ocean-like guru
   c) calm as the sea
   d) spiritual leader.
2. Tensin Gyatso was recognized as Dalai Lama at the age of:
   a) 2
   b) 5
   c) 10
   d) 15.
3. A Catholic who gives up going to church is known as:
   a) lazy
   b) lapsed
   c) liberal
   d) left-wing.
4. Rule by a religious group is called a:
   a) democracy
   b) theocracy
   c) oligarchy
   d) theogarchy.

5. How many monasteries did the Chinese find in Tibet?
   a) 6257
   b) 6258
   c) 6259
   d) 6260.

6. Guru and rabbi both mean the same thing. The meaning is:
   a) teacher
   b) pacifist
   c) learned
   d) leader.

7. The Maharishi Mahesh Yogi's most famous pupil/s was/were:
   a) Richard Gere
   b) President Clinton
   c) The Beatles
   d) The Rolling Stones.

8. The majority of people in the UK:
   a) are members of an organized religion
   b) are Christian
   c) do not attend church
   d) intend to travel to Dharamsala.

9. The Panchen Lama is an incarnation of:
   a) The Buddha
   b) Tensin Gyatso
   c) Buddha Amitabha
   d) The Dalai Lama.

10. The Chinese invaded Tibet in:
    a) 1949
    b) 1959
    c) 1969
    d) 1979.

ACTIVITY 1

- In small groups, make a list of world religions. Make notes for each explaining their main principles and any features of life for a believer.

- Could you imagine becoming a convert to any of these religions? What aspect of them would convince you?

- Are there any factors which appear to be common to all beliefs? Try to take 'the best bits' from all the religions and construct one ideal belief system.

- Is there anything in all or some of these religions that turn you away from any kind of personal religious belief?

ACTIVITY 2

Choose one religion and list five points that you could use in an argument to convince someone to convert to that religion. Now list five points against it. Choose people at random in your group to try to convince the rest of the group either

- to join a particular religion

- to oppose a particular religion.

05 The Celtic tiger – social and economic changes in Ireland

Preview

For generations, Ireland was an isolated country with a less-than-booming economy. The Irish tourist authorities promoted the country as a place where daily life was more traditional and quieter than people from most other countries were used to. Then in the late 1980s Ireland, around the capital Dublin at least, suddenly 'woke up'. Largely because of the quality of its college graduates, the government realized it has a powerful, skilled but woefully under-employed workforce. Ireland has a very young population, many of whom traditionally went abroad to live and work. The government encouraged them to stay at home by convincing companies from other countries to invest in Ireland.

The face and feel of Dublin was transformed: from a rather poor, conservative city, to a throbbing European capital with many new businesses, soaring house prices and a vibrant night life.

But change is not universally welcomed. In this fictional script, an older Irish man returns to his family in a small, more traditional village in the country after spending a few days in the 'new Dublin'. Such discussions could happen in any country that has rapidly shrugged off its old image and economy for a new global one.

In a recent survey of 50 Western nations, the Republic of Ireland came out as the most 'globalized' economy of all. This was just after the introduction of the euro, which Ireland adopted.

THE GOOD OLD DAYS?

Cast: **Boyle**, a man from the country, 50s; **Mary**, his wife; **Jack**, his son, 20s

BOYLE: And the names of the shops are all gone and changed! It used be MaCarthy's this and O'Hagan's that. Traditional shops, run by local Dublin people. Now, in the centre by the river, there's a shop that sells coffee from America and a restaurant that says its from Covent Garden. Where's that, for god's sake?

JACK: London.

BOYLE: London! I tell you son, Dublin's just like London now. Not a spit of difference.

MARY: Well now, is that so wrong? I always liked London.

JACK: It's bloody brilliant if you ask me.

BOYLE: Not in all ways, not at all. Dublin is Ireland's capital. It should look like an Irish city.

MARY: Some new shops in Dublin would be nice. Brighter ones, you know. More up to the minute. Selling things like you see in the magazines. The old ones were never too good on the latest fashions. There were always things you couldn't get.

BOYLE: There's difference between get and want. Look at all the adverts now telling you to buy this, and you must have that. We're bombarded. Children especially. Trainers! What's wrong with plimsolls?

JACK: You'll be telling us that people shouldn't want to have new things. Who decides, eh? Who decides what we can and cannot have? The government used to try to do that and it never worked. The reason the economy is on a roll now is because people want things, have money and there've got to be companies to provide it all. Wanting things has transformed this country.

MARY: For the better if you ask me.

BOYLE: For those who can afford it. Don't forget, not everyone's a winner in this boom time. There's always those who miss the boat. Didn't the English find that, all that 1980s 'greed is good' stuff with their Maggie Thatcher. What happened? A lot of yuppies got rich and a lot of factories closed.

JACK: If people are losing out, then they just have to try harder.

MARY: That's hard. Irish people have always had respect for education and hard work. But not everyone can succeed. That's why there're so many coming into this country, to help out with the new jobs.

BOYLE: Hardly an Irish voice in some of the streets nowadays.

MARY: Tourists, that's nice. I mean, don't we get a lot of the tourists here in the village? Looking at the scenery.

BOYLE: But when they come out here, it's to see Ireland, the real Ireland. In Dublin, it's like they don't want to leave home so the city's been all changed to suit them.

JACK: Globalization.

BOYLE: So the papers tell us. And a good thing it's all supposed to be. World markets, people going all over for work, sending things all over the world for people to buy.

JACK: You can't fight it. It's the way of the world. Don't you drive a Nissan?

BOYLE: And if it goes on then the whole world will be just the same all over. Do we really want that? I tell you, you'll get on a plane and fly to New York, get out and find exactly the same shops there that you left in Dublin. People wearing the same clothes, which have probably been run up in Indonesia or Portugal anyway.

MARY: Oh yes, and you with your old-style shirts made by the little old man in County Galway.

BOYLE: It's good Irish cloth and cut, and I'm keeping the man there in his work.

MARY: [Sadly] No chance of you becoming a fashionable dresser.

JACK: International companies have invested in Ireland. That's why people are doing so well in Dublin. Their lives have been changed. The new shops and all are part of global companies. They have a brand identity. There are burger joints in Russia now. Is that wrong? Don't the Russians have the right to buy a burger if they want one? You'll still be able to get shirts from Galway just like your grandad wore.

BOYLE: Sure, but they'll be all marketed like tourist things. Novelties. Shouldn't ordinary Irish people have the right to keep some of the old life, the real life of our country? Without it becoming something to sell the tourists. And if we end up just the same as New York, why will the Yanks bother to fly all the way across the Atlantic just to see it?

MARY: Ireland will always be special. Every place in the world has something special about it. Always will.

BOYLE: But it becomes smaller. Less important. It becomes a tourist feature, not the 'real life' of the place.

JACK: The government does a good job of presenting Dublin's image to the world. Don't worry, they won't let the international chains turn all the old bars into cocktail lounges. They'll still be places where you can get a pint of stout with the old boys in their flat caps. And be served by a miserable barman.

BOYLE: It'll probably be some theme bar. I don't want that.

JACK: Or is it that you don't want to share the bar with people from all over the world? Is that not your real problem? You don't like all the different people and races in your dear old city. You can't turn back the clocks. Cities like Dublin are world cities now. Like London, Paris, New York. All sorts of people from all over the world visiting. And not just visiting, living and working too. You remember Dick Creeley from this village? He's in Dublin now, and going to be married to an Italian girl.

BOYLE: At least she'll be a Catholic then.

JACK: Would it matter if she were a Buddhist?

MARY: I think all that international thing is quite nice. Last time I went up to Dublin I had a curry! And there was a lovely Indian woman in one of those sari things, all gold and floaty. I asked her where she was from and she said Howth [A Dublin Suburb.] No, I says, where were yous born? And she says 'Howth'. I think that's nice.

JACK: What about you then da? Is that wrong? Hindus in Howth? OK, the shops have different names, non-Irish names. What about people? You're on dangerous ground now. Dublin for the Irish only is it?

BOYLE: Of course not. The Irish have always welcomed people.

JACK: For years and years didn't we have governments that wanted to keep this country frozen into an old image of itself that was hopelessly out of date? Things had to move on. There's a lot of very traditionally minded people here, so the government knew they couldn't move things on by trying to get them to change their ways of thinking. Then economics takes over. Companies start wanting to invest, to develop new things, in Dublin anyway. And new international companies bring international ideas. Liberal ideas. Soon, money is flowing and people relax and see that new ideas from outside might not be so bad after all. Now we're doing so well there's people having to come to Ireland to work to keep it all rolling. For generations it was us that had to leave, to go all over the world to find work. Now, they come to us.

TIPS FOR FURTHER RESEARCH

Look up 'globalization' and find out what elements are used to judge whether a country is 'globalized' or not. Would you use the same elements or do other things matter more?

Redevelopment is transforming Ireland's capital city

A Dublin street in the 1950s

Read the articles on the World Trade Organization (page 186) and on Europe (page 148) in order to bring an extra dimension of knowledge to your essay.

WEB LINKS

www.ireland-information.com/engine/

Questions for discussion

1. What signs of globalization are there in your local area?

2. Should governments have the right to stop international companies taking over national and local industries and businesses?

3. Do people have the right to want everything that the advertising industries offer? Do governments have a duty to protect the way of life of a country even if that means denying some consumer rights or wishes?

4. 'Globalization makes everywhere the same.' Do you think this is true? Does it matter?

5. Irish governments tried hard to keep Ireland isolated from the rest of Europe until the 1960s, but economics, not changes in policy, defeated this aim. Does the fact that it was business, not government, that changed attitudes matter?

Examiners will look for the following in your written answer:

- Evidence that you have understood the source material and can make appropriate use of it.
- You need to be able to make value judgements based on it and support these with evidence or interpretation.
- You need to have something of your own to say and to be able to state it clearly.
- You need to show you can relate this work to other relevant areas of study.

Questions for written answer

1. Tourism is one of the major industries in Britain, employing more people than manufacturing and reaching almost all parts of the country. What are the advantages of having such a powerful tourist industry, and what are the dangers? Think about economics and the practical effects on life in the country.

2. From time to time the British government debates ideas about how immigrants can be better assimilated into UK society. Should people migrating into a new country make positive efforts to adopt the lifestyle of that country? How much of their old culture should they be prepared to give up?

3. Do you think a multicultural society is the necessary and inevitable ideal for the Western nations to work towards? What are the advantages and disadvantages of a society that is created from the diverse cultural heritages of different people settling in a country?

4. Many major companies are global operations. They are hugely powerful and not elected by populations. They provide more people with more goods and services than at any time in history. What do you think are the advantages and disadvantages of this system of global capitalism?

ACTIVITY 1

Write another scene with Boyle, Mary and Jack, in which Jack announces he is giving up his job teaching in the village school to teach languages to international students in Dublin. His salary will be double what he gets in the village. How do the family react? What issues does his decision raise for each character? Try to develop issues that cropped up in the scene in this unit.

ACTIVITY 2

List the clothes that you wore last weekend. How many of these were global brands? How many are really global brands but disguised as something else ('skater', 'board' and 'surf' wear are particular culprits). Think about what you did. How many global brands came into your choice of food, drink, entertainment? Discuss what you think this says about globalization in general.

Crowds and silence: the Vermeer exhibition as a cultural event

Preview

Jan (or Johannes) Vermeer van Delft was born in October 1632 and died in December 1675. Little is known of the life of this Dutch painter who lived and worked in Delft, except that he created some of the most exquisite paintings in Western art. He gained some recognition in his lifetime in Holland, but made little effort to sell the relatively small number of paintings he completed. As a result, his art was forgotten until nineteenth-century art historians re-established his reputation. He painted mainly small, detailed domestic interiors, notable for their use of perspective and treatment of the various tones of daylight.

Today his works are rare, and hugely valuable. About 35 or 36 paintings are now generally attributed to him (agreed by the experts to have been painted by him) and most are on display as 'prize works' in major world-class art galleries. All his works are admired for the sensitivity with which he rendered effects of light and colour and for the poetic quality of his images.

> Vermeer gained little recognition in his lifetime, even though he was master painter and headman to the Guild of St Luke in Delft. He did, however, succeed in making a living from his painting during his lifetime – unlike many other artists.

Vermeer's *Girl with a Pearl Earring*

An unlikely star?

Unlike the great Italian painter Michelangelo's work, Vermeer's small, detailed scenes of Dutch domestic life do not 'leap off' the walls of galleries and amaze you. Unlike Caravaggio (Italian painter, 1571–1610), whose turbulent and sensual life is reflected in his paintings, Vermeer does not reveal anything of his personality in his pictures (except perhaps that he was neat and thorough and engrossed by the everyday). Yet Vermeer's work created a cultural phenomenon when a special, 'greatest ever' exhibition was announced in the mid-1990s. This was a showing of the greatest number of surviving Vermeer works ever gathered together. It took place at The Hague in his home country, The Netherlands. Tickets were snapped up months before the show opened. Why?

Performances and pictures

Fine art differs from other art forms in the way it is shown and sold. With performance arts (drama, music, dance, film) the assumption is that artists want their work to be available to as wide an audience as possible. Film is the most accessible. Once a film is 'in the can' it can be transported easily and shown relatively cheaply in any cinema in the world. After decades of declining audience figures, cinema in the UK is on a roll of popularity. Audience figures are up enormously from say the 1980s. More and better cinemas are being built.

Live events – theatre, dance and music – generally cost more than film to see. There are fewer theatres and concert venues around the country, but most people are within range of one for a night out. The assumption is that artists and performers want to perform to the public, as many of them as possible.

Painting is different. The work of very famous painters, usually of painters long dead, is bought by trusts and museums and displayed for the public to see in public galleries in major cities. Or not. Some end up in the hands of private collectors, others in the boardrooms of large companies. The paintings are not for sale. Many are worth millions.

But the works of most living painters trying to establish their careers are shown in private galleries. These are essentially shops that exhibit paintings for sale. Most private gallery owners say they welcome the public in, but their business is selling. The work of even a middle ranking modern painter slowly developing a reputation can cost thousands. Galleries want to attract the sort of people who can afford that sort of money, so many appear quite up-market places, daunting to the passer-by who wants to go in and look at a few pictures with no intention of ever buying.

Public taste

The public are often accused by artists and art critics of failing to understand and appreciate modern art. These people seem to forget that for the average member of the public it is much easier to see traditional paintings, as they are bought and exhibited by public galleries and museums. (Curators spending public money, taxpayers' money, don't like to risk buying modern paintings by artists who may not yet have established a reputation.)

But the public do like looking at pictures. Art galleries are some of the top tourist attractions in the world's major cities. Go to famous galleries like the Louvre in Paris, the Metropolitan in New York or the Uffizi in Florence and every room will be jam packed. Most people go to see the standard collections that these galleries have acquired. Galleries don't like sending very valuable paintings off for exhibits abroad. Generally speaking the tourists go to the painting, not the other way round! Insurance costs for paintings that are hundreds of years old and worth millions are enormous. When the Vermeer paintings that were owned by American galleries were being flown to The Hague each painting travelled on a separate plane. If there were a crash, only one painting would be lost.

Stars on tour

Despite these cost problems, many galleries were prepared through the 1980s and 1990s to mount big exhibitions of works gathered together from round the world. The reason was that the public seemed to have a growing appetite for queuing for hours and paying quite a lot of money as an entry fee to crowded exhibitions of world class art. Sometimes it was the work of a single painter, sometimes paintings of a school of artists or particular period.

The major exhibition of Pre-Raphaelite art in London in the late 1980s was possibly the first 'big hit'. The newspapers took photos of queues snaking all round the gallery. There was a slight sense that everyone had been surprised by the public demand to see the pictures. But the Pre-Raphaelite artists painted very accessible paintings, and their works had been reprinted on posters that had been best-sellers among a whole generation of students. At least some of the paintings were well known before the exhibition opened.

Then the special exhibition idea just seemed to grow and grow. Travelling exhibitions were lavishly advertised. The public were advised to buy tickets well in advance, strictly for entry at a specific hour on a specific day to keep the crowds moving. Galleries were making big money, though most of this was needed to pay the huge insurance fees demanded to allow the masterpieces to be hung in public. The big exhibitions became something to talk about having seen, or having got tickets for. A cultural version of the 'big match' in many ways.

TIPS FOR FURTHER RESEARCH

Visit your local municipal (or nearest major) art gallery and either discuss or write up the experience. Has it altered your view on art?

Vermeer's *Maid with Milk Jug*

But Vermeer was still the biggest surprise. His works are small and needed careful study. His paintings use symbols to add extra meaning. Although traditional, these various symbols were obscure to most members of the public not familiar with the iconography of paintings. For example, Vermeer might include an apple, which can be used to refer to the Bible, or a snake, which symbolizes the devil. An apple and a snake together therefore symbolize the temptation that exists between god and the devil.

The right reasons?

Vermeer's paintings are 'quiet' and many people who trudged round the packed galleries at The Hague struggled to catch a glimpse of the 30 or so small canvases. Many people criticized the public for creating a demand in which the paintings had to be seen in this way.

TIPS FOR FURTHER RESEARCH

Look up Henricus van Meegeren. What contribution do you think his forgeries made to the establishment of Vermeer's reputation?

Other more formal and 'serious' critics complained that the public were flocking to the paintings for the 'wrong reasons': they were attracted by the fuss the media had drummed up, by the event rather than the pictures. This may have been true: some people go to cultural events for all sorts of reasons not directly linked to a burning desire to see the event. Some people go to the opera just to be seen by other people.

People also go to things because they might experience something new, discover an area of human creativity they didn't know about before. This learning experience might be purely incidental, it might even surprise the person. If the Vermeer exhibition in The Hague surprised even a few people who took advantage of the package deals that were offered at the time (a couple of days enjoying Holland with guaranteed tickets to the exhibition), surely that's a good thing.

Of course the one person whose answer would really be worth hearing is Vermeer, but he's not around. Given the quiet life he led and the placid style of his paintings, he would certainly have been surprised by the crowds that thronged The Hague to look at his works.

Questions for discussion

1. Do you think there is always a right or wrong reason for going to a creative or cultural event?

2. Paintings are worth money because people buy and sell them. They are unique objects: there is only ever one original. What are the problems and advantages of having creative works worth so much money?

3. Why do you think so many people who never go to a gallery at home spend time on their holidays going round galleries abroad?

4. Have there been any cultural events in the last couple of years that have become more important as events than for the art or performance itself.

5. Why do you think that large companies and corporations buy works of art?

Questions for written answer

Examiners will look for the following in your written answer:

• Evidence that you have understood the source material and can make appropriate use of it.
• You need to be able to make value judgements based on it and support these with evidence or interpretation.
• You need to have something of your own to say and to be able to state it clearly.
• You need to show you can relate this work to other relevant areas of study.

1. Can great works of art (paintings, drama, poems, etc.) from the past teach us anything about the present? Why should people go and look at things created hundreds of years ago in a very different world? Pick an artist or a type of art (painting, drama, etc.) and say what, if anything, about the work still has relevance, and why.

2. Good marketing is essential to any cultural event. Without publicity there is unlikely to be an audience! But too much demand can destroy the quality of the event. Do you think 'bums on seats' at any price is the best way, or should the number of people who can attend an event be deliberately limited? Why? How would you restrict attendance? Give examples of how your ideas might work for different types of event.

3. Are there right and wrong, good and bad, reasons for attending cultural events? Can you identify any general principles, and give particular

examples. (Think about 'corporate tickets', where companies buy up the best seats for a show to give to visiting clients, etc.)

4. Any art form is only a form of entertainment. As such they are of no use to society. Discuss this view with reference to more than one art form.

5. Modern art is often criticized for not being 'art' at all, except in the eyes of critics. What, therefore, is art? Do you think that there can ever be an objective view of art, or is it always going to be subjective?

? Quiz

1. What are Vermeer's dates?

2. Who was Caravaggio?

3. Where was the Vermeer Exhibition held?

4. What is van Meegeren famous for?

5. Name three famous art galleries.

A CTIVITY

A hoard of very early photographs depicting scenes in your town have been discovered. They are unusual because there are so many of them showing every aspect of life in mid-Victorian England, and because the photographer was both very talented and a woman (in a time when almost all photographers were men).

The council are sending the photos on a national tour. They hope the tour will make money! Imagine you are planning publicity for the tour. What could the attraction of the photos be to the general public? How would you make them sound like something worth paying money to visit? Think about targeting different types of potential visitor? Make notes of your ideas.

What types of support material (catalogues, educational material, etc.) could be produced for such a collection of pictures? Make notes of your ideas.

Use a computer program to produce a page (or more) from such a catalogue.

Why do we put people in prison?

Preview

Every country in the world operates some sort of penal system, whereby people who break the law are punished for their crimes, usually by being put in prison. Being incarcerated is not just a removal of liberty: it has been argued at various times that prison is supposed to deter, reform, to punish in some degree or other, and remove a wrong-doer from the rest of law-abiding society.

But do we take the idea of sending wrong-doers to jail for granted? How exactly is it justified? Does it work? And what are our real reasons for locking people away?

The American model

Britain is said to enjoy a 'special relationship' with the USA in many aspects of life. This dates from the Second World War when British and American forces fought side by side to defeat Fascism. We are closely joined to America politically. We are influenced by American culture far more than most other European countries.

America sends a greater percentage of its population to jail than any other Western nation, and imposes generally longer sentences for crimes. The government in the UK in the 1990s advocated more custodial sentences by courts and demanded a growth in building new prisons. Are we following the way America has gone? Does this make it even more important to be clear about exactly why we want to send law-breakers to jail?

The 'three Rs' – justifications for punishment

Punishing criminals is an emotive issue and it is sometimes hard to think logically about the reasons for jailing a person who has committed some shocking crime. There are some basic reasons that have been used to justify the prison system. Let's begin by looking at three possible justifications. We will start with the most emotive, reactive and simplest justification and end with the most generous and liberal one.

- Retribution – this argument says simply that society needs to 'get its own back' on people who abuse it by breaking the agreed rules or laws. It is a legalized form of revenge: indeed the victims of crime, or their relatives, are often reported as saying 'justice has been done' at the end of the trial where

Judges have a range of sentences, ranging from the size of a fine to the number of years to be spent in jail, which they can administer if a prisoner is found guilty. They can decide not only whether or not to jail someone, but can take the circumstances of the crime into consideration when imposing a 'light' or 'heavy' sentence.

the wrong-doer is sent to jail. It is a condition of this argument that jail is at least uncomfortable, preferably unpleasant, so that retribution is exacted.

- Redress – this argument is a slightly less direct, less easily emotion-filled version of retribution. Instead of focusing on the individual criminal and victim, it looks at the whole of society. People function in societies only by agreeing to obey rules. When a criminal breaks the basic social rules, they take what is not theirs, harm innocent people, etc. If they are seen to get away with this, or, if caught, receive only minimal punishment, then the balance of rules and freedoms that make society work is seen to have broken down. For this argument to work the punishment must be fair, and must reflect the severity of the crime. The punishment must be seen by others in society so that it will act as a warning, and make the law-abiding feel right in their decision to remain so.

- Rehabilitation – this is the most 'forgiving' theory for justifying a penal system. Prison should punish by taking away liberty, but it should not brutalize by being a cruel place. Instead, it should encourage criminals to learn new skills, to come to see the error of their ways, and to become, when they leave prison, better people with more chance to succeed in society. The balance between prison as a place of cruel restrictions and a place where inmates can attend adult learning classes, etc., has been an ongoing issue in the Prison Service, in government and society generally for generations. As conditions in most prisons have gradually 'softened' over the years, some people have complained that prisons have become more like hotels.

So, it seems there is no shortage of good reasons to justify sending people to prison for breaking the law. But let's look again at these three common arguments.

A traditional English courtroom scene from the film *10 Rillington Place*

'White collar' crime (such as tax evasion, insurance fraud, accountancy and company fraud) are often given 'white collar' sentences – shorter prison sentences and 'time' served in an open prison. On the other hand, some crimes (particularly those involving children and sex) are seen as so terrible that a guilty party may have to be segregated from other prisoners.

The 'three Rs' – a few problems

- Retribution – we see the wrong doer 'get their just desserts' and it makes us feel good. But does this justify satisfying a society's or an individual's anger? The criminal is unlikely to emerge from jail wanting to be a better person, wanting to fit into a society that took away their freedom simply to 'get their own back'.

  How far do you go in making the punishment fit the crime? If we believe in retribution, encoded in a state system, the way could be open for all sorts of ghastly punishments to really make people feel retribution is being handed out. The Old Testament urges 'eye for eye, tooth for tooth'. Islamic Sharia law specifies symbolic punishments such as cutting off the hands of thieves. America, having a death penalty that is used more and more regularly, appears to see a fair trade-off in killing murderers.

  Given that in a civilized society it is generally considered unacceptable to inflict on the criminal the same sort of pain or anguish they inflicted on their victim, a balance has to be struck between the severity of the crime and the amount of the criminal's life that will be spent in jail 'paying' for their misdeeds. Again, victims of crime and their relatives often feel this trade-off is never going to be fair, and are often heard urging the prison to 'lock them [the criminal] up and throw away the key'.

- Redress – for redress to be a valid argument for punishing criminals, the link between the crime and the degree or type of punishment must be clear, and seen by everyone to be fair and justified. But people have argued for generations about which crimes should incur what kinds and degree of punishments. Rarely has any agreement been reached. Some criminals who have stolen big sums of money have been given longer sentences than some murderers. There are always elements of society who want harsher punishments across the whole range of crimes, while others take a more moderate view.

  Given the complex circumstances surrounding most crimes, it is impossible for society to watch the judicial system in action and say that it is working well in every case, demonstrating clear redress by society against those who break its rules. With the possible exception of fines imposed then paid to victims to replace money extracted or stolen by the criminal (where figures might be 'made to balance'), redress as a justification doesn't really work.

- Rehabilitation – the evidence from some research has shown that most people who go to prison re-offend, often pretty quickly. Only a small minority of prisoners are rehabilitated by their experience of prison. In fact some people argue that, far from offering a chance of rehabilitation, prison provides a perfect training ground for young criminals, giving them the opportunity to meet and learn from older habitual criminals.

WEB LINKS

Check the web for the Howard League for Penal Reform, a group that focuses on prison issues and prisoners' interests. Both The Red Cross and Amnesty International also concern themselves with the conditions in which prisoners are held.

Revenge wins the day

That leaves retribution or revenge as the only operating justification of the three so far discussed. Yet most people would feel a bit uncomfortable in saying that the whole system of punishing wrong-doers is, ultimately, based on society's simple desire to 'get its own back'. It doesn't sound very civilized. But you can't just let people commit crimes and be seen to go unpunished. Society would quickly collapse.

Another option is to say that prison acts as a deterrent. People contemplating breaking the law see what happens to those who do, and stop! It sounds good, but then, in theory at least, there are no safeguards in this system. You could punish anyone to any degree of severity, as a warning to others. You could choose someone who may or may not have actually committed a crime, but who will, for whatever reasons of character or position, really act as a warning when they are punished. A society that is held together by fear not agreement will eventually rebel or become unhealthy and destroy itself. The chance for civil liberties to be abused under a punishment system based purely on deterrent is huge.

Camp X – America's terrorist prison – ancient or modern?

In America, many sentences are reduced by the practice of 'plea bargaining'. An accused either gives evidence or otherwise co-operates with an investigation in order to face reduced charges or sentence. In some cases, evidence is considered so valuable that an accused might be given immunity from prosecution.

Watch someone die?

Some societies have less of a problem stating that their prison system is designed to make life visibly unpleasant for those who break its laws. They may even be maimed or executed for certain crimes. This can be done publicly as a special warning to others. In America there must be witnesses to the carrying out of a death sentence, and relatives of victims of the condemned person's crimes are sometimes invited to sit in and see 'justice being done'.

We may shrink away from what we regard as such barbaric practices, but ultimately the retribution or revenge on which they are founded is the one justification for punishing criminals that operates with the best logic. This also means that the system will come under pressure to be more severe, more visible in causing distress to the criminal, as society reacts with shock and outrage to new crimes. If we accept the somewhat basic, even potentially bloody, justification of revenge as the basis for a criminal justice system, then at least we can take care to look out for forces that try to make it more vengeful.

Questions for discussion

1. Which of the three 'r's in the article do you think provides the best general justification for punishing criminals?

2. Should prison be a harsh and punishing experience? How harsh? What practical things should go on there?

3. Brainstorm a list of rules you think fair to impose on adult prisoners serving sentences for 'middle-weight' offences (robbery of large sums of money, actual bodily harm, repeated car stealing, forgery, etc.). Think about access to communications to the outside, visitors, level of privacy or surveillance, etc.

4. Do you think murderers should be punished differently from other types of criminal? Why?

Questions for written answer

1. In the UK most punishment of criminals consists of locking then up in cells for up to 23 hours a day. Is this a good use of their time and the government's money? How else could prisoners be punished? Think about ways that might involve less public cost, or better use of the prisoners' time. Think about different types of prisons. Give full reasons for your ideas.

2. 'If the penal system was harsh and sentences known to be long, people would think twice about breaking the law.' Do you think this is true? Make a detailed case to either support the statement, or to argue that the causes of why people commit crimes need to be looked at before the way we go about punishing them.

3. Should the same crime, e.g. assault, always incur the same punishment? If the sentence varies, this could lead to claims of unfairness or victimization. Imagine you were a judge. Brainstorm a list of things that might influence

Examiners will look for the following in your written answer:

- Evidence that you have understood the source material and can make appropriate use of it.
- You need to be able to make value judgements based on it and support these with evidence or interpretation.
- You need to have something of your own to say and to be able to state it clearly.
- You need to show you can relate this work to other relevant areas of study.

the sentence you would hand out if the following guilty cases come up before you: a man convicted of fighting outside a pub at closing time, a woman caught shoplifting, a man who has worked out a way to defraud car insurance companies, and a man caught writing racist graffiti. (Use your imagination to build up possible details of the crimes, the characters and histories of the people involved.)

4. One American law is called 'three strikes and you're out' meaning that the sentence for a third crime committed – however petty – will be 25 years to life. Another law, giving householders the right to shoot intruders dead is called the 'make my day' law. In your opinion, how important is it for (a) judges to have freedom of choice when sentencing and (b) criminals to be brought to justice rather than have summary justice meted out on them?

ACTIVITY

You need groups of four people for this activity.

- As a whole group discuss the death penalty. Think about the effect it can have as a deterrent, the various ways it could be carried out, what might happen if there is a miscarriage of justice, etc.

- Now role-play two couples. Andy and Jane are British tourists visiting America. They meet Josh and Cathy, an American couple. They end up discussing the death penalty. Josh and Cathy think it is a good thing and that Britain should have it. Andy and Jane disagree.

- Devise a scene in which they discuss their views. (Think about gender possibilities: would women be more forgiving, less vengeful than men?)

08 The man who was Private Widdle

Preview

'The Man Who Was Private Widdle' is the eye-catching title of a newspaper review of a book published in the autumn of 2001, a biography of Charles Hawtrey. Hawtrey was an actor who was one of the longest serving members of the cast who played in nearly 30 *Carry On* films. He was a Victorian army private – Private Widdle – in the film *Carry On Up The Khyber*, in which the 'stiff upper lip' British do battle with the 'native ruler' the Kharsi of Kalabar. 'Kharsi' was 1960s slang for toilet: toilet–widdle, geddit? Welcome to the world of *Carry On* films.

What makes us say something is funny? Why does so much old humour get recycled? As a nation, are we predisposed to a certain sort of humour? Or do we laugh at what we are given?

Carrying on ...

In fact, for more or less the same reasons as another, better-known *Carry On* regular, Kenneth Williams, Hawtrey's life is depressing and rather thin material for a biographer. Like Williams, Hawtrey believed that the formulaic, smutty farce style of the *Carry On* films was an insult to him. But they both needed the money. Both were also homosexual, and oddly camp, at a time when gay men were either mocked or loathed by British society. At the time, gay sex, even between consenting adults, was an illegal and imprisonable offence.

Charles Hawtrey and Hattie Jacques in a scene from *Carry On Matron*

WEB LINKS

www.carryonline.com/ – home of the Carry On films.

www.carryonlaughing.co.uk/ presents a personal view of the genre.

Carry On Sergeant was the first of the *Carry On* film series, released in 1958. It is described by Leslie Halliwell, in his definitive and encyclopaedic guide to films, as, 'A shabby farce with humdrum script and slack direction, saved by energetic performances', a damning observation that pretty much sums up the views of serious film critics to the whole series. The films always seemed curiously outdated, their view of the world hopelessly at odds with what really existed. The lead characters were usually grotesque exaggerations – leering men, sexually repressed matrons and mincing, effeminate men never actually identified as gay – the sort of figures that might have appeared in musical halls, a form of live entertainment that had all but died out when the film series started.

And on ...

Yet the biography of Kenneth Williams was something of a publishing event when it came out in the mid-1990s. It was widely reviewed in newspapers and was discussed on arts talk shows on BBC radio. The whole *Carry On* series was released on video in the late 1990s. *Carry On* films are still shown on television (although no longer in prime-time slots). In 2000, ITV broadcast a two-hour drama on the (generally unhappy) working and private lives of several of the *Carry On* regulars – including, to sum up their usual roles, the lewd, sexually predatory Sid James, the 'dim-witted man-mountain' Bernard Breslaw and bubbly, big-breasted 'sex bomb' Barbara Windsor (now a television soap opera queen in *EastEnders*).

This was a series of cheaply made films that were generally poorly reviewed when they first came out, were thought by almost everyone to have lost all contact with public taste long before the series finally gave up the ghost in the early 1970s, and featured a bunch of actors who were both unhappy with what they were doing but hopelessly locked into the routine of churning out on average two *Carry On* films a year. So why the media fuss in the 1990s? Why does anyone watch a *Carry On* film in the new millennium?

Irony

Humour is intensely personal. It is impossible to persuade someone to genuinely laugh at something they just don't intuitively find amusing. Much has been written about the nature of humour, from learned philosophical investigations to observations by comedians into what works to make an audience laugh.

Many people explain the continuing interest in such dated and disconnected (to current popular culture) humour as is found in the *Carry On* films on a sophisticated sense of irony. 'Of course,' we can say, 'these films are shoddy, full

Radio comedies were the precursors of many of the most successful TV comedy shows. Kenneth Horne's *Round the Horne*, Peter Cook and Dudley Moore's dialogues and *I'm Sorry I'll Read That Again* (with a cast including Tim Brooke-Taylor, Graeme Garden, Jo Kendall and John Cleese) were all hugely successful despite never being able to do any visual gags. Conversely, great comedians like Charlie Chaplin had to rely almost totally on sight gags.

Barbara Windsor, from *Carry On* to soap star

of dated and limp sexual innuendo, the acting is weak and the technical competence of the crew questionable. But that's the whole point! The things we genuinely find funny are a million miles away from this creaky farce, but the act of indulging ourselves in this rubbish is what makes the rubbish funny. When we say we find a camp little actor playing a character called Private Widdle amusing, we are being ironic, which is itself a form of humour.'

'Cultural glue'

Comedy, especially television comedy that probably gains a viewing audience of millions, is a key part of the 'cultural glue' that binds together and succinctly epitomizes eras in popular culture. Great works of art may endure whole shifts in culture and keep their freshness and appeal over centuries, but comedy too can have some sort of life after the first laugh. But it changes, and so does our relationship to it. A catch-phrase first becomes out of date; then it becomes part of our nostalgia.

Nostalgia makes the humour of our childhood and youth seem funnier than it might actually be, because we remember it from first time around and feel some ownership of it. This is an easier explanation than a sophisticated sense of irony for the continuing interest in *Carry On* films, except that some people who watch them now were not born when the last in the series was released.

Real life

British comedy films have always appeared out of touch with the real world. Until the recent past, they leant too heavily on exaggeration of character. They were usually cheaply made. In the case of the *Carry On* films, this has one passing benefit. They give us a sporadic but interesting view of Britain from the

Shakespeare's *The Taming of The Shrew* in which Katharina is taught to be pliant and dutiful and *The Merchant of Venice* in which a black-hearted Jew gets his comeuppance at the hands of noble Christians are both billed as 'comedies'. Why were they seen as comedies in Shakespeare's time? Would they be comedies today?

What is your favourite joke? Tell it to a friend who hasn't heard it before. Now come up with a joke that has no sexist, racist or other politically incorrect characters or themes. Is this possible?

late 1950s through to the early 1970s. Made gross by exaggeration certain attitudes in the film might be, but they do reflect some starting point in actual public thinking and feeling of the time. Britain was a tight-lipped and dourly reactive and puritanical society for most of the so-called 'swinging sixties'. Flower power and all the rest may have happened in London and a few other cities, but the world of Saturday-night pictures, dreary pubs and young women in tasteless versions of 'swinging' fashions was the reality for most young people growing up in most provincial towns in the 1960s. Because they couldn't afford specially constructed sets, *Carry On* films, and the even more sexually lewd *Confessions of …* series of 'sex romps', were shot on location and snap-shot what the country really looked like at domestic and street level.

National humour?

Now we are much more sophisticated. We watch huge amounts of American television comedy. Every angle on the situation comedy has been exploited: every permutation of family, house-sharers, neighbours and work colleagues has been used as a vehicle for television comedy.

And yet so much has not changed. As a nation, we still like humour that deals with toilets and bodily functions. When it comes to sex, the writing in most television comedies is still of the 'nudge nudge' dirty joke type. A gay man is usually camp and used as an easy vehicle for lots of 'gay jokes', and presumably people do laugh because the device is still used. Really different comedy programmes are very rare, but their effect tends to be long lasting.

Americans cannot understand our love of farting and bottom jokes. Recently an English journalist speaking on American public broadcasting radio ('serious' radio) was trying to explain why British readers find *Viz* magazine so funny. The American host was literally unable to comprehend why 'Johnny Fartpants – there's always a commotion in his underwear' was so funny, nor why 'Brits' fall about at the antics of the Gestapo-like Bottom Inspectors.

Americans are also largely confused by our love of absurdist humour. This really started with *Monty Python* in the late 1960s. Many other programmes have extended the surreal humour this show began. Americans have never attempted to copy it.

Now we apparently watch *Carry On* films in an ironic way, and *Monty Python* because it is still genuinely funny and influenced other absurdist shows still being made. This, and toilets and farting, is the mainstay of our national humour perhaps. We also watch 'wise-cracking' American comedy which generally avoids two things that have been characteristic to the style of our humour: slapstick/physical violence and sexual innuendo.

Our comedy programme makers don't seek to imitate *Frasier* or *Seinfeld*, two hugely popular American shows. There is clearly a national taste in humour operating. Apart from anything else, these two American shows are 'star vehicles' for their leading actors. In Britain, it seems we care less about the star than the characters they create.

TIPS FOR FURTHER
RESEARCH

Investigate what is currently seen as 'funny' on the stage, at the cinema, and on the television. Try reading an ancient Greek comedy like Aristophanes' *The Birds* (set in CloudCuckooLand). What devices are used by the writer? Do they still work?

CULTURE, MORALITY, ARTS AND HUMANITIES

Questions for discussion

1. Think of a television or film comedy that you have found funny. Can you say what the key elements of it are that make it amusing to you? (Think about plot, characters, style, performances, etc.)

2. Discuss and give examples of how the following can be used to create comedy:
   • mistaken identity
   • confusion of purpose
   • jokes and punch lines
   • comedy based on a clash of cultures, beliefs or opinions
   • physical acting and appearance.

3. What makes a good joke? Think about creating a sense of anticipation in the listener, looking at something in an absurd way, taking some little trait or thing that happens in the real world and blowing it up to absurd extremes, etc. Make a list of key ingredients for good jokes.

4. Apart from *Carry On* films, can you think of other examples of humour, shows or characters from the past that still have appeal, to you or to the public generally? Discuss why you think the appeal still holds. Do you think the show/character is still liked today for the same reasons that made them popular years ago?

5. Why do you think that someone suffering physical hurt is often seen as funny? Examples could include 'person falling down an open manhole'; 'person hit with a plank'; object (e.g. paint pot, hammer, bucket of water) being dropped on person. Extreme violence of this kind is often seen in cartoons (such as *Tom and Jerry, Sylvester and Tweety Pie*). Why does this make it more acceptable (but still funny)?

Questions for written answer

Examiners will look for the following in your written answer:

• Evidence that you have understood the source material and can make appropriate use of it.
• You need to be able to make value judgements based on it and support these with evidence or interpretation.
• You need to have something of your own to say and to be able to state it clearly.
• You need to show you can relate this work to other relevant areas of study.

1. Are there only so many things it is possible to laugh at, and ways to make things funny? Has television and film used up all the good ones, and will new comedy really just be new versions of old ideas? Identify, describe and explain 'standard' comic ideas or themes.

2. How does comedy fit into popular culture? What can it reveal about society? How can it connect to public life and thought? Pick examples of current popular comedy (especially television and film) and examine what they might reveal about contemporary society.

3. 'All comedy is cruel.' Do you think this is true? How can comedy be cruel? Give examples. Are there some things that it would be 'too cruel' to make into the subject of humour? What are they and why should we not use them in comedy?

4. Why, in a world of almost instant global communications and cultures that cross frontiers, should there still be national characteristics in comedy? Think of how popular culture reflects society and explain your ideas. Or do you think there is only one type of humour now, that appeals to people across the world?

Quiz

1. Name five actors who were regulars in *Carry On* films.

2. What were the usual roles for each of the five?

3. What was the first *Carry On* film and when was it released?

4. When was the last *Carry On* film made?

5. Shakespeare wrote 12 comedies (divided into early, middle and 'dark' comedies). How many can you name?

6. Describe what is meant by irony.

7. What is said to make the humour of our childhood funnier?

8. What is meant by a 'situation comedy'?

9. Who or what is *Viz*?

10. Name three successful early radio comedy programmes.

Activity

- In small groups, give examples of times when you have been watching a comedy programme or film and found it almost unbearable to see a character do something totally embarrassing or self-destructive. How do these moments operate? Why is it so painful to watch, when you know the character is only an actor playing a part in a script?

- Two things tend to happen at moments like this. First we put ourselves in the place of the character and imagine how awful to would be if we behaved in the way they are. Secondly, the character is usually breaking some 'unspoken rule' of behaviour, or is blind to something that all the other characters can see.

- Devise a short scene to illustrate this sort of painful embarrassment. Set the scene, make a short cast list (no more than four characters), then make brief notes describing what happens.

- Use the notes to rehearse and develop the scene.

- A small group should play the scene to the rest of your class or group to see if they find it funny.

09 The 'creative industries': a career choice?

Preview

The image of hundreds of men streaming out of a big factory at the end of the shift now almost belongs to history in this country. Once, Britain was the world's most industrialized nation, now, apart from a few car plants, some steel mills and a couple of ship-yards struggling on, heavy industry has disappeared from huge areas of the UK. Where it does linger, mechanization and robots have vastly reduced the number of men working together in manual labour. For young men leaving school in particular, the change has been profound. Britain at the start of the twenty-first century has a thriving, although to some people confusing, post-industrial economy based heavily on creative and service industries.

What do we do now?

Job and career opportunities have changed enormously in the space of one or two generations. The decline of labour-intensive, heavy manual jobs has contributed to equality between the sexes in many areas of work. The major employer in a medium-sized British town is more likely to be a call centre than a factory. Tourism is a huge employer, as is catering. But many jobs in these sectors are low-skill and badly paid, leading one famous American economist to coin the term a 'McJob': low paid and with little chance of meaningful promotion. Social observers and politicians may argue that people today are pleased to be defined by the job they do and are generally working in situations where equality and responsibility are valued, but for many workers on the national minimum wage, this just isn't true.

But some people, especially young people, have decided on a more dynamic approach to their career by joining an area of employment known as the 'creative industries'. These are broadly professions with a core creative element:

The music industry offers a range of creative careers

Table 1 *The creative industries – UK national overview (1998)*

Industry sector	Estimated revenue (£ millions)	Numbers employed
Advertising	4000	96,000
Architecture	1500	30,000
Arts and antiques	2200	39,700
Crafts	400	25,000
Design	12,000	23,000
Designer fashion	600	11,500
Film	900	33,000
Interactive leisure software	1200	27,000
Music	3600	160,000
Performing arts	900	60,000
Publishing	16,300	125,000
Software	7500	272,000
TV and radio	6400	63,500
Total	£57 billion	~1 million

(*Source*: Department of Culture Media and Science, Creative Industries Mapping Document, 1998.)

ranging from artists making pictures, writing books or playing music at one extreme, to designers thinking creatively to build new computer software at the other. Government research defined the 'creative industries' as those industries that have their origin in individual creativity, skill and talent, which have the potential for wealth and job creation through the exploitation of creative property.

Often people go into these areas of work to harness skills and interests they already have. The term 'industry', suggesting monolithic profit-driven companies, may at first seem inappropriate to say, running a recording studio or designing furniture, but think about these few general figures:

- In 1998 in the UK, the creative industries generated revenue of approximately £60 billion – far more than any old-style manufacturing industry.

- Four per cent of the country's economy is driven by the creative industries.

- It is the fastest growing sector of the economy (in terms of money earned and jobs created).

- By 2000, over one-and-a-half million people worked in the creative industries.

Table 1 lists what the term 'creative industry' broadly defines, and shows how much each sector earned and how many people they employed.

It sounds too good to be true! Here is government research basically praising young people for developing their own creative interests. Visits to the Careers Adviser will never be the same again. You think being a DJ is a good career move: government research thinks so too. Forget about a job at the local insurance company! Learn to design new computer games! Work can be creative, and fun!

But in 1999 the government was so worried about what might happen to this most successful area of the economy that it set up a task force to investigate a problem that was looming on the horizon.

Skills shortage

The problem was that many organizations in the creative industries could not find the number of trained young people they needed to help them expand and develop. People just didn't leave school knowing how to operate a sound recording studio. They did not have the right sort of IT skills, such as how to use industry-standard desktop publishing systems like Quark. The task force reported that if the creative industries continued growing at the rate they were, there would be a huge skills shortage. Young people, exactly the sort of people who would be attracted to the generally more relaxed and informal style of workplace typical in the creative industries, just weren't getting the training they needed. Worse, many didn't even know, weren't being told, that the creative industries were a career option.

TIPS FOR FURTHER RESEARCH

Investigate ways of surveying the creative industries on your local area. Contact local Business Enterprise Councils, Chambers of Commerce, etc. for listings of local companies, then identify which of them fit in the categories included in the creative industries sector table.

No more apprentices

A generation or two ago, many young men became apprentices when they left school. They basically learnt a trade – plumbing, cabinet-making, ship-building – by working alongside an older experienced tradesman. For other types of employment, people went to special post-16 training schools or colleges. Many women trained as secretaries and hairdressers in this way. Why don't the creative industries train their own new workers? Why don't colleges offer appropriate courses?

The answer to the first question is that the typical firm in the creative industries sector is very small, sometimes just a person working alone as an artist, photographer, etc., sometimes just a small group of people working in an open-plan workshop designing software, clothes, furniture. They don't have the resources to take time to train people.

At the high-tech end of the creative industries, time is definitely money. Even a basic professional grade-recording studio has tens of thousands of pounds worth of equipment in it and it has to earn money. Studios cost from £50 to many thousands of pounds an hour, and it isn't viable to shut them to customers and train a couple of new inexperienced young people to be sound engineers one day a week.

A further problem with firms within the creative industries sector providing regular and standardized training is that they often operate on a contract-to-contract basis. Being small, often riding precariously on the wave of fashion or innovation – and perhaps because they are managed by people who are more creative than business orientated! – they don't want to be tied down to offering regular training. Much of the creative industries' success is down to speed, in delivering new ideas to customers, exploiting technology, etc., and training young people in the basics just isn't so exciting.

New college courses

Colleges are trying to meet the challenge. But it takes time for a college to set up a course, even if they can find a partner from the local creative industries to help them. The high-tech creative industries use equipment that is cutting edge, specialized and usually very expensive, and colleges often do not have the resources to provide it for training.

And maybe, just maybe, hidden somewhere in the minds of perhaps older teachers, lecturers, parents and society as a whole, is the idea that a course training people to be DJs or sound mixers in a music recording studio is not 'real education'. Maybe, they think, this is all just fashion, and the possibility of making a living from this sort of work will not exist for very long. Using computers to build new games software can't be a serious learning experience! It's just too much fun to be proper career training!

WEB LINKS

The DCMS (Department of Culture Media and Science) has published several major papers and reports on the creative industries and extracts from these appear on various DCMS websites: www.open.gov-dcms

But all the evidence suggests that people who hold these views will have to change their minds. British music earns far more in 'exports' that many old-style manufacturing industries, but it is still hard for some people to see that British-run clubs in Ibiza and Ayia Napa are more valuable to our economy than some old 'metal-bashing' firm struggling to export products in the face of world competition. It is hard to realize that more people earn a living from making curry in the UK than from building cars.

Someone, incidentally, worked out that the amount of chicken tikka masala consumed in Britain in an average year would fill six supertankers, and that if all the poppadoms eaten annually were put on one plate, the pile would reach to the moon! These comic images are actually based on hard economic research, and are another example, like the creative industries, of people failing to realize just how big a sector of the 'new' economy, in this case Indian catering, can grow. It's not until someone does some serious research that changes in the economic make-up of the country are revealed.

Questions for discussion

1. Look at the list of creative industries in the table. Are there any that you don't think fit the description? Have some professions been left out that you think should be part of the sector? Discuss your ideas.

2. In the 1970s someone conducted a survey, asking year 11 school students what their favourite out-of-school activity was. It was listening to music. When the same students were asked what their least favourite school subject was, it was music. Why do you think this was? How could the creative industries as a career choice today help students see school subjects differently? How do school subjects need to change?

3. What are the possible dangers for a young person's career of working for a small, informal creative company that surfs from contract to contract, as opposed to settling for a job in bank?

Questions for written answer

1. If Britain manufactures less and less, and more people are employed in the creative, service and financial services sectors, how does the economy keep going? Where do the things we have in our homes, etc. come from? How does this new sort of economy work? Discuss your ideas, then write an essay explaining how Britain's economy operates as part of a larger global one.

2. Should colleges invest in courses and expensive equipment to try and train potential entrants to the creative industries? What are the risks for colleges? Should the firms within the sector be forced to realize that they have to do their own training? How could they provide this? Discuss your ideas, then write an essay giving both sides of the argument for and against college based, therefore publicly funded, training for the creative industries.

Examiners will look for the following in your written answer:

- Evidence that you have understood the source material and can make appropriate use of it.
- You need to be able to make value judgements based on it and support these with evidence or interpretation.
- You need to have something of your own to say and to be able to state it clearly.
- You need to show you can relate this work to other relevant areas of study.

ACTIVITY 1

You will need either three or six people for this role-playing activity. You are going to devise two short dramas, each based on an interview.

In the first it is Britain in the 1960s. Hogsbreathe & Dimmock, paint manufacturers, are interviewing a candidate for a vacancy in the paint development department of this 100-year-old firm. The research offices are above the factory. The candidate is to be interviewed by two people from the firm:

- the personnel manager (who will say things like 'a uniform is provided and this is a steady job for life')
- the paint research manager ('we don't want anything too modern or unusual').

The candidate really wants/needs the job.

Role-play the scene, bringing out the differences between characters by exaggeration.

The other scene is in the present: an interview for new, highly style conscious company, Zingbatz, that digitally manipulate photographs, etc. on computers. The two interviewers are:

- the company's incredibly cool founder and owner (it has been established nearly a year on business loans)
- the computer-mad head of program development (who is 19 years old).

The candidate really wants the job, but there are things about the company that challenge them. What might they be?

Role-play this scene, again bringing out the differences between characters by exaggeration.

A possible extension of this activity is for the two candidates to time travel and meet each other. They discuss why they wanted the jobs they went for. This will be a meeting of people with different views of the world.

ACTIVITY 2

Using the figures shown in Table 1 on page 52, make a graph or chart to show the contribution of each of the creative industries to the UK economy. It should clearly show which is most and which is least important. Research some figures for more traditional industries (a good starting point is the Department of Trade and Industry's website at www.open.gov.dti/) and construct a further chart to compare the traditional industries with the new ones.

Reputations: 'Das Boot'

Preview

Reputations was a recent television series that set out each week to 're-appraise' the careers of public figures. Usually the subjects chosen have enjoyed general public acclaim. If not heroes, they have been well regarded. Some are important historical figures who contributed to world-shaping politics or military events. Others were film stars, or even 'celebrity' intellectuals.

But often the reason for why this good regard was gained in the first place has been forgotten. We just accept that so-and-so was a 'good guy' because that's always been how they have been thought of. But perhaps a politician was great because his supporters at the time made sure the historians remembered him that way. An entertainer can become 'one of the greats' through a curious process whereby someone usually now out of fashion becomes iconic through a mix of nostalgia and historical soft-focus.

Is this constant re-appraising of the reputations of public figures a good thing? It keeps our perspective on history alive and stops us just accepting the word of other people. On the other hand, re-appraisal was one of the elements of Stalin's terrible purges in Soviet Russia, where 'heroes' were suddenly revealed to be subversives and sent off to exile, or executed.

The underdogs make good art

British and US war films of the 1950s and 1960s were generally moving-image versions of the endless strip cartoon war stories that were published around the same time. Chisel-jawed British and American troops fought, and always overcame, 'Jerry' or the 'Krauts' in violent, but curiously bloodless battles.

Slightly more informative and less-biased books on the war focused on the joint heroism of the ordinary soldier whether they were fighting on the Allied or Axis (supporters of Germany) side. But there were many parts of the Nazi war machine that it was not considered healthy to dwell on too far. There has always been a slightly questionable interest in certain German military uniforms by some people, and the activities of less straightforward fighting units (the SS, the Gestapo, etc.) were not the stuff to linger over in books designed to tell young people about the Second World War. Among the taboo groups of German combatants, or at least number one in the 'evil, ruthless and tricky' list, were the U-boats ('Unterseeboats', or submarines) and their crews.

Not real sailors?

Wartime opinion held that these men were not real sailors, they had no feel for the rules and honour of seafarers. Their vessels were not real boats, just killing machines that slunk about under the waves torpedoing defenceless merchant conveys. They were at best murderously sly, at worst vicious killers preying on unarmed ships. How much of this is likely to be true?

WEB LINKS

www.bwb.net/dasboot
Part of the Movie Treasury site. The *Das Boot* pages give full details of the film, with video images.

Then, in 1982 when films about a war that had been over for nearly 40 years were definitely not in fashion, along came a small budget, German language film adaptation of an obscure novel, that has become what many critics regard as one of the greatest films of all time. *Das Boot* is about a German U-boat. In its full version it runs for six hours. The crew do all the things they were traditionally infamous for. They torpedo British merchant ships and leave the struggling crews to drown or burn in the blazing, oil-slicked waters of the mid-Atlantic. Some of the crew are loyal to Hitler. They all want to destroy British ships. But audiences were moved to expressions of pity for the U-boat crew when the film was first shown (admittedly on limited 'art-house' release) in the UK.

Harsh facts

The film begins with a short notice that, of the 40,000 U-boatmen who went to sea during the war 30,000 died in their boats. Britain had broken the German naval Enigma code by the mid-point of the war and often knew exactly where to find the submerged U-boat packs. Improved technology, such as echo-sounding, meant that submarines could be pursued and depth charged. In the morale-boosting British naval films of the 1940s and 1950s (all duffle coats and cheery cockney ratings making mugs of cocoa!), we usually see the explosions of depth charges in the wake of the British destroyer, followed by a cheer from the bridge as a plume of water comes up black with oil, indicating that the U-boat has been hit.

In *Das Boot* we are inside the submarine, while for hours it is blasted and wrenched by near misses. Men sweat and cry in the darkness, water bursts in: a man goes insane cowering in the oil pit between the engines in the stern of the vessel, the one place from which it was known that escape was absolutely impossible.

A scene from *Das Boot*

The film's director, Wolfgang Petersen, did not set out to make the U-boatmen heroes or victims. He wanted to show what war could do to ordinary people, what appalling extremes it can force them into. Made for the German market, it may have told older Germans what they already knew, that the U-boat service was a place of slaughter and horror. What was remarkable was the film's success in countries that were enemies of Germany during the war. Such was the artistic and dramatic qualities of the film that the 'pity of war' overcame any lingering issues of national right and wrong. And choosing a wing of the German military that had (in Britain anyway) been picked out for demonization for so long added to the effect that Petersen wanted his film to have.

Churchill's humour

In Britain, the re-appraisal of famous figures by the media has created almost a whole industry around the country's war-time leader Winston Churchill. Long revered, especially by the generation that had lived through the Second World War, as a hero of mythic proportions, it seemed that a new, more cynical group of people, who had perhaps grown up in the supposedly revolutionary 1960s, were out to cut Churchill down to size. His drinking, snobbery and refusal to co-operate at times were all areas for attack. In fact, his image appears to come out rather well. His famous rudeness has become something of a source of humour. (Once when drunk in the House of Commons he was reprimanded by a woman Labour MP, Bessie Braddock: 'Sir, you are drunk', she opined. He replied, 'Yes madam, and you are ugly; but I shall be sober in the morning'.)

Another example of Churchill's rudeness as humour: in a contretemps with the American-born Conservative MP Nancy Astor she stated 'If I were your wife I would put poison in your coffee!' To which he replied 'If I were your husband I would drink it'.

TIPS FOR FURTHER RESEARCH

Investigate the law on privacy and how it should protect popular figures. Think about how the desire to know 'the real facts' about media celebrities maintains a whole range of weekly magazines. Look at some of these. Are they harmless gossip, or do they invade people's privacy?

Entertainers

'Re-appraising' the careers and personalities of famous entertainers and media figures – usually by finding something ugly behind the professional smile – is a major part of the drive to 'honestly re-evaluate' public figures. Often entertainers were so keen to build cheery personas that revealing a less attractive truth is too tempting to avoid. Kenneth Williams, the star of the *Carry On* comedy films, is a good example. His miserable private life and self-torturing soul has been so publicized in the form of startling 'revelations after his death' that it is almost impossible to regard him now as the public figure he spent his whole career trying to perfect (see Chapter 8). Does it matter that we know how he felt the stock camp role he had to play in every film debased his talents? Is it important we see the 'real man' behind the actor's mask?

Villains

The case for revealing the true person behind the public mask is far less important for entertainers than it is for historical figures on whose reputations, even posthumously, many more ideas depend. As such figures are, one after another, held up by the media for investigation, and in almost every case the great person is found to have a previously unseen flaw or secret, it is curious that the media are not so brave as to try the process in reverse.

No-one seems keen to make films about villains, from recent history at least, and show them to have been misrepresented. Perhaps villainy is a more honest drive. Perhaps villains don't have to hide their good points behind a mask of evil, because they don't have any!

In fact, in contrast to the *Reputations* series, some channels have run series on senior Nazi figures. In almost every case research has shown the reality of the characters to be at least as bad, usually worse, than the simplified view of 'monsters in a mad and violent time' that history hands down to us. No-one wants to re-appraise Goebbels, to find some good things about him. No-one wants to find anything to seriously support the now punchline remark made about Mussolini, 'At least he made the trains run on time'. These men were just evil. Or is it that the media doesn't have the courage to risk huge unpopularity by trying to find good things to say about even minor villains?

Joseph Goebbels became Minister for Propaganda in Nazi Germany. While Hitler looked after the conduct of the war, Goebbels virtually ran the country. He remained Hitler's most loyal ally and died, by his own hand and after despatching his wife and six children, in Hitler's bunker in 1945.

Only the good get to be bad

So the media's love of re-appraising reputations is apparently a one-sided affair. The good can be bought down a peg or two, or even utterly discredited, but the bad are off limits because it's not good ratings to try and change peoples' views about a villainous character.

'Hitler youth' meeting their leader

Questions for discussion

1. 'History is written by the victors.' What does this quote mean? Do you agree with it?

2. Is it right to constantly challenge received ideas handed down as part of history? What is the danger of doing this? What is the danger of not questioning historical 'truths'?

3. Some famous people, especially writers, publish their diaries while they are still alive. Others leave a note in their will to have their diaries destroyed. Imagine you were famous. Which option do you think you would go for? Why?

4. Can you think of any person or group of people that you think have got a 'raw deal' in the public reputation stakes and should be 're-appraised' to be seen in a better light? Give reasons for your choice(s), i.e. say why they are not as bad as people seem to think they are.

Questions for written answer

1. Do you think 'stars' and celebrities alive today should be protected from the sort of investigation that allows people to 're-appraise' them? Or should they accept that, by putting themselves in the public gaze, they have given up some rights to a private life. Where would you draw the line at investigating a celebrity's private life? Explain your ideas with reasons, and show both sides of the argument for and against a celebrity's right to privacy.

2. 'Those who do not remember the past are condemned to relive it.' Explain the meaning of this quote, then write a detailed explanation, with examples, of why we should know about certain things (what things?) that have happened in history and how exactly we might learn from them.

3. Pick one character who has been very powerful, successful or famous in any walk of life in the past 100 years. Research them (use the school or college library and the internet), building up two lists of their good and bad sides; their successes and their failures. Now write a detailed and balanced account of the person you have researched. Imagine you are writing for an audience that has never heard of the person.

ACTIVITY

This activity can only be attempted once question 3 from 'Questions for written answer' has been completed.

Director Robert Altman made a film in which famous figures, including Albert Einstein and Marilyn Monroe met in a motel room. He imagined how they would react to one another, what they would want to know, what agreements and disagreements they might have based on their public faces as we know them.

Work in groups of four to six and do the same with the characters you have written about. Make notes on how each might react to the others, and of what arguments or discussions might develop. Use your imaginations but try to keep the details of each character as the centre of the drama you devise together.

CULTURE, MORALITY, ARTS AND HUMANITIES

11 Are there only so many good stories?

Preview

One of Shakespeare's gifts was his ability to take existing stories and rework them into plays that, while keeping the basic ideas and plots of the originals, soared above them in scope, style and characterization. And since Shakespeare, writers and film-makers have used his plots to make new versions of his plays. The musical *West Side Story*, set among street gangs in 1950s New York, is a pretty straight retelling of *Romeo and Juliet*. In the early 1990s The Royal Shakespeare Company did a community production of Macbeth on a housing estate where the nobles were portrayed as local gang leaders, their castles were tower blocks, etc. Shakespeare's original language was used and the story worked perfectly.

Why do so many writers rework stories from other earlier writers or from myths and legend? Are they being lazy or are there only so many basic good stories, and they've all been done at least once.

Driving to Midnight

In this fictional interview, a dramatist defends his decision to write a version of the Doctor Faustus legend – the man who sells his soul to the devil for a certain period of power and pleasure on earth before having to give himself up to eternity in hell – to a critic who thinks modern dramatists should think up new stories. The play is set in Northern Ireland and is called *Driving to Midnight*.

TIPS FOR FURTHER RESEARCH

Find a 'literary companion' in your school or college library. Such books will often contain brief outlines of plots in novels and plays. You could also find a guide to classical music or to the opera; again, précis of the plots of operas can be found. Compare the story lines. Is it true to say that there are only so many good stories?

CAST: W, A WRITER, AUTHOR OF *DRIVING TO MIDNIGHT*; X, A CRITIC.

X: Let me get this right. The basic story, a man who sells his soul to the devil in return for a period of time on earth when he will enjoy special-powers, really first appears in English as the play by Christopher Marlowe in 1588, just about when Shakespeare was starting out. But Marlowe based his play on a medieval legend, which was written down in a German collection of stories about 10 years earlier. The story involves magic, pacts with the devil and all sorts of things that are hardly part of life to day. So what did you do with the story?

W: I've set it in Northern Ireland during the Troubles. But my version, *Driving to Midnight*, is not a realistic piece about exactly what went on during that violent time. It is, in a sense, a modern myth or fairy tale. It still has magic in it, and supernatural events, such as the man who is the devil coming back unscathed after being blown up by a bomb.

X: How can you make such things convincing in a modern version of such an old story?

W: In Marlowe's stage version of the story, Faustus is a highly intelligent man, who is bored. He wants to do something new. The devil appears and offers him mysterious powers to do this, but only on condition that, after a certain period of enjoying diabolic power on earth, Faustus gives his soul to the devil. This is a terrible pact, because it commits Faustus to something awful beyond even death.

X: Of course we don't all believe in the after-life today, so that's a problem for a modern version.

W: The man who is the Faustus figure in my play doesn't ever fully understand the conditions of the pact he makes. It is not explicit. But that's sort of a part of so much thinking today. We pretend to be rational, many of us profess no belief in any sort of god, but we all hanker after something that is bigger than just the things we do in our lives. We want a spiritual dimension. But we are not clear what it is we want or believe. Danny, my Faustus figure, is like that.

X: Why bother with trying to match the structure of a modern story set in a highly charged political situation to the form of a medieval legend?

W: Once you start planning your version, using the original as a sort of template, it's amazing how things start to fall into place and ideas come to you that you might not have had if you were writing the plot from scratch. This is the thing about the great stories, they seem to be universal, you can set them in almost any place and time and the details seem to work themselves out. You get a whole new story, but with the underlying thematic power of the original. The actual original story is a small part of the new play.

X: In Marlowe's *Faustus*, the devil appears from the pits of hell and carries Faustus off at midnight at the end of their pact. How do you do that in a play set in Northern Ireland?

W: Danny/Faustus is blown up by a bomb at exactly midnight. The devil has come to him in the form of a mysterious leader of a paramilitary group. Such is the secrecy surrounding it that Danny is never actually sure which side he is working for. In Marlowe's play, Faustus is a learned doctor, a sort of philosopher and alchemist. In mine, Danny is a gifted science research student. Faustus is corrupted by the devil, Danny is persuaded, by huge rewards, to use his skills to devise bombs and terrorists devices. One of these finally kills him. [*X leans forwards, suddenly more aggressive.*]

X: But why bother?

W: What?

X: Isn't it just being lazy? Surely a good writer, a really original one, is one who thinks up a new story.

W: Each version of a great 'standard' story is a new story.

X: If the writers who wrote them in the first place had thought that, they wouldn't have bothered. They'd just have looked about for even older stories to play about with.

W: Some people say there are archetypal stories, old stories that have been retold in many forms, but whose basic ideas, often just the very general outline, is so crucial and basic to our culture that we can't help wanting to

W EB LINKS

Use the search term 'literary companion' on www.google.com and you will come across many different types of the genre. A similar search on 'librettos' will open up the world of opera plots.

make new versions of them. The idea of people going off on a quest for something and facing all sorts of trials and dangers before returning home, that's a very simple outline for a type of story that goes right back to the Greek myths.

X: And the Greeks invented these myths?

W: Maybe they collected them from even earlier oral stories or traveller's tales or whatever. The Greek myths are where we look for them because the Greeks wrote them down and they survived.

X: Then those ancient Greeks were better writers than us because they were creating new material.

W: They were creating the culture. We have had a couple of thousand years of basic Western or European culture since then. It was part of the founding process of our culture to set down the basic stock of stories.

X: So is that it? Has the basic work been done and the rest is always going to be adaptations?

W: Of course not. Writers respond to the world they live in. Literature of any age reflects the age in which it is created. But the great stories do seem to fit so well with any age, it's like they have something special.

X: Don't writers want to find a new 'great story'?

W: Some say they do. Willy Russell's musical *Blood Brothers* is about twins who are separated soon after birth and grow up as best friends but never knowing they are actually brothers. They only learn the truth on the day when one kills the other in a fit of jealousy and is then killed himself. Willy Russell says that, as far as he knows, this very mythic, elemental plot has not existed before.

X: That seems more creative than re-hashing old stories.

W: It's different that's all. People wouldn't have flocked to see the film *Romeo + Juliet* if it was just a 're-hash'. They wouldn't go to see all the new versions of Shakespeare plays that appear in theatres every year if all they really wanted was to see a completely new story. The great stories have a basic drive in them that strikes a cord with people.

X: Well that's all we have time for tonight, thank you.

West Side Story, which transfers the role of the Montagus and Capulets in Verona to the rival gangs of the Sharks and the Jets in New York is just one adaptation of *Romeo and Juliet*. How many other adaptations (into film, musical, etc.) of Shakespeare plays can you find?

Blaise Pascal, a seventeenth-century French moralist, scientist and philosopher, saw all art as vain copying of originals. For example, he had this to say about painting: 'Quelle vanite que la peinture, qui attire l'admiration par la resemblance des choses don't on n'admire point les originaux'. ('How vain is painting, exciting admiration by its resemblance to things even though we do not admire the originals.')

Questions for discussion

1. Do you know of any films, stories, etc. that are versions of traditional great stories? How did they use the original in a new way?

2. Do you think every writer (for stage, screen or a novelist) should try to find a completely new story, or can great works be written as new versions of old tales?

3. Romeo and Juliet were 'star-crossed lovers' who eventually died because their families hated one another. In the musical *West Side Story* this becomes a racial issue. Tony (Romeo) is a Polish immigrant to New York, Maria (Juliet) a Puerto Rican immigrant. Can you think of other settings for this story?

4. Which would you rather see, a traditional play performed in a traditional way ('tights and swords'), or a modern or unusual adaptation? Give reasons for your opinions.

A scene from a traditional theatre production of *Romeo and Juliet*

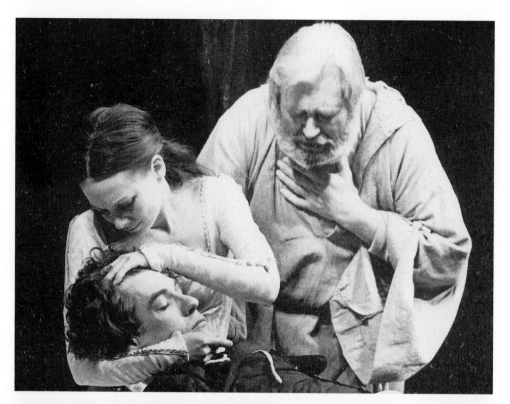

A scene from *West Side Story*, composer Leonard Bernstein's 1958 musical version of *Romeo and Juliet*

Questions for written answer

1. Painters don't often take the works of the old masters and rework them in a modern style. What might be the difference between writing and telling stories and painting pictures that accounts for this? Think about the way a painter works alone on a canvas to hang on a wall, and a groups of actors, the writer, director, etc getting together to put on a show for a theatre full of people.

2. 'Those who do not remember the past are condemned to relive it.' Explain how this maxim might connect to a writer knowing, or not knowing, the great stories that have been part of our culture for centuries. Could starting completely fresh, with no knowledge of what writers in earlier ages wrote, be a good or bad thing?

3. Do you think different cultures and races have different and distinct repertoires of great stories that permeate their cultures? Or are people the same all over the world and likely to have the same drives and desires that will come out in basically similar stories? Think about the effect religions and social customs might have on the types of stories a culture creates.

4. Many works of art (not just plays, but also paintings, films, even operas) are designed to put forward a particular political or social viewpoint. Choose one work which has influenced your own philosophy of life and explain how it has had an impact on you.

ACTIVITY 1

There are many successful works based on the idea of a 'quest' for something. One of the originals was the search for the golden fleece; in the Middle Ages, knights sought the holy grail (the cup that Jesus was said to have drunk from at the last supper). Sometimes quests are not even to find things – Frodo Baggins, in Tolkien's *Lord of the Rings* has a mission to destroy the evil ring of power.

In small groups devise your own new version of the quest story that originates in Greek myths. The thing sought must not just be valuable, it must be symbolic in some way. What is it? Where do you go to look for it, and who are 'you'? Why do you and your companions set off on this quest? (It should not just be for personal gain.) What dangers do you encounter and are you successful? (Don't assume success is necessary to the story.)

Recount the philosophy of your quest and its main features and stages to the rest of your class or group. You could use flip charts or computer presentation, or put together a storyboard to show how the story would progress.

When all groups have presented you should look at the main features of them and see what is common to more than one story and what features are unique. What does this tell you about the viewpoint of the writer in the article?

Finally you should decide which of the stories is the best one, and why.

ACTIVITY 2

Look at this week's pop music charts. How many of the top 20 hits are original works; how many are either re-releases or copies of earlier works? What does this tell you about original music?

Preview

The first four Harry Potter books for children have, like their author, become the stuff of myths. Not the sort of myths that Harry might come across in the world of Hogwart's school and its magical characters; but the sort of media, public relations and marketing legends that have been created around the enormous success of the books. The scale of operations that have grown up to promote, market and now film Harry Potter astounds even an industry used to promoting 'the best ever', 'the most amazing', etc. Warner Bros, who have made the first of what may be a whole series of film versions of the books, have established no less that 107 internet sites (in 2002) for dealing with the publicity, merchandising, etc., that the films will generate.

But can JK Rowling's vision of the curious, rather gentle world of Harry Potter, and the imaginations of the millions of children who create the world of Hogwart's in their minds through the words alone, survive this type of media hype, film development and merchandising?

The author emerges

At the start of the whole phenomenon, JK Rowling was, like most authors, relatively unknown. Publishers do not generally bother to expose their authors to the limelight. Writers might secretly want the media attention that actors get, but their role is to stay at home writing. But as the publishers realized what a demand there was for the first and second of the Harry Potter books, JK was gradually developed as a public figure. They turned her apparent ordinariness into a story of success triumphing over difficulty. Hers was a struggle typical of late twentieth-century Britain, one that many of the parents who bought her books could understand.

Joanne Rowling was born in 1965. She gained a degree from Exeter University, and became a teacher. She then married, had a daughter, got divorced and found herself a single parent struggling to pay the bills. The official publicist's story is that she begins writing the first Harry Potter book at a café table during her infant daughter's naps. Then, success! London publisher Bloomsbury reads the manuscript, a story that could have been written for children 50 years ago, with wizards, a boarding school and a hero called 'Potter', and decided to take a risk. Within four years Harry Potter became a world-wide phenomenon.

Old fashioned?

In every respect the books appear to hark back to another age of children's fiction: when reading was a major leisure activity, before multichannel television, computer games and the web. The books are large by current children's fiction standard, requiring a commitment of time and effort to read.

> Struggling authors, artists, etc. always make better stories than rich or non-struggling ones. Which other artists or authors can you find that have had to struggle to become successful?

Rowling does not work with an illustrator like many children's writers do, using images to support text. Her books are strictly 'a good read'.

The style and content of the books are also somewhat old-fashioned. 'Harry Potter' is a deliberately uncool, dated sort of name. The stories contain 'good versus evil' plots. Not the violent, science-fiction fantasy worlds derived from the imagery of computer games, nor the 'dungeons and dragons' style of gothic hero stories, but a gentler, more traditional world of wizards and almost domestic magic. This is one of the 'hooks' that draw young people into the stories. A young reader identifies more easily with a hero their own age going on a shopping trip to buy a wand than they can with a muscle-bound space cadet who wrests a sword from a block of radioactive kryptonite!

Boarding school

Most notably, Harry goes to boarding school. There was a whole genre of boarding school fiction for boys and girls throughout the first half of the twentieth century. The cast of these books were inevitably middle or upper class, and the plots were based on the sort of experiences real boarders might have had at school. Hogwart's school is obviously a completely different sort of setting, a fantasy world where the stories are located, but Rowling has, deliberately or not, carried on some of the traditions and images of boarding school fiction. Harry goes to school by train, an old-fashioned steam train of course. The school is divided, like most English public schools, into houses that compete against one another. It may teach magic and spells, but Hogwart's has the structure of an English boarding school of perhaps 40 years ago.

A scene from Harry Potter and the Philosopher's Stone

TIPS FOR FURTHER RESEARCH

Identify other popular cultural phenomena that have started small then been taken up by the media and developed. Has the development always been a good thing? Has the original charm been lost?

Despite these elements, the books have, at the time of writing, sold over 65 million copies world-wide – a figure that is ever increasing. For Rowling is a very good writer, she creates a style that utterly enchants most children – and many adults. As some grown-ups wanted to read the books but felt embarrassed being seen reading 'children's' books in public, the publishers bought out special editions with more 'adult' covers.

Control

The scale of the success of the first book probably surprised everyone. Booksellers saw the slightly odd, dated tale of *Harry Potter and the Philosopher's Stone* as a one-off novelty publication. But Rowling had already told Bloomsbury that she planned a series of seven books, one for every year of Harry's time at Hogwart's, from age 11 to 18. Unusually, she wanted Harry to grow up with each passing year and for both the style and content of the books to reflect this. This is something publishers like to avoid with children's fiction. They prefer the formula to stay the same, the protagonists to remain the same age. It follows that Rowling's books will only be accessible, even appealing, to older children as the years go by and Harry ages.

So how did she fare when Hollywood giants came along?

Hollywood giants

Children's films are big business in America. As the first four Harry Potter books climbed one after the other to the top of bestseller lists around the world, Hollywood studios must have been watching carefully. However, none of them made a move to gain exclusive film rights to the Harry Potter stories until the first book hit the top of the US best-sellers list in January 1999. Hollywood was now very interested. American children had picked up on the Rowling magic.

A monster movie, or a movie monster?

WEB LINKS

Search the web using 'Harry Potter' and step back! Most of the dozens of sites that you will find are either shops trying to sell you the books, or sites created by fans. Make a list of three or four that offer genuine information about the books, the film, and JK Rowling. Try, for example, www.sffworld.com/authors/r/rowling

Hollywood may have the resources to throw huge sums of money into film projects, but it doesn't always have the sensitivity to retain the original charm or style of the story it is adapting. Warner Bros agreed that this should be a no-expense-spared project.

With Harry Potter they knew they had to keep the gentle, very English overtones that colour the fantasy world of Hogwart's. The first film was shot in England at a rumoured cost of over £100 million, although the director, Chris Columbus is American.

A deeper and darker magic: did the film of *The Lord of the Rings* need so much promotion?

The film of *The Lord of the Rings* – depicting a deeper and darker magic – was released at around the same time as the first Harry Potter film. Both were heavily promoted. Why do you think that *The Lord of the Rings* was more successful at the box office?

Do things speed up and die?

Children are notoriously difficult to please. The media usually creates a 'must have' Christmas present for children every year, sending exhausted parents dashing around shops in fruitless searches for a toy or novelty that is deliberately held in tight supply to keep prices, and market interest, up. The same novelty is usually abandoned by the spring. The kids have had so much of the marketing for whatever it was stuffed in their faces that they have moved on to something new, something less obvious and more exciting because of that.

The Harry Potter books appear slowly; they take a long time to write. And children are re-discovering what young people in previous, more reading-oriented generations knew: that books are a special, private experience, a locked world of words that only bursts into life when you sit down and read.

Every child has a different Hogwart's in their head. They see Harry as a different character according to their own imagination. Do film versions of the books change this experience?

Killing the magic?

A Sunday newspaper took the unprecedented step of issuing an 80-page special supplement about the Harry Potter film, before it was even released. There were pictures of all the main characters, a plan of the school, and dozens of stills from the film. Harry now has one face, that of Daniel Radcliffe, the 12-year-old chosen to play the hero. Rubeus Hagrid, the keeper of keys and grounds at Hogwart's, is clearly Robbie Coltraine behind a beard.

The film was released in time for Christmas 2001 and was a huge success, endlessly playing 'at cinemas everywhere' (although competition from the first of *The Lord of the Rings* trilogy, released soon afterwards, was fierce). The publicity for Harry Potter was enormous, with posters covering high-street billboards like wallpaper. Kids could see Harry staring down at them every time they went to school. The marketers' fear was 'will they start to get bored?' 'Will they start to look for something more exclusive, newer, less in the public gaze of adults?'

Coca-Cola paid a reported £103 million for film-related marketing rights, and for that they weren't allowed to put Harry's face on the bottles. A Hogwart's express train set was one of the Christmas 'must haves'. The potential list of merchandise that can be created is huge. The investment made by companies to buy licences to make and sell it means they will try to squeeze every last opportunity from Harry Potter.

Questions for discussion

1. Publishers don't usually try to present their authors to the public. Do you think they should? Would you be interested in knowing what the author of a book you had read was like? Would you go to hear them speak about their books?

2. Do you think there are specific stories or types of story that can only work either as film or as a book? Give examples, or give suggestions for general principles about the best way to tell different types of story: in moving images or words.

3. Can you think of cases where over selling by the media has killed a cultural or entertainment phenomenon?

Questions for written answer

1. How exactly can a film spoil the magic of a book? Think about the experience of reading a book and compare it to watching a film. What things can the book do better than the film? What can the film do that the words on the page can't?

2. Think of a scene from a film that really impressed you and stuck in your mind. Write a brief description of the scene: where it took place, how it was shot, who was in it, what happened. Now imagine you are an author writing a book in which this same scene takes place. Write the scene as if it were a chapter or episode in the book. (Use as much style as you can to really bring it to life. Don't worry about explaining what happens before or comes next: this is an exercise in style.)

3. '*Harry Potter and the Philosopher's Stone* does not have as strong a moral message as *The Lord of the Rings: The Fellowship of the Ring*.' If you are familiar with the two works, how far do you think this is true? If not, compare two works with which you are familiar and compare the moral message of each. Do you think that having such a message is an essential element of a good story?

ACTIVITY 1

Work in small groups.

JK Rowling and Harry Potter came to the publisher out of the blue. She wrote the first book then sent it off to see what people might think. In the music industry things are much more manipulated. Some bands are created by executives who have an idea for a certain sound and image, then audition for people to form the band.

You are a group of publishers and film script agents who are planning to create a new successful series of children's books. You are going to draw up a list of ingredients that you think will make a winning formula, then find an author to knock it all together!

Make that list. Think about time, location, characters, possible plots, and beside your ideas give a few lines explaining the reasons for your choice.

Compare your list with those of other groups. Whose do you think will be most successful? Compile a 'master list' from the separate lists of the items that you think are most important.

ACTIVITY 2

Draw up a table or chart to show which people in your class or group have read one or all of the Harry Potter books or seen the Harry Potter film. You could categorize them like this:

- refused to read the book (usually because it's seen as pandering to 'fashion' or because it's too 'young')
- refused to watch the film (for similar reasons)
- read the book and watched the film
- read the book and refused to watch the film (because it would spoil the magic)
- watched the film and been encouraged to read the book
- watched the film and been discouraged from reading the book.

Area 2

SCIENCE AND TECHNOLOGY

Preview

The main difference between the ideas of Isaac Newton and those of Albert Einstein is the way they dealt with the idea of time. Everyone has had some kind of idea about time and space. It may have been a simple question about how Santa Claus managed to get round everyone on Christmas Eve or that time drags (in an examination) or speeds past (on holiday). It may have been an introduction to ideas of time in science fiction writing. Masters of this genre are writers such as Arthur C Clarke and Isaac Asimov, who go into a fair amount of technical detail. Television has picked up on time with series like *Dr Who*, *Star Trek* and *Red Dwarf*. Even light-hearted works such as *The Hitchhiker's Guide to the Galaxy* or Terry Pratchett's *Discworld* novels deal with ideas about time in some depth. The point is, you will have met a lot of highly technical ideas already in one form or another. It is just a matter of drawing the line between ideas based on scientific research and the step into imagination that fiction writers have taken. Newton gave us the physics that we use and are familiar with. Einstein opened the door to the universe, and his ideas on time were a key factor.

Can we travel in time? Can we visit other galaxies?

Not with our current technology. Three hundred years ago Newton developed the scientific ideas available at the time, put them all together and we are still using his laws of physics today. His view was that the universe had basic rules that would not change. Newton seemed to believe that all creation was a bit like a clockwork mechanism and God's role was like that of a watchmaker. God put it together, set it going and could make minor adjustments if needed. By the start of this century some scientists were finding that Newton's laws did not explain everything. Various strange theories were advanced. One theory was that a layer of 'ether' was everywhere and it was this layer that allowed light and other electromagnetic waves to travel. The theory was wrong, but we still read about 'messages moving through the ether'. We now know that matter is made up of atoms. Finally it was accepted that Newton's laws only applied for the things we can detect with our senses. The world of atoms, the speed of light and the nature of time itself needed to be explored and explained. This was the manifestation of Einstein's genius.

TIPS FOR FURTHER RESEARCH

Research the idea of the 'ether' being around the Earth. How was this theory proved to be wrong? What other 'scientific' theories can you find out about that gained common currency but were eventually discarded. The 'music of the spheres' or 'the humours of the body' could be good starting points.

New theories need new ways of thinking

Albert Einstein

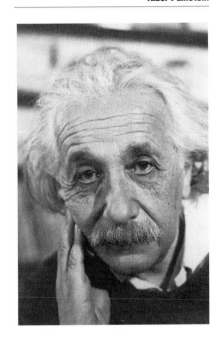

The new scientific theories were about the world of atoms and molecules, which are too small to be seen by the human eye. In 1897 JJ Thompson showed that when metal was hot, 'cathode rays' came off it and they had a mass and a charge. These were electrons – part of an atom. So not only was the atom the smallest thing that could exist on its own, but it was made up of even smaller parts. These cathode rays are used to produce the picture on a television screen. In 1911 Ernest Rutherford discovered a central core to the atom, the nucleus. Later Einstein used this research to explain the photoelectric effect – how light and electrons interact. According to Einstein, light is composed of photons, each photon being a sort of packet of energy. We know that electrons are emitted from a surface – usually a metallic one – when it is hit by light. Einstein said a single quantum of light is like a packet of energy that can eject a single electron from the metal. The energy of the quantum is proportional to the frequency. The higher the frequency, the greater the energy. Einstein said that the existing idea that light energy was one continuous stream of bits was wrong and that light had both the properties of a wave, that has no mass, and also the properties of a small quantity of mass. This is called wave–particle duality. In the widest sense this theory had important effects as it opened the way to quantum theory.

Theory of relativity

Einstein never achieved his life's work of formulating a unified field theory to include electromagnetism, relativity, quantum mechanics and gravitation. He did, however, foresee the possibility of nuclear weapons and wrote to President Roosevelt in 1939 about the military potential of nuclear energy. He spoke out strongly against the atom bomb after the war.

Albert Einstein took Newton's theories a stage further. Einstein made connections between scientific ideas that had not been connected before. Physicists are able to measure what happens but then need a theory to explain why it happens. Einstein produced a theory to explain how things like atoms worked and how the forces in space behaved. For example, he said that acceleration was equivalent to gravity. So if you were in a space station then a force pulling you down could be due to gravity or it could be due to the station spinning round. He said that we can only measure in a particular 'frame of reference'. Everything that happens follows the laws of science as long as you are inside the 'frame of reference', but you cannot assume there is a universal standard outside of your frame of reference. In *The Special Theory of Relativity* published in 1905, he explained how Newtonian physics did not apply at high velocities getting close to the speed of light:

- first, observers can never detect their uniform motion except relative to other objects

- secondly, the speed of light is the same for all observers regardless of their relative motion.

ⓦEB LINKS

Search under the following headings:
general theory of relativity, Isaac
Newton, Albert Einstein. Einstein;
relativity. A good starting point is
www.westegg.com/einstein/
which has links to many other
Einstein-related sites.

If these two are accepted then it follows that the speed of light is the limit for matter and mass increases with velocity. This means lengths contract as objects move and mass and energy are interchangeable. Einstein showed that the mass of a body is a measure of its energy content. He said that energy and mass are linked by the formula $E = mc^2$, where E is energy, m is the mass and c is the speed of light.

This means that energy can create matter and matter can be destroyed to produce huge amounts of energy. This is the theory behind nuclear power (and nuclear weaponry). In a nuclear power-station uranium nuclei are split and a small amount of mass is destroyed and replaced by a huge mass of energy which is released. Einstein provided the theory behind the experiments to make an atom bomb. He also said because of the equivalence of energy and mass the closer a mass got to the speed of light the greater the mass would become. This has been proved using electron accelerators. Scientists are able to accelerate electrons near to the speed of light and they find the mass of the electrons increases.

What about time?

Einstein said that we exist in a space–time continuum. This means we measure the 'normal' three dimensions that we always use but also have to take the fourth dimension of time into account. So time is not the same everywhere. The time for someone on a star will be different from that of someone at a distance from it because of the gravitational field of the star. In his *General Theory of Relativity*, published in 1916, he said that gravitation is not a force but is a curved field in the space–time continuum which was created by the presence of mass. This space–time is a four-dimensional space, the fourth dimension being time. Einstein said that therefore gravitational fields bend light. This was not accepted by a lot of scientists until the British astronomer Arthur Eddington measured it during an eclipse in 1925. As light from a star went past the sun it was bent by the mass of the sun. In the *General Theory of Relativity* Einstein suggested that gravity was not a force like other forces but a consequence of space–time being warped. Bodies like the Earth do not move on curved orbits as they move through space by a force called gravity, instead they follow the nearest thing they can to a straight line but in a curved space – called a geodesic. It is often compared to a planet being like a heavy ball resting on a stretched sheet of elastic and the elastic is space.

The 'ball on the rubber mat' analogy illustrates Einstein's gravitational theories

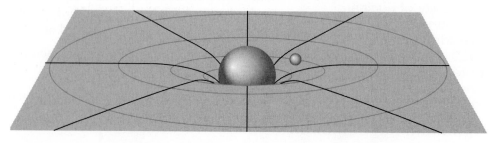

You could extend your understanding by looking up the following key terms: atoms, molecules, photons, frame of reference, ether, cathode rays, photoelectric effect, wave–particle duality, space–time continuum, geodesic, weak and strong atomic forces.

So we can travel in time then?

Another prediction based on the general theory is that time should appear to run slower near a massive body (like Earth) as there is a relation between the energy of light and its frequency. The greater the energy, the higher the frequency. So as light travels away from Earth's gravity it loses energy, so its frequency goes down. Therefore its wavelength is longer and this means that time changes. This is used in space travel. The difference in the speed of clocks at different heights is important for satellite navigation systems. In general, we can say that for Newton, motion is along curved lines in a flat space, but for Einstein, motion is along straight lines in a curved space. Einstein thought all forces could be explained this geometrical way. In theory, there is a possibility of time travel but other factors would also change.

Conclusion

So Einstein brought in some very different ideas to the simpler model that Newton had developed. Einstein's main points are that:

- light has mass as a photon of electromagnetic energy, as well as being a wave

- space has curvature

- gravity affects time.

Einstein spent the rest of his life trying to find a unified theory of forces but without success. There are four forces that we know of: gravity, electromagnetism, weak atomic forces and strong atomic forces. The overall theory would be one that connected gravity and electromagnetism. Scientists are still looking for it, but one view is that only God has the answer.

Questions for discussion

1. Science brought you television. What would you do without it?

2. Do you think most scientists believe in God? Why? What are your views?

3. What are the most important parts of a good scientific idea? How can you identify a bad scientific idea?

4. Einstein's theories ultimately led to the development of the atom bomb. How much responsibility should he take? (He eventually supported the pacifist movement.) How much 'blame' can any scientist take for the way his or her ideas are used or misused?

5. $E = mc^2$. What does it stand for? What does it mean? What did the science mean for the 'art' of war?

Questions for written answer

1. What are the main differences in the idea of our universe between Newton's theories and Einstein's? Write a paragraph on each.

2. What problems do you think each major world religion might have with the ideas of science? Identify and discuss the areas where you think there can be an agreement and where you think there could be a conflict. How might a religious scientist resolve such a conflict?

3. Explain why you think the ideas of both Einstein and Newton were accepted so quickly and completely while other theorists have struggled to gain acceptance. For example, Mendel's theory on genetics (see Chapter 18) was correct but ignored until long after he died.

4. Explain the main differences in the way the idea of time is treated in Newtonian mechanics compared to the way that Einstein treats it.

5. In Germany in the 1930s Einstein's ideas were not accepted as they said he was a Bolshevik Jew. What effect do think this might have had on the outcome of the Second World War and on the formation of subsequent power blocs?

? Quiz

1. What are Newton's three laws of motion?
2. Why was Newton wrong about light?
3. What did Newton discover about colour?
4. What are cathode rays and what are they used for?
5. What is wave–particle duality?
6. What are the three main points of the theory of relativity?
7. Who discovered the nucleus of the atom?
8. Where does the energy come from in a nuclear explosion?
9. Is the time in a satellite the same as on Earth?
10. Why were Einstein's ideas not accepted in Germany at the time he made them?

 ## CTIVITY

Read the introduction to HG Wells' *The Time Machine* in which the time traveller explains his ideas of the fourth dimension. Remember that this was first published in 1895 when Einstein was only around your age (he was born in 1879 so would have been 16 or 17 years old). Do you think he read the story? In pairs, script a chance meeting between Wells and the boy Einstein and be prepared to perform this to the rest of the class.

How much science fiction has become science fact? (For example, what is the difference between Captain Kirk's hand-held communicator and your mobile phone?) What other ideas of the imagination do you think will be realized? Watch an episode of *Star Trek*, *Farscape*, *Dr Who* or similar or an extract from a film such as *Star Wars* or *Alien* and start by making a list of all the technology which the writers have assumed but which did not actually exist. Does any of it now exist? Have the ideas been superseded by science?

Common sense and nonsense

Preview

We are bombarded with views and opinions and all of them claim to be right. Teenagers are told they have silly ideas as they have 'no common sense'. How can you sort out good ideas from bad, is it enough to 'stick to the facts'? Is common sense a good guide? Three hundred years ago philosophers and mathematicians like Descartes, Leibniz and Hume were trying to find answers to the question 'of what can we be certain?'. While mathematics could provide definite answers, was anything else as reliable? Questions about the theory of knowledge are called epistemological questions. The various answers that were given by these mathematicians and philosophers made it clear that they thought we could only be certain of a very small number of things. These were called axioms: an axiom is an accepted general truth or principle. Descartes (1596–1650) is well known for his statement that he was certain of only one thing: 'Cogito ergo sum' which means 'I think therefore I am'. Descartes' approach to science was to question everything and his ideas were the foundation of modern scientific investigation. This developed into a school of thought called positivism. This was that only experience and knowledge based on observation could be relied on. This is probably where the belief in 'reliable facts' and 'I will believe it when I can see it' started. However even that was considered doubtful by some. One famous scientist said that if ever an extraterrestrial landed on Earth they would probably look at our science and say that we had got $2 + 2 = 4$ right but the rest was a load of nonsense!

What can we be sure of?

> You could extend your understanding by considering areas of common sense that are no longer believed. Examples could be that women were created to serve men or that a world of spirits exist (as believed in Shakespeare's time). Why did these common-sense views change?

Without going deeper into the area of philosophy, is it reasonable to say there is very little that we can be certain of? Surely science, mathematics and a bit of common sense will provide the reliable answers we need. The term 'common sense' is one we often use to deal with the experiences of everyday life. So how far can common sense be trusted? Most people would say that we could be certain of a lot of things and rely on 'experts' to add certainty to other areas. However history shows that many so-called experts are often wrong. In 1956 the British Astronomer Royal said the thought of space travel was 'utter bilge' then in 1957 the Russians launched the *Sputnik* satellite. History is full of theories to explain the world that have been proved wrong. Everything we 'make sense of' or understand is due to a theory or 'perspective' that we have. A perspective means a set of ideas that can be used to put information into an order of importance so they make sense to us. A perspective can stop you from being able to appreciate another point of view. The philosopher Auguste Comte said 'No real observation of any kind of phenomena is possible except in so far it is first directed and then finally intercepted by some theory'.

Do we live in a scientific world where the facts speak for themselves?

In science and mathematics we try to be objective. To be objective is to study a topic without allowing your own values, moral beliefs or ideology to influence you. The general view is that science and mathematics can provide us with certainty as they are objective. Using a scientific method of working is when experiments are carried out then people verify that they are accurate and reliable so that we can then trust them to predict what will happen the next time. Experience tells me that when I push a switch down on the wall in my room, a light will come on. Science tells me why and that it will always happen (assuming nothing breaks). Even this would be challenged by some, Sir Karl Popper (1902–1994) for example. He said that no scientific theory can be conclusively established. He also believed that the future cannot be accurately predicted from the study of history. In simple terms it is like the turkey that visits the farmer's kitchen door and gets fed extra food. After a while the turkey uses the theory that going to the door equals extra food. The theory only held up to 24 December. Popper said good scientific theory must be able to make a testable prediction (hypothesis) and is only good up to the point just before it fails.

Sir Karl Popper

Can science be relied on?

So do scientists really use 'scientific methods'? This is where the observed facts lead to a theory which is then tested out – in experiments – to see if it explains other facts. This then leads to a more detailed theory. Often there are certain observations which will not fit, often referred to as 'the exception that proves the rule'. A good scientific theory will include the possibility of being proved wrong. Once a theory is accepted, scientists usually hang on to it until the conflicting evidence is overwhelming. They do not like to challenge the accepted truth, which has become an axiom. A good example of this is the '24th chromosome'. In 1923 an important American zoologist called Painter said that there were definitely 24 pairs of chromosomes in a human cell. For the next 30 years this was treated as a 'fact'. If you counted 23 you were wrong. Then in 1956 it was clearly shown that there were only 23 pairs. For 30 years no-one had challenged the accepted 'fact' even though the evidence was there.

Fact or fiction?

So does this mean that scientists just set out to prove the ideas they already have are correct? This would be like a detective deciding you were guilty and only collecting the evidence that made you look guilty and ignoring the rest. In other words the facts never just speak for themselves, they must be interpreted through ideas. When Louis and Mary Leakey went to Africa in search of our ancestors, they did not have some existing data to investigate, they went because of Darwin's theory of evolution and they therefore believed we were closely related to the great apes. The great apes live in Africa so that was the logical place for the fossil remains to be found. They went because of an idea they already had which they wanted to be proved or disproved. This was a hypothesis. The data followed and confirmed the theory, which is the very opposite of how we think science works.

Is common sense based on the axioms we have?

Scientific understanding, theories and ideas can change dramatically and rapidly. When Albert Einstein was a student in the 1890s he was taught that the universe was filled with 'ether' and that the idea of atoms was silly. By the time he won the Nobel Prize in 1922 the idea of 'ether' was seen as silly and atoms had become a fact of life. His work had been a major part of the movement to bring in ideas that would have been unthinkable 50 years before. The importance of trusting mathematics was shown by a major error made by Einstein. In 1915 he worked on his new theory of general relativity. The ideas then held as 'common sense' about the planets and universe were that we were in a static universe. He was not happy to find that according to his equations the universe was anything but static. He therefore set about fiddling his

A Russian scientist called TD Lysenko did not believe in Mendelian genetics and as a result Russian agriculture was a disaster between the two world wars. Why was he believed when better-qualified scientists were ignored?
Can you identify someone who was believed just because of their personal qualities and not because of what they said? Think about recent dictators.

TIPS FOR FURTHER RESEARCH

Look up the following scientists: René Descartes, Auguste Comte, David Hume, Gottfried Willhelm Leibniz, Karl Popper, Louis and Mary Leakey, Edwin Hubble.

equations until they gave the 'right' answer of an unchanging universe. This 'fiddle factor' was called the cosmological constant. Subsequent studies of distant galaxies by Edwin Hubble showed that they were racing away from each other. Einstein's original equations had been right all along. He later told colleagues that by failing to trust them he had made the biggest blunder of his life. Einstein's failure to predict the expansion of the universe is a lesson which is now fundamental to all scientists. The lesson is clear: when it comes to understanding the universe, don't think – calculate.

Are there any methods for being certain?

Science does have one advantage in that it has a self-correcting mechanism. This is that someone will eventually find the error and shoot the theory down. Science history is a collection of defeated theories. A thesis is a theory with evidence to support it. The philosopher Hegel put forward the view that in order to identify the truth we should construct a thesis, then balance it against the opposite view, an antithesis, and from what is left develop a synthesis that is the best of both. This is then the new thesis and the process continues. This process of progress from a conflict of opposite views is called the dialectic. Often we judge the person rather than the idea itself. Governments have tried to use that view. In the 1930s the German Nazi Party rejected any Jewish science; they said the truth could only come from Aryan scientists. Albert Einstein and many other Jewish scientists left to work in the USA. One outcome of this was the development of the atom bomb by the USA. If the Germans had produced it first they could have defeated the allies and won the war.

In conclusion – there must be some basic facts we can rely on?

You could extend your understanding by looking up the following terms: philosopher, philosophy, objective, axiom, positivism, reliable, chromosomes, theory, thesis, hypothesis, synthesis, cosmology, data, epistemology, verification, dialectic.

Last of all, can we then trust pure mathematics? Statisticians can use mathematics to prove almost anything. By only showing part of the full evidence they can easily mislead. One recent example was when a government department said that statistics showed that smaller classes did not lead to better GCSE results. This ignored the evidence that schools try to have difficult students in small classes so they can be managed better. Staff shortages then mean that the more able are in bigger classes. The figures the government department used were correct but part of the evidence had been ignored to give a misleading conclusion. To be sure of something you need to have all of the evidence and have it in the correct order of importance.

Questions for discussion

1. 'It is not possible for scientists to be objective'. Briefly outline reasons both for and against this view.

2. Where does our common sense understanding come from? Can it be trusted? Pick out a 'common sense' view you have been told, that you did not follow, then analyse it.

3. Working in a small group, identify a 'common sense' view that you feel is not accurate and give reasons. Then compare your findings with another group.

4. Can you always rely on experts when they are telling us scientific facts? List the reasons why you should and then try to put an opposite view for each one.

5. Give an example of where statistics are often used, can be mathematically correct but are misleading. Opinion polls in newspapers can be misleading, why is this?

Questions for a written answer

1. What is a 'scientific method'? Make a list of everything that needs to be included.

2. Should scientists be guided by mathematics even when the answers seem to be wrong? Give examples in favour of this and against it.

3. Scientists are seldom objective therefore science needs to be under the control of politicians. Discuss.

4. Explain an experiment you did in science that proved something, why was it 'proof'?

5. Possible evidence has been published to show that there is life on Mars. Explain what is generally understood by 'life' and what scientists might mean by 'life on another planet'. Discuss any evidence which you know of that supports the view that life exists elsewhere in the universe. Be careful to distinguish between 'fact' (evidence) and 'opinion' (supposition).

Examiners will look for the following in your written answer:

- Evidence that you have understood the source material and can make appropriate use of it.
- You need to be able to make value judgements based on it and support these with evidence or interpretation.
- You need to have something of your own to say and to be able to state it clearly.
- You need to show you can relate this work to other relevant areas of study.

❓ Quiz

1. What does 'cogito ergo sum' mean?
2. What is epistemology?
3. What was Sir Karl Popper's views on scientific facts?
4. How many pairs of chromosomes do we have?
5. What was the contribution to science made by the Leakeys?
6. What was the big mistake that Einstein admitted to?
7. What is the way to discover the truth according to Hegel?
8. Why did Germany expel Albert Einstein?
9. What is an axiom?
10. What is the 'dialectic'?

Were women made to serve men?

ACTIVITY 1

In pairs think of a common-sense assumption, one that is taken to be an axiom, a self-evident truth. Then discuss where it started and why it is not questioned. There are differences between men and women that are taken as being self-evident – are they? We evolved from an ape-like creature millions of years ago – or did we?

'A lower speed limit will reduce death on the road.' Is this self-evident or can it be challenged?

Make a list of five axioms that appear to be self-evident.

Present your axioms to the rest of your class or group. You could use flip charts or computer software to do this. The rest of the group should challenge your axioms and you should be prepared to defend them.

What does the outcome of this exercise tell you about the nature of axioms in general?

ACTIVITY 2

A perspective is one way of organizing evidence. Divide into two groups. One group is to take the perspective that school uniforms are necessary and the second to argue against them.

On a board, list the evidence for both sides of the argument.

Both groups must argue using the same evidence – that which is on the board – no other evidence may be introduced.

15 Does unlocking DNA mean perfection or problems?

Preview

On Monday 12 February 2001 the *New York Times* published the news that two competing groups had mapped the human genome. There was a world-wide reaction to the news and wonderful claims were made for the importance of this 'book of the entire human genetic code'. It was hailed as being a bigger scientific breakthrough than the discovery of antibiotics and comparable to the landing on the moon. We were told that its impact on all of us would be rapid and dramatic because cancer, ageing and congenital disease would all soon disappear. The then President of the United States, Bill Clinton said: 'Today we are learning the language in which God created life, we are gaining ever more awe for the complexity, the beauty, the wonder of God's most divine and sacred gift'.

The science behind it

Genes are the instructions in a cell nucleus to make cells do a particular job. Genes are inherited from both parents and the full genetic code is three billion letters long. Inside the nucleus of humans are 23 pairs of chromosomes. One chromosome from the mother paired with one from the father. The parts are then 'shuffled', a bit like playing cards, so a baby is dealt a selection and an individual is created from it. Each chromosome contains DNA, a coiled double-stranded molecule. Genes are a particular length of DNA found on our chromosomes and affect a particular characteristic, such as eye colour. Some of our characteristics are polygenic, which means they are due to a combination of genes, for example being athletic. Humans have approximately 100,000 genes. The human genome is the full set of genetic information carried by an individual. Most of the DNA we have (99%) is identical in everybody. However the other 1% of it makes us different from one another. Some types of DNA differ so much between individuals that each person is effectively unique. So DNA sampling, or genetic fingerprinting, is being used by police forces in forensic investigations to identify people with a certainty that was previously impossible.

TIPS FOR FURTHER RESEARCH

You could extend your research by looking at the history of eugenics from 1883 onwards. An English scientist called Francis Galton put forward ideas on improving intelligence and behaviour.

Is it as important as it is claimed?

The potential benefits are certainly impressive. One in three of us will get cancer, one in five die of it. There are over 200 types of cancer genes. Cancer genes have a growth instruction that is faulty. If genetic engineering could turn off that instruction then that, on its own, would be enough to justify the excitement. There are believed to be over 1600 diseases that can be linked to a single gene. More people now die of genetic disease than deaths caused by war, disease or starvation. Typical diseases are diabetes, liver failure, kidney disease, Alzheimer's and Parkinson's diseases. It may also be able to reverse the ageing process. Almost all the cells in our body contain inbuilt 'clocks' called telemores. These are like a 'tail' of DNA that gets shorter every time it replicates. Eventually there is no more left and the cell dies. If this could be reversed then you would have an 'immortal' cell. If these immortal genes could be identified and controlled then ageing would stop. If you asked most people if they wanted to live forever the answer would probably be no, but if people were asked if they wanted to stay physically at their best for longer the answer would be an emphatic yes. Most people dread old age because of infirmity and a reduced quality of life. Currently scientists are saying that genetics could give everyone a life expectancy of 150. This would be a much more attractive option if you could stay young as well.

The Queen Mother – born in 1900, died in 2002: what genetic (or other) factors do you think contributed to such longevity?

W EB LINKS

Try http://vector.cshl.org/genetic for further information or search using key terms such as 'human genome'.

Are there any problems?

Genes only specify the sequence of amino acids that are linked together. These are part of the manufacture of a molecule that folds up to become a protein. We are still not sure about the way genes make particular proteins and exactly how this affects an individual. There are millions of non-gene stretches of DNA. These may also reveal information, for example about the way we evolved or even the potential for further evolutionary development. The problem is that genetic engineering may interfere with a process that is only partly understood. Making changes could have unexpected results in future generations.

Genes are relatively simple compared to proteins which have a three-dimensional structure. If we assume that humans have 32,000 genes it is not a lot compared to a mustard weed which has 26,000 or the nematode worm that has 18,000. If the difference between a weed and us is only that we have 25% more genes then a number of scientists have said that there must be more to it than that. There are a lot more proteins than there are genes and proteins are a lot more complex. Perhaps that is where we should be looking. There are about 3500 million base pairs in the human genome. We are not sure what a lot of them do nor are we sure exactly how the proteins work that are made as a consequence.

If there are problems then are there dangers?

Is it possible or likely that genetic engineering could present a threat? It is certainly possible that gradual scientific advances could eventually result in major changes. It would start with the – very desirable – removal of known genetic disease. For example Tay–Sachs disease causes the brain to degenerate in the first few years of life. Currently those at risk are genetically tested and offered an abortion if it is present in a foetus. Soon it may be possible to offer to change the DNA so the child will be born without the disease. Down's syndrome is due to a duplicate copy of chromosome 21 being present so it could also be eliminated before the child is born. It is only a small step to then have minor improvements for children, a little bit taller or removal of short-sightedness for example. Some parents would then want their children to have more intelligence or have the best possible physique. You are then in an area where other parents are faced with a choice of their child being at a disadvantage compared to others. Just try to think of a law that tells people they cannot spend their money to give their child 'the best chance' in life. Another area of 'improvement' would be if genetic engineers could introduce DNA sequences from outside of that individual. People could be made with the aggressive traits removed for example, or DNA from another species could be introduced. Athletic ability or eyesight could be improved by using DNA from another source in the animal kingdom. A very narrow line separates repair and improvement in genetic engineering.

HG Wells' *Time Machine* describes the Eloi and the Morlocks. How could this type of divided society be brought about by genetic manipulation?

Transgenic means a foreign gene has been added to it. Another term used is chimera, which is a creature made when cells from one organism are implanted into the embryo of another. A chimera was a mythological creature with a lion's head, a goat's body and a serpent's tail.

Is this being used already?

Animal experiments are providing a lot of evidence and commercial applications are already becoming apparent. They have found that they can accelerate the growth rate by 12% and create adult animals 50% bigger than usual with a much higher proportion of muscle. Other firms have developed salmon that grow faster and bigger and there are a flock of 120 transgenic sheep that produce much more wool than usual but only eat the same amount of grass as unaltered sheep. Animals could have human cells implanted so their organs could be used for transplants in to people.

Is it likely to affect most people?

An example of how this research could have far-reaching consequences is that men may become redundant. Researchers at Monash University in Australia say it may be possible to produce an embryo from a female egg by 'fertilizing' it with a reprogrammed female cell. It is more complicated to try to do it with two male cells as there is a problem of 'imprinting'. Some genes appear to be switched on or off depending on whether they are passed down from the mother or the father but this area is not yet fully understood. If women do not need men to have a baby, what do you think could be the long-term effects on society?

A chimera. Ancient mythology often put different animals together in order to draw on the perceived strengths of each

SCIENCE AND TECHNOLOGY

Another problem is the possible disadvantages for people who already have genetic disorders. The Department of Health and the Association of British Insurers have been discussing plans to allow insurers to use gene tests to see if there is a family history of certain illnesses which could develop later in life. These would include Huntingdon's disease, cystic fibrosis, Alzheimer's, sickle-cell anaemia and a form of breast cancer. An underclass of uninsurable people could be created.

Conclusion

Can we say with confidence that if it is a medical advance then it will benefit most people? The history of using scientific ideas to improve the human race does not make good reading. Eugenics was suggested by many leading figures all around the world in the early 1900s. This was the way the physical and mental quality of a people could be improved by selective breeding. It was the basis for the Nazi party to exterminate millions of people and try to create a master race during the Second World War. The ideas are still here. In Singapore in 1986 extra money was promised to women graduates when they had a child and housing grants were offered to non-graduate women if they were sterilized after their first or second child. The benefits of genetic engineering are clear but the dangers are also very real. Perhaps it is a question of how it should be controlled?

Questions for discussion

1. If you were about to become a parent and you knew your child would be smaller than average with weak eyesight would you pay to have a genetic improvement? Divide into groups and discuss it with one group in favour and the other group against.

2. What sort of rules do you think should be made to control genetic engineering? Explain your choice to your group and identify the areas you all agree on.

3. Some politicians and members of the police force would like everyone to have an ID card and a DNA profile. Do you think this is a good idea?

4. Do you think most people would want to live to 150 years old? Put forward views for and against this. What would make such great age more/less attractive?

Questions for written answer

1. Explain the term 'unlocking the human genome'.

2. Why could genetic engineering used in the next five years be a threat to future generations?

3. Would you agree to having a DNA profile? List the possible advantages and disadvantages.

4. How important is religion in deciding how to control genetic research on people?

TIPS FOR FURTHER RESEARCH

The ideas of 'ethnic cleansing' have been present for much of our history. It is the basis of anti-Semitism. This is an area that could be researched in considerable detail. The recent conflicts in Serbia and Croatia are examples of this idea being imposed.

Examiners will look for the following in your written answer:

- Evidence that you have understood the source material and can make appropriate use of it.
- You need to be able to make value judgements based on it and support these with evidence or interpretation.
- You need to have something of your own to say and to be able to state it clearly.
- You need to show you can relate this work to other relevant areas of study.

5. Do you think a society of perfect humans would be a good idea?

6. Animals have been improved by selective breeding for a long time, is genetic engineering just a more modern version of the same thing? Explain your views.

7. If people could live longer and be in good health, how do you think it would change the world?

8. Do you think governments should pay well educated people to have more children and unemployed people to have less? Explain your reasons.

9. The average lifespan in developed countries has been predicted to increase further in the foreseeable future. How far do you consider increased longevity to be a good thing?

? Quiz

1. What is a gene?
2. What is a chromosome?
3. What is forensic science?
4. What happens when someone has Alzheimer's disease?
5. Why should we research proteins instead of DNA?
6. What is a Chimera? Give an example of one that would benefit people.
7. What DNA research could end two-parent families?
8. How could DNA research end Down's syndrome?
9. If you could not get any life insurance, what effect might it have on your life?
10. How did the Nazi party adopt the theory of eugenics?

ACTIVITY

Prepare a debate on the view 'The development of the human race'. One group are to prepare arguments for identifying undesirable qualities in embryos and preventing them going full term. This could be by genetic manipulation or termination. The end product would be an end to extremely violent personalities and many disabilities. Humanity would then continue to evolve. The second group are to argue against this as it threatens personal freedom and could be abused. The definition of a civilized society is the way it cares for minority and disadvantaged groups.

There is a quotation attributed to Churchill which goes something like this (he was speaking to a female MP):

Churchill: Would you sleep with me for a million pounds?

MP: Well, I suppose I would.

Churchill: Would you sleep with me for a penny?

MP: Certainly not!

Churchill: Oh come on, we've established the principle, why haggle about the price!

Think about this in the context of your discussion – what exact diseases, personality disorders or problems would you outlaw? Cancer is an obvious contender at one end of the scale, teenage spots at the other. But who would decide? And would the treatments be for everyone or just those who can afford it?

SCIENCE AND TECHNOLOGY

16 Genetically modified crops and the nature of progress

Preview

Is the reaction to genetically modified (GM) crops comparable to the reaction to the machinery that replaced the traditional loom? In areas around Nottingham and parts of Yorkshire in the early 1800s a group of factory workers went round smashing up machinery as they were objecting to it being used to make textiles. They were trying to halt progress and they lost. The jobs they had and the way of life they were used to all changed with the new technology. Recently people have been burning GM crops as they say they are a threat. The argument is that GM crops are part of the same unstoppable process – progress.

Why do we need GM crops?

Pick up a paper on any day and you read about somewhere having a shortage of food, pictures of stick-like children and a part of the world where starvation is happening to thousands of people. Lack of food is a major killer somewhere in the world. GM crops are able to produce more food from the same fields.

But surely, you ask, we have fertilizers, pesticides and insecticides to help to grow more food, why use GM crops? You often get news items about the poor quality of our food, BSE and infected foods. For example, a recent inspection by the government's pesticides residue committee of food in major supermarkets found high levels of pesticides, some over the legal limit. Overall, 56% of lettuces sampled contained some residues with multiple residues in 42%. A sample of pears from one of the biggest food retailers was found to contain chlomequat – a pesticide that is not approved for use in the UK. The report went on to mention 26% of Spanish cucumbers and 23% of plums contained pesticide residues. A government spokesman said that only 79% were free of residues. So every day you may be eating food containing very toxic chemicals, ones designed to kill insects or microbes. What effect will it have on your digestive system?

What are GM crops and why not use them?

The planet needs to produce more food and at affordable prices. Genetic engineering offers one way out of the problems. Genetic engineering is the deliberate manipulation of genetic material in the nucleus of living cells using biochemical techniques. This would alter plants or animals so that they are free of the diseases that often kill them. It could alter crops so they produce a bigger yield and more food will be available. We have been improving plants for thousands of years, so why not just carry on with it, why isn't GM being used more widely?

How to make a GM plant

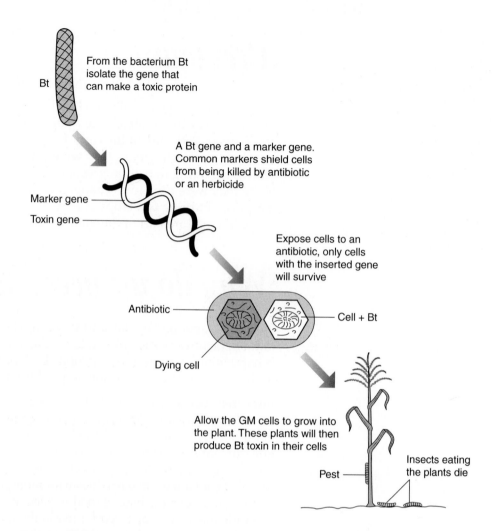

Bt

From the bacterium Bt isolate the gene that can make a toxic protein

A Bt gene and a marker gene. Common markers shield cells from being killed by antibiotic or an herbicide

Marker gene

Toxin gene

Expose cells to an antibiotic, only cells with the inserted gene will survive

Antibiotic

Cell + Bt

Dying cell

Allow the GM cells to grow into the plant. These plants will then produce Bt toxin in their cells

Pest

Insects eating the plants die

The problem is that as soon as GM food is mentioned a mass fear appears, people march in the streets to oppose it and some even set fire to farmers' crops. That is why they are compared to the workers who smashed the looms. Horror stories of deformed children and long-term risks to health are quoted. Are we just frightened of a new technology or is industry in danger of harming mankind in its pursuit of money? It has happened in the past. Are the risks as bad as some people claim, are the benefits as real? Is there a middle ground?

The points in favour of GM crops

Genetic modification is said to be just a more sophisticated advance on the breeding we have been doing for centuries. Gardeners often graft one plant on to another or cross-pollinate to improve the plant. So is the current GM technique so very different? The answer is yes, it is. In simple terms strawberries will only be affected by other strawberries, but modern science could put part of an elephant gene in a strawberry. As a matter of interest, humans share 50% of their genes with bananas. Changes can now be made that could never occur in nature even with major mutations. However GM only introduces a few carefully selected genes whereas cross-breeding introduces thousands of genes.

TIPS FOR FURTHER RESEARCH

Look up any government reports on food. Read articles in journals such as the *Scientific American* and the *New Scientist*. Research Dr Vandana Shiva's Reith Lectures, May 2000. Read Tony Trewavas in the journal *Nature*, March 2001 and Paul Heiney, author of *Home Farm*.

A gene is a length of the DNA inside the nucleus of every living cell. DNA are the chemical instructions to the cell, to tell it its job. Since the 1980s we have the technical ability to transfer 'foreign' genes into plants and animals. Any living organism that has had a foreign gene added to it is called transgenic. Species of plants have been made resistant to weed killers so only the weeds are killed off. A bacterial gene can be introduced that makes plants resistant to insects that would normally eat them. Insecticides are then no longer needed. Insecticides and pesticides do a lot of environmental damage and they can work through the food chain. It may be that insecticides present a bigger threat to our well-being than GM food. Every year US growers use 440 million kilograms of pesticides on crops. These stay on the crops, enter the soil and are eaten by wildlife. In Africa a GM sweet potato has been developed that shows resistance to the disease that normally causes the loss of between 20% and 80% of the crop. GM crops can produce higher yields, in less favourable climates, with less ploughing, less fertilizer, and need less insecticide. This means less pollution, less soil erosion, fewer chemicals in the food chain and less work for farmers in the developing world. It is claimed that the developing world in particular has benefited from it. GM foods have been around for over 10 years and are being widely used, for example, fatless chips, calorie-free sugars and so on. It is estimated that over 60% of processed food sold in the USA contain a GM ingredient especially soy, corn, or canola; some fresh vegetables are altered as well.

The argument against GM crops

There are three main concerns:

- That innocent creatures will be hurt by insecticides built into many GM crops. Laboratory tests where massive overdoses are used do show harm to insects, but field trials using more normal amounts do not. Bugs, birds and worms will all come into contact with GM crops.

- Superweeds could easily arise as most GM crops have a 'weedy' relative and cross-pollination could accidentally occur as GM and non-GM could interact in an unchecked way. You then have a weed you cannot control. This is a real issue and restrictions are in place concerning what grows where. Herbicide-resistant weeds are already being reported in Canada.

- The GM crops will suddenly fail because insects will evolve tolerance. Evolution is probably the biggest worry as agriculture is like an evolutionary race between protection and pests. In the same way virus-resistant GM crops could evolve. There is already evidence of diseases like the 'super'-flu virus that evolve and are resistant to any treatment. If we got 'superweeds' and 'superbugs' it could put present famines in the category of a mild headache in comparison to the plague.

- We do not know the long-term effect on people. Do you trust big business to fully research the effect of chemicals before they are sold? If you do, then research the thalidomide drug and its effects in the 1960s.

Some opponents of GM in plants and in animals use a religious argument. They say GM breaks the bounds between species and is unnatural; that man is playing God and that the new technology meddles with the divine order.

The middle ground

We seem to be stuck between starvation and a risk of a global disaster. Is there a middle way; is genetic engineering the only answer or even the best answer? Consider the following:

- The first is that there are areas of food surplus as well as shortage. It's just a question of having the money to move the food to where it is needed. Trade policy and reducing developing world debt along with information on better farming methods could provide a better long-term solution to famine.

- Integrated farm management can often offer other solutions by using mixed crops instead of concentrating on one cash crop. Research has shown that small farms with a wide range of crops produce more food than large, industrial monocultures. Greenfly can be killed off by ladybirds instead of chemicals.

- Piped water can bring more food production than GM seeds.

It is still not very clear why some people get so emotional about GM. Perhaps it is the language that puts people off? 'Genetically engineered strawberries' would probably stop many people from buying, whereas 'organically grown strawberries' would probably sell for a higher price. Instead we could try 'improved strawberries' compared to 'fruit grown in animal excrement' and see what happened.

As Darwin said: 'It is not the strongest of the species that survive, nor the most intelligent, but the one most responsive to change'.

Questions for discussion

1. Are pesticides and insecticides any more of a risk than GM crops?
2. What would be the advantages of reducing Third World debt instead of using GM crops.
3. What are the religious objections to genetic engineering? Do you agree or disagree with these objections?
4. Briefly explain three ways of improving food production without using GM crops.
5. Testing of GM crops has been taking place for 10 years. Is this long enough? Explain your answer.
6. How would the introduction of GM crops indirectly reduce pollution?
7. Many people are afraid of genetic modifications. Explain why: (a) from a religious point of view and (b) from a long-term medical view. Evaluate the reasons.

Examiners will look for the following in your written answer:

- Evidence that you have understood the source material and can make appropriate use of it.
- You need to be able to make value judgements based on it and support these with evidence or interpretation.
- You need to have something of your own to say and to be able to state it clearly.
- You need to show you can relate this work to other relevant areas of study.

Questions for written answer

1. Explain what is meant by genetic modification of food. Discuss the issues which arise from this practice, outlining for and against its continuing development and use.

2. Explain what a GM crop is and identify where it is different to traditional methods for improving crops. Outline the problems of testing GM crops. How do you think that they could be safely tested?

3. Discuss three possible benefits and three possible dangers of GM crops. In each case, explain to whom it would be a danger or a benefit. Then draw a balanced conclusion to say whether you think GM crops should be allowed.

4. Since GM food was first invented and tested it has thrown up moral dilemmas while legislation has often been slow to catch up. Using any scientific or medical advance with which you are familiar:

   - briefly describe the meaning of the medical or scientific progress
   - discuss the rights of the parties involved, highlighting what problems may arise
   - discuss the possible regulation that could be introduced and how it would be enforced
   - argue whether you believe that the threat to civil liberties, or the rights of the parties involved, is greater than the benefits from the innovation.

5. What is progress? How would you define it? What might stop an innovation or advance being 'progress' in your opinion?

? Multiple-choice questions

1. Chlomequat is an illegal pesticide that was found in the UK on:
   a) pears
   b) apples
   c) oranges
   d) grapes.

2. Which of the following has been found to contain pesticide residues in the UK? i) lettuces, ii) plums, iii) pears.
   a) i and ii only
   b) i and iii only
   c) none of these
   d) all of these.

3. Which of the following is not used to kill something in agriculture?
   a) pesticide
   b) insecticide
   c) fertilizer
   d) herbicide.

4. According to a government report, how much of the food bought in UK supermarkets has toxic residues in it?
   a) less than 10%
   b) between 10 and 25%
   c) between 25 and 50%
   d) over 50%.

5. Approximately what proportion of American foodstuffs has GM ingredients?
   a) less than 25%
   b) between 25% and 50%
   c) between 50% and 75%
   d) over 75%.

6. Genetic modification mostly involves which branch of science?
   a) biology
   b) botany
   c) chemistry
   d) biochemistry.

7. Humans and bananas – how similar are they in genetic terms?
   a) 25% of genes the same
   b) 50% of genes the same
   c) 75% of genes the same
   d) 99% of genes the same.

8. Which of these GM foods are sold in the USA? i) soy, ii) canola, iii) corn.
   a) i and ii only
   b) i and iii only
   c) none of these
   d) all of these.

ACTIVITY

A farmer, under contract to a chemical firm, is doing trials of a GM crop just outside the village, town or city where you live. Assume an attempt had been made to (illegally) burn the farmers' crops.

Divide into small groups. Each group should write two newspaper articles, one supporting GM crops, the other opposing their introduction. Each article should be between 300–400 words long and contain as much evidence as you can find (use the library and the internet) to support your case. Each should be presented in as biased a way as possible.

Examples of evidence could be that the GM crop could improve maize and be used in the developing world where they currently have only subsistence farming or that the GM crop has long-term unknown effects on people and farmers in the developing world could be helped in other ways such as using clean water, introduced insects or natural methods.

The articles should be passed around, or put on the wall, so that everyone has a chance to read everyone else's.

The class will then be divided into two groups to represent the two opposing sides at an international conference. One group is to argue for the use of GM crops, the other for their destruction or, at least, control. You must come to an agreed conclusion and issue a joint communiqué (in the manner of such groups) saying what you have agreed.

SCIENCE AND TECHNOLOGY

An experience that changes your life ...?

17

Preview

Recently there was a big rush of investment into businesses based on the internet, which were called 'dot.com' companies. Some of these entrepreneurs became millionaires in hours without their companies earning a penny. Then, a few months later, the market in them crashed and lot of money was lost. So is it just 'over-hyped' technology? Grand claims for new technology are often made; television is full of advertising for washing machines that it is claimed 'will change your life', for example. The question is, will the internet and its development change the way we live or is it just another useful piece of technology like the mobile phone?

From Pentagon to supermarket

The internet started in the 1970s as a way of storing military information. 'Arpanet' linked US Defense Department Pentagon computers to university ones so that data could be both moved and stored without the enemy (at the time, the Soviet Union) accessing it. However, there was nothing to stop any computer from linking to the net with the result that it grew and was made public property in 1984. There was little further growth until the World Wide Web was launched in 1993 and the first usable 'browser' – Netscape Navigator – made it possible for anyone to access it. From this standing start a huge growth surge saw, by 1995, about five million computers connected. By 2000 this had grown to over 100 million computers.

In the USA selling on the internet is worth $3.5 billion a year and showing a steady growth. However, this growth has been lower than predicted. Online shopping, for example, has not grown as forecast. The current figure is closer to 1% and growth is slow. There are about six million internet shoppers now world-wide, three times more than in 1999. The conclusion is that people are not as attracted to its use as experts thought. Of course, there is a big problem with shopping online – online ordering is really no more technologically advanced than ringing an order in – the problem is that the purchases still have to be physically delivered.

Getting the information in

Perhaps it is people that are the main reason for slow growth, not the technology. If it is, then it could take 10 or 20 years to grow to a maximum. We all know of households with a computer that is only used for games or the odd item of homework. The general public are not willing to keep up with the latest computer technology. Many adults are very cautious about learning to use a

The QWERTY keyboard was originally developed to slow typists down. The letters were placed so that, on a mechanical typewriter, they were less likely to jam. Other keyboards have been introduced, but none has taken off.

computer and only use it if they have to in the course of their work. Most of the people who do use it only make use of the e-mail and to look for information about things they intend to buy. Statistics have been reported that indicate that 80% of the 12 million people who use the net in the UK access only 20% of the available websites. Perhaps the growth in the internet will only occur when using computers is much more user-friendly. How far can this go? The main way of inputting information is still the typewriter keyboard – but how long can this last?

The general belief in the industry is that computing capacity will double every 18 months, this is called Moore's law. So by 2025 we may have computers as 'intelligent' as people. Voice-activated systems are already in place in numerous applications and the next generation of computer games will have far more voice activated functions. The problem that will still remain is that most of our speech is almost totally lacking in logic when it is in sentences. Word recognition when dictating to a word processor does not present a problem. However, anything more than a simple sentence is very difficult for a computer to understand and then reply to. We understand other people from sentences spoken to us partly from the meaning of the words being used, partly from the context in which the sentence is placed and partly from our knowledge of the person speaking and the meanings they are likely to give to a set of words. We use a kind of inspired guesswork a lot of the time, called intuition, to understand each other. Whether a computer will be able to unscramble that in a reliable way will be a major task. One area of research is called 'fuzzy logic' – trying to teach computers to think more like humans in an effort to solve the problem.

A fictional 'supercomputer'

In 1999 the US had around 60% of households connected to the internet; Europe had around 25%, Asia and the Pacific Rim 15%, Latin America 5% and Africa and the Middle East insignificant amounts. The biggest potential area for growth is China. (*Source:* Neil Denby, *Teach Yourself E-Commerce*, Hodder & Stoughton, 2001.)

Lessons from history

Science fiction writer Arthur C Clarke said everyone overestimates technology in the short term and underestimates it in the long term. There are many experts who are sure that while it may be off to a slow start, using the internet will quickly accelerate for the majority of people. Other technology was slow to be accepted at first but eventually raced ahead. Looking back, the telephone and television were slow to be used, then suddenly everyone was converted to using one and it became considered a necessity. In 1959 Xerox released its first photocopier. Their market research said 3000 might be sold. Over 200,000 were sold and by 1986 over 200 billion copies of documents were being made. Mobile phones are a good example of how an item of technology rapidly became as important as wearing shoes.

Changing the way we live

One widely held view is that computers, and the internet, will not be any more important than mobile phones have become: they are useful and convenient but no one lives any differently since they became available. Interaction between people is a fundamental part of our nature; while some internet shopping will probably be a part of everyday life, it is unlikely to completely replace the social side of going shopping with other people. Being able to squeeze a piece of fruit or stroke a piece of cloth cannot be simulated by a computer. Working from home is now possible for a lot of occupations, especially those linked to computer applications – examples include CAD work, writing, database management, architecture, office work. However, the social interactions in everyday work are something most people seem unwilling to give up. This would suggest the internet will not alter society any more than television or telephones did.

TIPS FOR FURTHER RESEARCH

Look up Bill Gates and his predictions of the information super-highway.

You could extend your understanding of how technology can change a society by researching how civilizations in the Mediterranean area developed as they moved into the Iron Age. In particular the way their day-to-day life altered and how the balance of power was changed between civilizations by ownership of the new technology.

The Oregon Trail

Bill Gates, who founded Microsoft, and Jim Clark, who founded Netscape, have shown that billions of dollars can be made very quickly with the right idea. Some analysts have predicted an Information Highway being developed from the internet. They compared the present internet to the Oregon Trail that opened up the American West. Their thought is that the Information Highway will develop from the internet as the dirt track that was the Oregon Trail developed to the modern six-lane highway that has replaced it. The Information Highway will make total communication available to everyone and this would change the way we live. If we have all the data available to us then the type of work people do will change for most of us. Soon people will be able to talk across distances with a three-dimensional hologram in front of them of the person they are talking to. The world of entertainment will change in unimaginable ways as we explore the technology of virtual reality. The television series *Red Dwarf* was based on this idea as are the 'holodecks' in *Star Trek*. In the future everyone could have their own interactive database that remembers everything about them and organizes their life.

Big Brother is watching you

Big Brother was not invented by a television station. Read George Orwell's *1984* to see the writer's version of a real 'Big Brother'.

One effect of this information highway could be advertising being directed at individuals rather than the television adverts or posters aimed at everyone. Billions of pounds are spent on advertising. Most advertising is wasted, most people find it a nuisance unless it is for the particular item they are interested in. Even amusing adverts are irritating after endless repeats. If business could build up a database of what each person buys and how much they have to spend then it could focus the advertising on individuals and the things they were likely to buy. This flow of information would be worth billions of dollars. The problem is that a detailed database of every individual could also mean that people could be manipulated in ways we currently find unacceptable. A 'Big Brother' government, watching your every move, could then be a real possibility.

You pays yer money ...

WEB LINKS
www.microsoft.com/billgates/ needs handling with care, as it is the official site of Gates.
Moore's law discussion is at www.intel.com/research/silicon/mooreslaw.htm
www.webpan.com/msauers/bibliography.html is a bibliography of Information Highway information.
www.generation5.org/fuzzyintro.shtml for fuzzy logic

So, computer technology will have more and more effect on us as it becomes more and more sophisticated and able to interact with us. It will take over more and more of our daily lives and quickly alter the way we live. The way people will earn a living will change, and our ideas on wealth and ownership will have to follow suit. For example, if total communication is possible then the best price for anything is just a mouse click away – the perfect market. The waste of food and over- (and under-) production of goods would end. Universal translators would mean no more misunderstandings and world peace.

Or perhaps the technology will just be another high-tech toy and be no more significant than a televised telephone service. The human being has lived together in family and social groups for several million years. It is human nature to live and interact with others on a personal basis, not an electronic one.

Questions for discussion

1. A Steven Spielberg film called *AI* was about an android with a supercomputer brain. A similar character was Commander Data in the *Star Trek: Next Generation* series. Do you think these androids could ever be more than just clever machines made to look like people? Argue both for and against the view they should be treated as living creatures.

2. Why do you think there was a big investment into 'dot.com' companies before they had made a profit? Why did many companies then crash? What does this say about the views of big business on the net?

3. Virtual reality can simulate shapes and sounds. When it can simulate touch, taste and smells do you think it will replace holidays? Explain the reasons for your answer.

4. If a database was made with all your likes and dislikes on it, would you welcome it or feel threatened by it? Would it be an intrusion into your personal privacy? Could propaganda be more effective if it was personalized?

Examiners will look for the following in your written answer:

- Evidence that you have understood the source material and can make appropriate use of it.
- You need to be able to make value judgements based on it and support these with evidence or interpretation.
- You need to have something of your own to say and to be able to state it clearly.
- You need to show you can relate this work to other relevant areas of study.

Questions for written answer

1. The 'millennium bug' threatened to crash computers world-wide. If the worst projections had been correct, what would have happened? What does this show about our dependency on computers?

2. What is the difference between using a personal computer and using the internet?

3. If you were going to try using the web to do your weekly shopping for a family, are there any reasons why you would still need to visit a shop?

4. Do you think the use of computers will increase at its present rate or will it rapidly take over most areas of our lives? Provide reasons for your views.

5. Consider how new technology advances could be used in a 'Big Brother' type way. Suggest developments that either have happened or could happen and discuss the implications of these for the safety and security of society as against the possible erosion of civil liberties.

? Quiz

1. Is the use of the internet growing faster or slower than expected?

2. Are some areas of internet sales more successful than others?

3. What factors may limit the growth of the internet?

4. What is Moore's law?

5. What is 'fuzzy logic'?

6. What is fibre-optic cable? Would it change anything?

7. Who coined the phrase Information Super Highway?

8. What was the name of the first usable browser?

9. Which countries do you think have the greatest potential for internet usage growth?

10. Who coined the phrase 'Big Brother'?

ACTIVITY 1

Work in small groups. Each group should prepare two sets of arguments as follows:

a) There should be a complete change in how education is delivered. Everyone will be working via computers from home. Experiences of anything can be recreated using virtual reality devices so there is no need for field trips or other visits. Even team games can be played in a virtual reality setting. Universal, free education should mean a computer permanently connected to the internet for every student.

b) Computers and the associated technology, however sophisticated, are still just gadgets that will change very little. They will have no effect on the basic family structure and none on education. Education is about interaction at a personal level and cannot be adequately provided remotely – however good the remote link.

Each group should then report its views back to the general group. A vote could be taken at the end of the discussion to see which view prevails.

ACTIVITY 2

People are often confused about the various definitions regarding the new technology. Make a list to define the following terms correctly: internet, intranet, World Wide Web, browser, web host, domain name, HTML, online shopping, hologram, input/output devices, B2B, B2C, B2G, EFTPOS, EDI, plus any other you can think of. Exchange lists with other members of the group both to check definitions and to add any additional definitions to your list.

ACTIVITY 3

Write down five sentences that you know you, and a friend, would understand but a computer would have difficulty with. An example could be: 'Melanie, I don't think that dress you're wearing really suits you, it's not your colour.' Work out why you think a computer would have difficulty understanding this. Now rephrase each question so that a computer would understand. Test each sentence (in both its original and modified form) on a partner.

Darwin: right or wrong?

Preview

When evolution is mentioned everyone seems to know about the basic idea, but you get the feeling they do not really believe it. Most people accept that the scientists are happy with evolution but many people do not seem convinced. People make comments on the lines of 'Oh yeah, something crawled out of the primeval swamp and a few million years later people turned up, second cousin to a chimp'. Some groups do not accept the theory at all, the 'Creationists' for example say that the theory denies the existence of God. Most of us are comfortable with the basic idea of a gradual improvement of living things of course and that humans are at the top of the development tree. The question is to decide if we are just another animal or are we specially created by God. Does accepting this scientific theory mean you cannot believe in God?

Charles Darwin

In 1859 Charles Darwin published his book *On the Origin of Species*. He said that over a very long period of time, millions of years at least, animals adapt to their surroundings in order to compete for food and living space. This competition causes a process called natural selection, so only the fittest, or best adapted, will survive. Every now and then random changes occur (that we now call mutations) and alter the way an organism works. Bones may be longer, or an extra part of an organ may develop. Where these mutations give a living thing an advantage then it will result in it being more successful. This means successful at staying alive, producing more young or feeding them and so passing on the advantage. Mutation is necessary for evolution to work – but it is not enough. Natural selection completes the process by making sure only helpful changes (helpful at that time) will continue.

All living things compete with each other for food and space, so a process of natural selection means the less successful die out and the more adaptive survive and prosper. Over a few thousand years the change is so small as to be unnoticeable but over millions of years it can result in a completely new species evolving. Darwin expected the process to be a tiny change over hundreds of thousands of years and only on those changes that give an advantage.

If we have evolved from the same base as other animals then the links between human behaviour and other animals could be explored by research in the area of sociobiology. Look in particular at the books by Robert Ardrey and David Barash.

Gregor Mendel

At the time he wrote his book Darwin did not know about Gregor Mendel's work. Mendel correctly identified the way genes pass on information. A particular gene is responsible for a particular part of the creature. So blue eyes are due to a particular gene, brown eyes from another. A blue-eyed parent together with a brown-eyed parent will produce a mix of brown- and blue-eyed children. Some genes are more dominant than others of course. The genes go into a collection of genes from parents, and other ancestors, in a sort of gene pool. Genes then emerge in individuals a bit like cards shuffled and then dealt to a hand. Modern molecular biology provides a lot of evidence that all known life forms share the same genetic code and therefore probably share a single common ancestor. At that point some Creationists might add 'and his name was Adam!'. Unfortunately it is not as simple as that: the ancestor was not a fully formed human. Modern molecular evidence has given support to this newer theory of evolution, which is called neo-Darwinism. It is not seriously challenged by scientists although there are a number of variations to consider.

The 'watchmaker' argument

Up to 200 years ago the general view was that God had created the different species as part of a mysterious plan. Species could develop and adapt, of course; racehorses were bred to run faster for example, but one species could not become another. Farm animals, horses and dogs have all been changed by selective breeding and developed in the direction we wanted. However no one had suggested that a mouse-like creature could develop into a horse or any other species. The most common objection to Darwinism is the 'watchmaker' argument. A Victorian scientist called William Paley said that if he found a rock on the ground he could accept it could have been made by the chance action of nature. But if he found a watch then he could not accept that anything so complex could possibly occur by undirected chance – even if odds of millions to one were accepted. Looking around at the wonders of nature it must mean a designer was responsible for it all. A particular example is the human eye. Mathematic probability would seem to make it impossible for it to evolve.

Richard Dawkins

The answer that neo-Darwinists like Richard Dawkins makes is that it is not pure chance, but instead cumulative advantage that produces the evolutionary change. A cell that responds to any light will give its owner an advantage over the totally blind. Incremental improvements then result in the eye thousands of generations later. It's a bit like someone saying how could anyone build a stone arch. Until the last stone is in place it is more likely to collapse than stay up. However, if you start with a pile of rubble and gradually remove the unwanted bits to leave behind the arch, then it is much easier to understand. Dawkins says that the watchmaker in the argument is a 'blind watchmaker' who learns by his mistakes!

WEB LINKS

www.wikipedia.com/wiki/Lamarck
http://geocities.com/Athens/5168/
aat/refs_books.html for publications
www.law.umkc.edu/faculty/projects/
ftrials/scopes/scopes.htm and
www.courttv.com/greatesttrials/
scopes/versus.html. for the Scopes
monkey trial.
www-bcs.mit.edu/-steve on instinct
or culture.

Evidence from fossils and odd parts

More support for evolution and one species evolving into another came when scientists began to identify common areas between species. Some of the connections between species were a bit surprising. Many creatures have spare bits that serve no purpose. We have an appendix for example in common with grass eaters. The appendix is for digesting the cellulose in grass. Whales have tiny buried hind-limbed bones that could have been the legs of their ancestors. Some fish have a buoyancy organ that is very much like a lung used by land dwellers. It would seem that some odd things have occurred along the evolutionary path, it has not been the totally logical progression that suggests a master design.

Fossils are an area that is debated with different groups claiming they prove different things for them. The record provided by fossils is by no means complete and new clues are being found all the time. Recently Dr Per Ahlberg found fragments of a 370 million-year-old creature that was part way between fish and mammal. All 2500 species of land animals share a common ancestor known as a tetrapod. It is thought to have looked a bit like a crocodile a little over a metre long with teeth. Not everyone accepts this record of evolution: Creationists say this fossil record does not show the unbroken move from one species to another so it does not support Darwinism. Some do not accept that things evolved over millions of years and say that the separate species were created in a much shorter time period. The Darwinists say the first fossils are 600 million years old, the first vertebrates 400 million years old and land-based animals began 250 million years ago. Dinosaurs became extinct 65 million years ago and the first human fossils have been found about two million years old.

Why were these created? Why then did they die out?

Read *The Scars of Evolution* by Elaine Morgan; *The Seven Daughters of Eve* by Bryan Sykes, *The Aquatic Ape: Fact or Fiction?* – a collection of 22 essays published by Souvenir Press. (A number of articles and even books are available online.)

Alternative views

There has always been a religious view that does not fully accept evolution. The main objection is that the theory of evolution means that humans evolved without any purpose or meaning other than simple survival. They say that if it is pure chance that produced humans then God can have no place in it. Different views have prevailed at different times:

- In 1925 there was a famous trial in Tennessee in the USA. A teacher called John Scopes was prosecuted for teaching evolutionary theory in a state school as the theory denied God. The trial was broadcast nationwide on the radio. Scopes was found guilty but released on a technicality.

- In the 1960s a book called *The Genesis Flood* was a bestseller. It said the Earth was created 10,000 years ago and Noah's Ark had held 17,500 kinds of creature. Shortly after this two American states ruled that it should be taught alongside Darwin's theory of evolution. It was overturned in 1982 when a judge said Creationism did not qualify as a scientific theory.

- In 1991 another best selling book called *Darwin on Trial* put forward the view that evolution was wrong.

There is no clear agreement between the different groups and even inside the broad group of Evolutionists there are variations of thought.

The trial of John Scopes: he argued that humans are descended from apes

TIPS FOR FURTHER RESEARCH

Look up and compare the Creationist theories of all the major modern world religions. Can you spot any significant similarities? Find out how the ancient Greeks, Romans, Egyptians, Celts, Aztecs and Incas thought that the world was created. Again, are there any significant similarities?

In 1972 Stephen Jay Gould presented a case to say that Darwin's idea of a slow and gradual rate of evolution is wrong. Gould believed it more likely that there would be long periods where no changes took place followed by a fairly rapid rate of change. By rapid he means around 100,000 years. This could be due to a climate change or a change in the geography of an area that caused a species to separate into distinct groups that lived in different conditions. He calls his theory that of 'punctuated equilibrium' and it is widely accepted. He also thought that the appearance of a new species is a separate process to the gradual evolution of adaptive changes within a species. This second part is in conflict with neo-Darwinism.

Conclusion

Is evolution just an example of scientists putting together a jumble of evidence and insisting on an answer when it is the mysterious working of a God whose plan is beyond our understanding? If we are the accidental result of biochemical reactions and simple survival then how do we explain our development with regard to truth, beauty and justice? Propagation of the species and survival of the fittest cannot explain Mother Theresa of Calcutta, Nelson Mandela and hundreds like them. Pope John Paul decided to accept evolution as an established scientific theory but this did not mean the Catholic Church thought science could produce a life force or deny the existence of the human soul.

Questions for discussion

1. Why is the timescale so important to supporters of Darwin's theory of evolution?

2. Read through the first chapter of Genesis in the Bible. How could this version of creation be correct?

3. What is the 'watchmaker' argument and what are your views on it.

4. It has been pointed out that a haemoglobin molecule is made of four chains of 146 amino acids. There are 20 different amino acids. The odds of one correct chain being made by chance are therefore 20 times itself 146 times. This is only one part of our system so pure chance could not produce it. How would a Darwinist answer this criticism?

5. If we are an accidental development then why should we have a moral code or any ideas about right or wrong? Do you think animals have ideas about truth, beauty or morality?

Questions for written answer

1. If you agree with the basic idea of evolution, do you think it is gradual or in the spurts that Gould has suggested? Explain your reasons.

2. Recently Professor Tim Crow proposed that there was a gene in humans (but not apes) that changed the way our brain developed and so gave us the ability to produce language. In what way would our evolution have altered if we only had the language range of a chimp or dolphin? Explain your reasoning.

3. If God created the different species, why are there so many different species in different parts of the world? Write down an argument to support this and one to oppose it.

4. 'If an animal uses a set of muscles a lot then this will be passed on to the next generation. This is how giraffes got long necks and families of blacksmiths strong arms.' This is wrong according to evolutionary theory. Explain why this is wrong. Research the ideas of the Chevalier de Lamarck to help you.

5. Draw up a set of rules for society designed for maximum survival, then compare this to the Christian Ten Commandments. Explain and justify any differences.

? Quiz

Define what is meant by the following terms:

1. evolution
2. creationists
3. species
4. mutations
5. natural selection
6. genes
7. genetic code
8. ancestor
9. selective breeding
10. cumulative advantage
11. incremental improvements
12. fossils
13. punctuated equilibrium
14. biochemical reactions
15. human soul.

Activity 1

For this activity you will need access to computers. Students download the image of any animal or organism that you wish from the internet or from a CD-ROM. (Going via www.google.co.uk and then searching under 'images' with the name of an organism will bring up numerous possibilities.) The first part of the exercise is to identify which features of the animal make it particularly suited to survival – is it, for example, a pack hunter, is it intelligent, does it live in communities, does it have special adaptations (teeth, claws and talons for predators, speed, camouflage and large numbers for prey)? The second part of the exercise is to introduce an outside influence (such as a global temperature change). Decide how the animal that you have chosen would best adapt to the new situation. You can 'design' your new organism and then justify its adaptations in discussion. Following this exercise, a discussion can take place as to what would happen if the adaptation did not take place.

Activity 2

Research the trial of John Scopes. Details can be found at www.law.umkc.edu/faculty/projects/ftrials/scopes/scopes.htm and www.courttv.com/greatesttrials/scopes/versus.html. Using the information that you find, recreate the famous 'monkey' trial. Choose a defendant that is willing (as was Scopes) and prosecution (Creationist) and defence (Evolutionist) teams. The rest of the group can act as jury. Do not limit yourselves to the arguments used at the trial but do introduce new arguments and reasoning.

19 Pollution: a consequence or a threat?

Preview

There have always been predictions about the world coming to an end, it seems to be part of our basic nature to expect it. HG Wells' book *War of the Worlds* was about alien invaders attacking Earth and trying to kill everyone. Douglas Adams' *The Hitchhiker's Guide to the Galaxy* told how Earth was destroyed to make way for an intergalactic highway. Many books and films have been made about meteors crashing into Earth, biological warfare germs infecting us or nuclear bomb devastation. Some disasters don't happen: over the past 25 years there were many warnings about a new ice age and its catastrophic consequences but few mention it now. Some disasters do happen: there were lots of warnings about over-farming in the American mid-west. Eventually it caused a huge dust bowl in the 1930s as the soil dried up and blew away. It happened across a huge area covering Kansas, Oklahoma, Texas and Colorado. Millions of people lost their homes and some areas of grassland are only now recovering. Warnings about terrorist threats were around for a long time, then the attack on the World Trade Center twin towers happened and was worse than anything fiction writers could have imagined. Scare stories are worrying because they may happen, however unlikely it may seem to most of us.

Why do we get pollution?

We are in no doubt that it is only people that cause pollution. Nature on its own uses the materials in the Earth but it all gets re-used eventually. This natural cycle is damaged by people creating things that cannot be recycled, like plastics, or destroying things that take them out of this cycle, like coal. This means the stocks of raw materials are being used up and there is no way to replace them. One of the main reasons this is done is to make energy, and most of it is electrical energy. Electricity allows us to convert the chemical energy in fuels to the light, heat, sound and kinetic energy used every day. We are using more and more electricity. As Third World countries develop and their living standards rise then their demand for electricity will also have to be met. We only have one way of making electricity – through the use of a generator – and energy is needed to spin it round.

The world needs lots of cheap electricity. The cost of energy is a large part of everything we buy. Therefore it seems clear that in the future the amount of energy we need will be much greater; for our wealth to increase we need it to be cheap energy. If we have plenty of cheap fuel then why is there a problem? Well this is where economics and ecology meet head on. An economist will build in costs for 'externalities' such as pollution, but that is all they are – costs to be paid. The ecologist looks at the long term damage to the environment. Providing and using energy creates problems for all of us, with industrial progress causing harm to the planet. The main environmental fears are that:

• natural resources are running out, oil being of particular concern

- the population continues to grow which leaves less and less food to go round
- species are becoming extinct in vast numbers; forests are disappearing and fish stocks are collapsing
- the planet's air and water are becoming ever more polluted
- natural protections (like the ozone layer) are being gradually eroded.

The end of this process would be the Earth becoming uninhabitable for humans.

Is pollution really a threat to life?

Some of these concerns can be answered easily. There is no indication that most of our natural resources are running out. Most are more plentiful than they were 25 years ago and their relative cost has fallen. New reserves are likely to be discovered and recycling has not been calculated into the equation.

The world population and food is another area of only limited concern. Over 170 years ago Thomas Malthus predicted that the world faced starvation as food production could only rise by a small percentage every year (arithmetically) while the world population was growing at an increasing rate (geometrically). A similar prediction was made by Dr Paul Ehrlich in his book *The Population Bomb* in 1968 (look on www.pbs.org/kqed/population_bomb/).

Fortunately both of them appear to have been wrong (although there is a counter-argument that both are right – it is just the timescale that is wrong). World population growth is currently slowing to less than 1.2%. Records show that, contrary to Malthus' predictions, as living standards rise population growth falls – even in China and India the rate of growth is reducing. More food is being produced world-wide than ever before as agriculture becomes more efficient. Starvation is often more due to political failure than agricultural failure.

Is something already being done about it?

A lot of evidence makes it clear that pollution is a major issue, both water and air pollution are now of world-wide concern. Some effective action has been taken already. The 1957 Clean Air Act in England did a great deal to reduce air pollution. CFCs are now banned and the damage to the ozone layer they did

WEB LINKS

There are numerous weblinks as this is a very popular area of study and discussion. Some starting points might be:
www.nature.com/nature
www.lancs.ac.uk/users/philosophy/mave/guide/gaia
www.epa.gov/globalwarming
www.weathervane.rff.org/pop/pop3
www.gcmd.gsfc.nasa.gov/pointers/glob_warm.html

TIPS FOR FURTHER RESEARCH

Research the 1997 Kyoto conference findings.
Also look at the problems of acid rain, the greenhouse effect and deforestation. Look at the alternative ways of generating electrical power. Find out what is meant by a 'carbon sink' and how countries would like to trade in carbon emissions.

Power without pain: harnessing solar power to run parking meters

has been limited. However, acid rain and the greenhouse effect due to too much carbon dioxide remain major problems. The nations of the world recognized the problem and sat down at a conference in Kyoto to see what could be done about pollution and the threat to the planet. In particular the conference said that as more fuel is burnt then more carbon dioxide gas, CO_2, is produced. The 1997 Kyoto Protocol was that all countries would reduce their emissions by half. The experts estimate that the world's temperature will rise by 2–3°C this century because of the 'greenhouse' warming effect of this CO_2.

Nearly half of the total increase in global CO_2 emissions since 1990 has come from the USA – exceeding the combined emissions growth of China, India, Africa and Latin America and the USA originally agreed to the Kyoto Accord. However, the incoming administration has refused to ratify the agreement with President Bush saying it harmed the US economy and placed an unfair burden on developed countries. Without the participation of the USA, the protocol is meaningless.

The US argument against the Kyoto conference recommendations is that for a much smaller cost other benefits such as clean water for developing countries or medical research could be paid for and save millions of lives. Reducing the man-made CO_2 emissions would slow down this rise in temperature but with an estimated cost to business of around \$500 billion – according to opponents of the idea. In comparison to this the total global-aid budget in 2001 is about \$50 billion. The US government says it is an enormous cost to industry for very little real benefit. In particular US President Bush wants to deal first with the energy crisis that caused electrical blackouts in California in 2001. More power-stations would increase the CO_2 emissions. There has been a big boom in the sale of solar panels fitted to houses in California recently, the voters are worried. The US has therefore rejected the Kyoto Protocol to reduce CO_2 emissions.

Is it only industry that is responsible?

As well as the huge costs some environmentalists also argue that global warming and cooling are a natural phenomena so the extra CO_2 from industry make very little difference. A number of other factors such as ocean currents, cloud cover and water vapour in the atmosphere also contribute to global warming. Therefore the effect of the CO_2 produced by industry being responsible for global warming is only a theory and not been proved as a fact. Despite this most countries are in agreement with the Kyoto Protocol and are trying to bring pressure to bear on the US to reduce the emissions and reduce their own emissions at a much faster rate than at present.

The energy in wind and waves is associated with the turning of the Earth. The transfer of energy from this source infinitesimally slows the speed of the Earth's rotation each year. Could this have dire effects in the future?

Present EU regulations forbid the disposal of old refrigerators in any way that might release CFCs into the atmosphere. Research what problems this legislation has caused.

Are there other solutions to the problem?

Huge areas of rainforest are cut down for wood or to grow cash crops so less CO_2 is absorbed by plants. This means different species of plant and animal life are threatened with extinction and the means to produce oxygen from photosynthesis are reduced. Plants in the oceans produce oxygen but the oceans are being increasingly polluted which reduces plant growth. Shoreline ecosystems are being damaged in many parts of the world and this is where coral reefs, mango swamps and seagrass are. The chemical pollution harms them and warmer water temperatures also harms them. One suggestion was that plants that can absorb high levels of carbon dioxide should be produced to grow in the ocean to reduce the levels of CO_2 in the air. Because of the higher levels of CO_2, the Earth warms up more causing more deserts, so there are fewer plants, water levels rise and less coastal land is available for growing, so less oxygen is made.

More people = more smoke and CO_2 = fewer plants = less oxygen to breathe = a very worrying future.

In conclusion – how serious is it?

If there is only a small increase in pollution will anyone notice, surely we can live with a small change? Many scientists believe that even a small change in the environment could lead to a major disaster for the Earth. There seems to be two main points of view.

One is that the rapid increase in industrialization and increased production of electricity will permanently upset the delicate balance that allows life to continue. Once the environment is damaged we could face extinction as a species and nothing is worth taking that risk. Perhaps we do not need all the technology we buy and could live with a more basic lifestyle. The question is: what can ordinary people do? As Edmund Burke said 'Nobody made a greater mistake than he who did nothing because he could do only a little.'

The second view is that while pollution has to be controlled it should not be allowed to reduce the rate of progress. As nations increase their standard of living the general population demands an improvement in their environment. Therefore increasing wealth will provide its own controls on pollution. Spending money on saving lives by providing clean water and better living conditions are more important than insignificant alterations in the atmosphere which is changing anyway due to nature. This view is that the dangers are exaggerated and mainly due to countries wanting the USA to reduce its industrial lead. This view is that a degree of pollution is the price to be paid for human progress.

Questions for written answer

1. Our planet is sometimes referred to as 'fragile Earth'. Discuss if the term 'fragile' is appropriate.

2. Make a list of the kinds of pollution that industrialized nations make compared to agricultural nations. What sort of responsibility do you think that industrial nations have to less developed ones, if any? Give reasons for your answer.

3. Research how copper is used. Does this cause pollution or damage the environment? Explain the processes that take place and consider whether the use of copper is either essential or moral.

4. If electricity was only provided by hydroelectricity and wind power it would be about one tenth of the amount we currently use. How would this effect your day-to-day life?

5. If the price of electricity was increased by five times in order to pay for the effects of pollution, how would it affect your lifestyle?

6. If the USA continues to increase its output of CO_2, what action could the rest of the world take to reduce CO_2 world-wide. Could they bring pressure to bear on the USA?

7. If aid to developing countries was increased instead of decreasing CO_2, how do you think it should be spent? Make a list of priorities and compare it with the rest of the class.

? Quiz

1. What is a scare story?

2. How does making electricity cause pollution?

3. What harm do CFCs do?

4. What effect does warming the oceans have?

5. How do solar panels work?

6. What is a shoreline ecosystem?

7. What could be done to absorb more carbon dioxide?

8. Why do Norway and Sweden have the problem of acid rain?

9. What were Thomas Malthus' predictions?

10. What is the 'more people ...' formula?

ACTIVITY 1

Divide into two groups and prepare a dialogue between:

- a US president who is under pressure from business interests and Californian voters to ignore the Kyoto conference recommendations and to build more power stations and

- the president of the Kyoto conference speaking on behalf of the world environmental groups.

List the points each would make and their probable response.

ACTIVITY 2

Write a newspaper article in the style of the *Sun* or the *Mirror* (popular tabloid newspapers) to explain to the average reader what the Kyoto Accord is all about. A sensationalist approach is to be encouraged. You can take the viewpoint that the Accord is unnecessary, unworkable and against American interests, or that it is marvellous and will help to save the world.

20 Technological determinism

Preview: what makes us behave the way we do?

Is technology the only thing to change our society, or is it only one of several factors? How important is it? Various kinds of 'determinism' feature in social science theories. Biological (or genetic) determinism says we are directed by our genetic codes. In contrast, the effect of our experiences (nurture) was seen by Jean-Jacques Rousseau as being the most important thing to affect us. The argument against these views would be that these factors would lead to a stable society and nothing would alter for thousands of years. History shows that many societies did not have any fundamental change until a new technology came along. Karl Marx is quoted as saying that 'The windmill gives you society with the feudal lord: the steam mill, society with the industrial capitalist'. This theory goes on to say that our personal relationships are determined by the way we work. If this is correct then the internet and computers are likely to change the way people work together and therefore change their personal relationships in families.

Only some things change

The way we live is changing rapidly. Newspapers often talk about people who live in 'the stone age' where day-to-day life hasn't changed for thousands of years and compare it to living in 'the space age' where life is changing rapidly. The way people keep themselves alive and the way people treat each other in families or the way they work together is very different in different countries. Alligators and other creatures haven't altered the way they live in millions of years, so why do humans change so much and so often? The social relationship between men and women appears to have changed a lot in the past 50 years in Britain: why? What was the cause for this change? The usual answer is that it is due to technology and science. Was the direction our society developed due to the technology someone invented or were other factors more important? Before technology was around, human life seemed to go on unchanged for thousands of years and only major climatic changes seemed to alter the way life was led. The evolution that Darwin explained takes hundreds of thousands of years. It seems to be that along came a technological change and the way people lived rapidly altered. Of course, the word 'rapidly' means different timescales at different times in history. The printing press took hundreds of years to make itself felt. In modern society five or even 10 years is short enough to see a change take place. We even list out history in terms of the main technology, stone age, iron age, agricultural age, industrial age and finally the present information age.

W EB LINKS

Try the following as starting points:
www.coe.missouri.edu/~pavtf311/
notes4.htm
http://cartoon.ecn.purdue.edu/
~birkhaus/
www.allsands.com/misc2/
technologicalde_ubp_gn
www.aber.ac.uk/media/documents/
tecdet

TIPS FOR FURTHER RESEARCH

Research the way family life changed as we moved from an agricultural economy to an industrial one. Imagine you are a young couple with two small children moving from a tied cottage on a farm to a factory job in 1810. What areas of family life do you think will change to most?

Research into the Wapping dispute between certain newspapers and the print and journalists unions. What happened? Why? With what consequences?

What does 'determinism' mean?

The view often put forward is that we do not have a free will or a free choice, but that our actions are decided for us (determined) by stronger forces outside of ourselves. Biologists say that evolution and the genetic makeup of our species is the cause of change. This view is that as our species develops we invent and accept the technology that we are ready to deal with. The need to compete for scarce resources is the reason for change and this comes from our genetic makeup. Most people say that their free will was used to decide how they lived their lives. However, the choices we can make are very limited. The consequences of 'stepping out of line' make sure we follow the rules of society. Some sociologists point to technology as being the cause of how we behave to each other, and the way we live together; this is called technological determinism. The question is do we have free will to decide how we develop or are we pushed and shaped by the mechanical, industrial and electronic devices we have invented? Karl Marx said the relationships people had at work were brought home and influenced the way that family relationships were formed.

Technology and society

Probably the first things to change life for the first humans would be the development of fire and the wheel, although some civilizations – notably South America – never developed the latter. Clearly these would have made a huge difference, but were they the main reason for change? Instead it could be argued that as humans evolved they invented technology to help them. Perhaps this is more a question of 'to what extent does technology change the way we live?' Simple technology like the plough (again not developed in South America) can have profound effects. Of course, technology makes changes in the way we live, but is it the main or only reason? Another major change would be that of moving from the flint and stone implements to melting the ore in rocks to make use of metals. Having metals to use meant it suddenly became much easier to plant crops, plough fields, hunt, cut and chop food so more would stay alive. Some civilizations were able to dominate others because of their technological superiority. Towns and cities could develop and along with them civilization.

Modern history and technology

Many sociologists would take the view that technology, and to a lesser extent science, are the central forces in our modern world. International conflicts, politics, differences in class and gender and even the distribution (or maldistribution) of wealth are all a consequence of technology.

Statements like 'the car created suburbia' or 'robots put riveters out of work' and ' typewriters altered the way men and women worked together' are common. This supports the theory that Karl Marx put forward that the work a person does has an enormous influence on the way they live all of their life. The values about what is considered good or bad, what is important or not is brought home by the worker and it affects their whole family. The way people work with machines or other people is largely controlled by technology. As technology changed, people moved out of agriculture into manufacturing. The industrial cities and the heavy industries of iron, coal or ship-building created types of communities with a particular lifestyle. They have now almost completely gone as the industry has been replaced. The way people ran their marriage and how communities worked together has also changed. Fifty years ago women stayed at home to have babies and look after men. Now everyone goes out to work and this has changed male–female relationships. Perhaps the modern communication and media will bring in a new change.

Information technology

The communications theory of technological determinism was moulded by Marshall McLuhan. His basic idea was that the way we live, our culture, is shaped by the way we communicate. As he said, 'We shape our tools, and they in turn shape us'. It is easy to agree that tribal life was shaped by the spoken word. As the written word was developed, in particular the printing press, then society and the way it worked were also changed. Ideas were spread so that progress and change were demanded and took place. McLuhan then says that the invention of the telegraph was the next technological development to change our world. The ability to instantly communicate using technology has allowed a sort of 'global village' to arrive. A hundred years ago the events and ideas in the Middle East, for example, would have made no difference in most of the Western world. Now they can be widely spread. While this argument seems to go along with common-sense views it is not to agree that all advances in communication technology have had similar effects. Natural evolution, politics, policies and the ideas of the main religions would claim to have shaped our thinking and therefore our lives more than gadgets.

How do we deal with technology?

People often act as if there is a life and personality to a machine, ships are called 'she' and cars can be objects of affection. When things go wrong it can be blamed on 'gremlins' that make the machines misbehave. Perhaps this is best shown by the Clarke-Trimble experiments of 1935. Clark-Trimble was not a physicist and his great discovery of the 'graduated hostility of things' was made

SCIENCE AND TECHNOLOGY

almost accidentally. During some research into the relation between periods of the day and human bad temper, Clark-Trimble, a leading Cambridge psychologist, came to the conclusion that low human dynamics in the early morning could not sufficiently explain the apparent hostility of things at the breakfast table – the way marmalade gets between the fingers and newspapers will not fold properly, etc. In the experiments that finally confirmed his views, and which he demonstrated before the Royal Society in London, Clark-Trimble arranged 400 pieces of carpet in ascending degrees of quality, from coarse matting to priceless Chinese silk. Pieces of toast and marmalade, graded, weighed and measured, were then dropped on each piece of carpet, and the marmalade-downwards incidence was statistically analysed. The toast fell right-side-up every time on the cheap carpet, except when the cheap carpet was screened from the rest (in which case the toast didn't know that Clark-Trimble had other and better carpets), and it fell marmalade side down every time on the Chinese silk carpet. Most remarkable of all, the marmalade-downwards incidence for the intermediate grades was found to vary exactly with the quality of the carpet. The success of the experiments led Clark-Trimble to investigate further in this area. It is believed this was the reason for the tragic and sudden end to his career when he trod on a garden rake at the Cambridge School of Agronomy (Jennings, 1960, p. 396). Followers of this school of thought are advised not to let the photocopier know how urgent their task is, if it does then a paper jam is certain.

Conclusion

The last significant revolt against technological change was probably the Luddites violent response to the introduction of new machinery. In different parts of the world (and for very different reasons) there are always groups of people who no longer wish to have anything to do with technology (often referred to as Luddites), but progress appears inexorable. Newspaper printers and compositors stood up against the new technology – the newspapers moved on without them. As we look to a future in the next 50 years where computers are as intelligent as people and robots will be able to carry out most human functions then we may have a cause for concern. When machines build machines they may not build in an 'off' switch.

Questions for discussion

1. If we do not have free will then why do we have democracy and religion?

2. Share a personal experience of 'gremlins' and explain why you think it happened.

3. Is sending a child away to boarding school the best way to educate them?

4. Bucolic societies are always pictured as serene and 'ideal'. Is this really the case?

5. What is your favourite gadget? Why?

Examiners will look for the following in your written answer:

- Evidence that you have understood the source material and can make appropriate use of it.
- You need to be able to make value judgements based on it and support these with evidence or interpretation.
- You need to have something of your own to say and to be able to state it clearly.
- You need to show you can relate this work to other relevant areas of study.

Questions for written answer

1. What does 'determinism' mean? Discuss the determinist point of view as opposed to the view that we have free will.

2. Is it free will that decides if you go to work or to school? Write down the consequences if you decided to stay at home.

3. Discuss the view that technology that can be used for mass destruction or crime (both the Omagh bombing and the 11 September World Trade Center attack were co-ordinated by mobile phone) should be either banned or licensed only for use by responsible bodies such as governments.

4. Advances in science and technology are now increasingly used to both prevent crime and to bring criminals to justice. Choose one such technological change (such as video-surveillance cameras, DNA testing or electronic tagging) and consider how far it is used and effective for its original purpose; how it can be misused and what implications you think it has for individual freedoms.

5. 'Advances in technology have moral repercussions'. Discuss this statement with a detailed analysis of any one technological change that you are familiar with.

? Multiple-choice questions

1. The belief that our actions are directed by our genetic code is called:

   a) biological determinism

   b) technological determinism

   c) indeterminism

   d) determination.

2. The belief that our actions are directed by changes in circumstances is called:

   a) biological determinism

   b) technological determinism

   c) indeterminism

   d) determination.

3. That our experiences are more important in determining actions led to the debate known as:

a) nature vs natural

b) nature vs nurture

c) nurture vs naturism

d) natural determinism.

4. According to Marx, the windmill leads to what sort of society?

a) communist

b) capitalist

c) feudal

d) socialist.

5. The correct order for: (i) information age, (ii) iron age, (iii) agricultural age is:

a) (i), (ii), (iii)

b) (ii), (iii), (i)

c) (i), (iii), (ii)

d) (iii), (ii), (i).

6. The correct order for : (i) stone age, (ii) industrial age, (iii) agricultural age is:

a) (i), (ii), (iii)

b) (ii), (iii), (i)

c) (i), (iii), (ii)

d) (iii), (ii), (i).

7. Marshall McLuhan's theory is called:

a) technological determinism

b) determined technology

c) universal hostility

d) technological hostility.

8. What is said to have created suburbia?

a) commuters

b) the car

c) trains

d) cities.

ACTIVITY 1

Divide into groups of two or three and select an item from the following list. Explain to the group how this advance could have affected relationships. How could it have changed the way a marriage works? (Think about partnership, responsibility, rights and obligations.) In Victorian times a middle-class father might give instructions regarding a new baby (and mean it) such as 'Bring it to me when it can hold a knife and fork'. (Others went further and said 'bring it to me when it can hold a conversation'!) It was also common practice to have children segregated in nurseries (with professional help) and then sent to a boarding school. Some of these practices still remain, but parent–child relations for most have changed. How do you think your chosen technological advance helped or caused this change?

- The printing press.
- Industrialization (from agriculture to manufacturing).
- Electricity and the electric light bulb.
- Radio, television and films.
- Public transport (bus and train).
- Free education for all.

ACTIVITY 2

Imagine a conversation with Jean Jacques Rousseau if you could go back in time. Rousseau thought that civilization corrupted the innocence and natural goodness of people. He would point to the horrors of the Second World War to say that technology had made people worse not better. How would you reply to this view? Hold a debate in which the two opposing points of view are put.

21 Quantum theory

Preview

Quantum theory is one of the two main theories in physics; the other one is Einstein's theory of relativity. Relativity explains how things happen in space and quantum theory explains how things happen at atomic level. They are both generally accepted as being correct, or at least the best explanation we have so far, but they do not agree. There is a missing link to complete a 'theory of everything'. Quantum theory (also called quantum mechanics or wave mechanics) has implications for science as if it is accepted in full then it appears to deny the existence of God or even the possibility of an ordered universe ruled by logical laws. If that is the case then what effect does this have on the way people think of themselves? If there is no God then what is special about humanity? Are we no better than a chattering animal? If science can predict the future then it will be able to predict human behaviour and therefore control it. The full implication of quantum theory would mean there is only uncertainty.

What is quantum theory?

Quantum theory started with the German physicist Max Planck. Planck demonstrated in 1900 that objects take in and give out energy, for example by heating or cooling. However this does not happen in a smoothly continuous way but in 'jumps' which we call 'quantum' changes. He wanted to find an explanation to connect the radiated power of a hot object to the frequencies it came off at and the temperature. He said that when radiation of frequency f exchanges energy with matter, the amount of energy exchanged E is given by the formula $E = hf$ (where h is Planck's constant and has a value of 6.626×10^{-34} joule-sec). Therefore, atoms can gain or lose energy only in multiples of hf. This idea has been developed to be quantum mechanics. This is the understanding that energy is soaked up or sent out in discontinuous bursts (lumps). This theory says that everything, particles, energy, the rate electrons spin at – they are all in discrete units and not a smooth continuous flow. Quantum is the Latin for 'so much' or 'bundle'. 'Mechanics ' is the old-fashioned way of talking about motion. So quantum mechanics is the study of the motion of things that come in little bundles. Scientists then began to question if electromagnetic radiation was a wave of pure energy or if it was a particle, a tiny lump of matter. We now work on the basis of it being a bit of both. Quantum theory is used in explaining how very small things like the atom works. The electrons that orbit the atom can only have certain precise energies and any 'quantum leap' between one orbit and another leads to the production or absorption of a photon which is also called quantum and is a short burst of electromagnetic energy. That is how energy is gained or lost by material objects.

The uncertainty principle

Another problem is that at molecular level you cannot measure something without changing it. This means you cannot be certain about how electrons are behaving if you want to measure their position and momentum for example. As soon as you measure the speed, then the action of measuring it will change the position of it. If you use light to see the electron then the energy from the light effects the electron as it adds energy to it and changes the speed. The more accurately you try to measure its position then the more uncertainty there is about its speed. This is called the uncertainty principle. It means there is a limit to how accurately we can predict the way a system will behave. A simple example is that if you put a thermometer in a hot liquid to measure the temperature then you will alter the temperature as it has to heat up the thermometer you are using, so you alter the thing you want to measure. The uncertainty principle means that science will not give complete answers, only possibilities or at best a probability. This conflicts with the idea of an ordered universe that follows the laws of physics, that may have been designed by God.

The Pyramids – 4000 years old – or are they?

SCIENCE AND TECHNOLOGY

EB LINKS

The basics of quantum theory can be found at
www.chembio.uoguelph.ca/educmat/chm386/rudiment/rudiment.htm
plato.stanford.edu/entries/qt-idind/ assesses the metaphysical implications of quantum theory at a fairly advanced level.

Religion and quantum theory

One of the important aspects of quantum theory is the doubt it raises over the part that God plays in science. While there are no exact statements from Einstein about God, several of his quotations refer to a belief in God, for example 'God does not play dice' in reply to the uncertainty principle developed from quantum theory. He said this even though he contributed a lot of the work towards quantum theory being developed. The religious view is that it is quite reasonable to believe that God created a logical set of laws that can predict the behaviour of the material word. This sees scientists as gradually uncovering the truth of a universe all put in place by a force greater than we are: God in other words. We may never be able to understand all of God's work. The question behind a lot of science is to decide if there is a master plan of a balanced universe or whether our world is the result of random events. Quantum theory suggests that we are just a brief rest from total chaos and our world is the result of chance, that there is no force or logic outside of mathematical probability. One religious view might be that we cannot understand God's work or we would be God. Therefore, the universe follows the ordered laws made by God and quantum theory must be wrong.

Can we be accurate about anything?

As far back as recorded history there have been investigations about the stars. Up to the Middle Ages it was thought to be where God, or the gods, lived. To try to understand how it worked and what it meant automatically involved timing the way the heavens moved. The idea of time has always given people a bit of a problem. According to the Jewish Talmud the world is to exist for 6000 years and each year has a number denoting the number of years since the giving of the Ten Commandments. Hindu and Greek traditions say there is an eternal universe that recycles itself. Muslims measure the years from the date the Prophet Mohammed left Mecca (CE 622). In Christian Europe the years began to be measured from the believed date of Christ's birth. A more accurate system was the Gregorian calendar which was introduced by a papal bull (an instruction to all Roman Catholics from the Pope) on 24 February 1582. This said the year began on 1 January. It also corrected errors by saying that Thursday 4 October would be followed by Friday 15 October. This caused riots by people who believed a part of their life had been taken away from them! The leap year was introduced to stop the 'slippage' of time, as a year is really 365.25 days. Time measurement has become a bit more accurate than 'bits of a day'. In 1991 the HP 5071A caesium-2 atomic clock was made. It is accurate to one second in 1.6 million years. The second is defined as 1/31,556,925.9747 of the time it takes for the Earth to circle the Sun.

Find out how the Chinese and the Jews measure the years. What year is it according to the Chinese calendar? According to the Jewish calendar? How can you square this with a biblical time period.

You could enhance your understanding by making sure that you know what the following words or phrases mean: frequency, quantum, photon, electromagnetic radiation, molecular level, momentum, electron, uncertainty principle, mathematical probability, random event, chaos theory.

Can we rely on time as a measure?

If we are using time to measure things, then the question is: when did time start? How did it all begin? Scientists, physicists in particular, are constantly arguing about this question. According to the Archbishop of Armagh (1581–1656) the world began at 6pm on Saturday 22 October 4004 BC and this was calculated by using the Bible. A rather more modern system of radioactive dating tells us that our Sun and its planets, including Earth, condensed 4.55 billion years ago from interstellar gas. The general scientific belief is that our universe emerged from a 'beginning' about 13 billion years ago. This start of our universe is called 'the Big Bang'. One theory is that there was a 'singularity' at that point. This means a point in space–time at which the known laws of physics break down. So no matter how accurately we measure time we cannot be certain of it, in a singularity it may not apply.

Conclusion

Huge amounts of money are being spent to find an explanation of how our world works. The basic idea is that if we can understand how our universe was created in the first fractions of a second, then that will tell us how the universe works. The belief is that if all factors are known, if all the scientific rules are understood, then we will be able to predict what will happen in the future and therefore be able to control it.

For most of us cosmic visions are a bit difficult to reconcile with the triviality of our daily lives: *The Hitchhiker's Guide to the Galaxy* said our world was an experiment being done by white mice and the universal answer to everything was 42. As Woody Allen put it: 'The universe is expanding – so why bother doing homework?'.

Questions for discussion

1. Modern science can destroy life on our planet or alter life, perhaps even create life. In the past we have had religion to provide a guide as to what is right and wrong. All religions have a broad agreement about right and wrong. If we find that our scientific research tells us that there is no God, just random chance, then how would you decide what was morally right and wrong?

2. If we discover the way our universe was created, does this mean there cannot be anything that can have a moral authority over us? Are our laws just the result of self-preservation?

3. If biologists can create life then are they the same as God? Is there no such thing as the human spirit or soul?

TIPS FOR FURTHER RESEARCH

To extend your understanding of quantum theory you should research the work done by Max Planck (1900), Albert Einstein, Neils Bohr, Erwin Schrödinger, Werner Heisenberg and Paul Dirac.

SCIENCE AND TECHNOLOGY

4. Carbon dating must be wrong – mustn't it?

5. Animals don't have souls … do they?

Questions for written answer

1. Discuss the connection between the study of time and the study of religion.

2. There are two main theories: relativity and quantum theory. If you agree with both can you still believe in God? Explain your answer. (By 'God' you could mean just the laws of nature or a religious view.)

3. If science cannot give a precise answer to the rules of physics then it can only calculate what will probably happen. Discuss how, if this is so, it can be used to predict the future or guide what we should do.

4. What is the evidence that there is a human spirit or soul? How can the quantum theory of science explain unselfish love, self sacrifice and our concept of beauty? Give reasons to support your views.

5. 'We are the result of chemical reactions and pure chance.' Discuss this statement using your knowledge of religion or other human codes of behaviour. Suggest and explain why we don't have a moral code based on the survival of the fittest.

Examiners will look for the following in your written answer:

- Evidence that you have understood the source material and can make appropriate use of it.
- You need to be able to make value judgements based on it and support these with evidence or interpretation.
- You need to have something of your own to say and to be able to state it clearly.
- You need to show you can relate this work to other relevant areas of study.

Quiz

1. What was special about the Gregorian calendar?

2. When does the Muslim calendar start? Why then?

3. What is the connection between energy given off and frequency?

4. What is another name for quantum mechanics?

5. What does the uncertainty principle state?

6. What does 'total chaos' mean?

7. What is a papal bull?

8. Who is the main proponent of chaos theory?

9. When did the world begin according to the Archbishop of Armagh?

10. What is the answer to the 'ultimate question of life, the universe and everything'?

ACTIVITY 1

Split in to two groups to debate the question of 'Our world is the result of pure chance, from the tens of millions of planets in the universe, it is a freak accident'. The second view would be that there must be a logical force behind it all, a force of nature or 'God' in the broadest sense. Write out the points you will make to support your view and try to anticipate the opposite view so that you have a reply to them.

ACTIVITY 2

In small groups try some simple 'scientific' experiments for yourselves. Some examples could be:

- Measuring the increase in heart rate after a 10-second on-the-spot run.
- Measuring the speed at which an object falls to the ground.
- Measuring the time it takes for a drop of water to make its way down a window.

From each of your experiments decide whether:

- You could frame any sort of rule or law.
- How accurate or 'universal' this law is likely to be (what other information would you need; what other parameters must you set; what else might affect your results).
- How you could test its universality.

Be prepared to question others in an attempt to prove them wrong and to defend your own assertions against such questioning.

Evaluate the activity by explaining what it tells us about the nature of scientific 'laws'.

Preview

After Einstein presented his theories there were a lot of new ideas developed about cosmology – the structure of the universe – but most agreed with his theory of relativity as it predicts the way light and time behave in space. The other main idea in this century was that of quantum theory. This began with the work done by Max Planck in 1900, it was added to by Einstein and then developed by Neils Bohr. The problem is that the theory of relativity and quantum theory do not totally support each other. As Stephen Hawking said: 'the eventual goal of science is to provide a single theory that describes the whole universe'. An enormous amount of research has gone into the pursuit of this 'grand theory for everything' to find a way of combining quantum theory and relativity. It is thought that a way to do this is to find out how our universe began. This would explain how atoms were formed and how energy keeps them together. In the next 10 years this may be discovered.

How do we know which theory is correct?

There are many conflicting theories in science. In order to decide which theory is best, scientists need to agree on what will count as evidence and then to try and find it. For example in 1989 NASA launched the cosmic background explorer satellite *COBE* to look for evidence of the Big Bang theory of how our universe was created. In 1992 it detected slight ripples in the strength of the background radiation in space. Therefore the 'Big Bang' is accepted as being something that actually took place and it is not just another theory. Most scientists agree there must have been a different set of rules in force for the first fractions of the first second of the 'Big Bang' when energy created matter, which is called a 'singularity'. To explain this, the idea of 'inflation' was put forward by Alan Guth in 1980. The inflationary theory says that the universe expanded very rapidly, faster than our present laws of physics would allow, faster than the speed of light, during the first fraction of a second of its existence and then settled down to a slower rate of expansion. So a different set of laws of physics were at work for the first tiny instants of time. A few seconds after the Big Bang the temperature would have fallen to that of the hottest stars and the usual laws of physics would then apply. The theory still left a question, this background radiation was too smooth to account for the 'lumpiness' of the currently observed universe. We have no general agreement as to why galaxies are clustered together with huge voids between them. Instruments are in place under the Antarctic icecaps and out in space trying to find evidence to support the different theories.

Why is the universe in 'lumps and clumps'?

According to Einstein's theory of general relativity, matter and energy will curve space–time. However, Big Bang theory cannot explain why it has become flat and not curved. Widely separated regions cluster together in much the same numbers and patterns on one side of the universe as the other. So the theories of physics do not explain what can be seen. Matter is just another form of energy and can be produced if the energy input is balanced by something else. That 'something else' could be negative energy in the gravitational field. We cannot detect it but it's a bit like digging a hole – you have a pile of dirt that you see (planets, etc.) and its balanced by a hole (a gravitation field) that we cannot see. The best guess so far is that 'invisible' dark matter may be an undiscovered mass in the universe. This then caused ordinary matter to pull into the pre-existing shape. Therefore new theories are needed beyond those of Einstein's relativity and Bohr's quantum mechanics. Most scientists expect a theory which will combine both of these theories rather than replace them.

The universe – what information will the coming years bring?

TIPS FOR FURTHER **RESEARCH**

Extend your knowledge by research on the following: Professor Stephen Hawking (whose own website is at www.hawking.org.uk/), Paul Dirac, Neils Bohr, NASA website (www.nasa.gov/).

Things we have not yet found

In the 1930s Paul Dirac predicted that for every kind of fundamental particle of matter there exists a particle with the same mass but opposite charge. These are described as anti-matter, and these anti-electrons are called positrons. Later observations showed that new particles and anti-particles could appear when there is a big enough supply of energy. So if a photon ceases to exist we would see an electron–positron pair produced. In the same way if they are destroyed they would be replaced by photons. Both of these support Einstein's $e = mc^2$ that predicted mass and energy are equivalent. Einstein pointed out that both wave and particle type behaviour can occur together. String theory is that the basic objects are not particles which occupy a single point in space, but things that have a length but no dimension. This is where the 'string' comes from, the objects may have ends or be in closed loops. A particle occupies one space at each instant of time. So its 'history' can be represented by a line in time and space. String theory goes some way to joining the two main theories of how material acts like a particle and energy behaves like a wave. It says each proton and neutron is made of particles called quarks and each particle has a minute loop energy vibrating inside it.

String theory

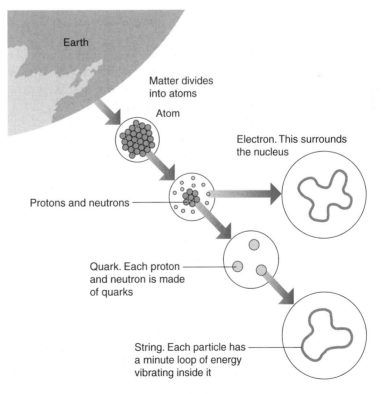

Earth

Matter divides into atoms

Atom

Electron. This surrounds the nucleus

Protons and neutrons

Quark. Each proton and neutron is made of quarks

String. Each particle has a minute loop of energy vibrating inside it

Everything, including light can be reduced to a vibrating loop

String theory can link quantum mechanics and Albert Einstein's theories of special and general relativity

W EB LINKS

www.nasa.gov/

www.hawking.org.uk/

For black holes look at

http://image.gsfc.nasa.gov/poetry/

ask/askmag.html

The universe as a bubble

But this still does not explain how the galaxies formed in 'lumps'. So the theories now explore the idea of a dark matter (light cannot escape from it). Ordinary matter would be attracted into regions of concentrated dark matter. If this theory is correct then over 90% of the universe consists of unseen matter. Other possibilities are of immense black holes, but how can we find them? Professor Hawking suggests that some black holes may emit radiation if we can develop the technology to detect it. He also put forward the idea that perhaps time and space together form a surface that was finite in size, but did not have any boundary or edge. This would be a universe like a huge bubble. Many scientists are undecided about the 'bubble' theory. It also means other universes could exist. This opens up the possibility of 'wormholes' between one universe and another.

Why stars are in 'lumps and clumps'

Dr Phil Mauskopf from Cardiff University led a British team that took part in an investigation to find evidence that there was a huge sound wave that went through the white-hot plasma gases generated in the Big Bang. The point is that this type of wave could concentrate matter in some areas and remove it from others, which is what we see in the galaxies. The evidence for this was found by suspending a 1500 kg telescope from a balloon over the Antarctic to measure fluctuations in the microwave radiation left behind by the acoustic (sound) wave. The team believe they have found the ripples of the sounds of the Big Bang that no one has detected before. This theory would fit in with the 'inflation' theory. So perhaps the universe started out less than the size of an atom and expanded faster than the speed of light – but only for an instant. When inflation suddenly stopped there would be a massive sound wave which would shape the universe into the galaxies we observe today. Sir Martin Rees, the astronomer royal, said the evidence confirmed the theory. It also confirmed that about 40% of the universe is made up of the so-called dark matter which cannot interact with light and so is invisible. Rees said: 'The research also adds weight to the strangest idea of all: that our universe, far from being unique, is one of an infinite number of universes'. Another recent theory is that another universe bumped into ours and this created the Big Bang which produced all the energy and matter.

Current research is suggesting there is a force which is anti-gravity and is called the cosmological constant. This force is the dark energy that is thought to be accelerating the expansion of the universe. The term 'cosmological constant' came from Einstein when he invented it as he had to 'fiddle' his equations to show a static universe. In June 2001 it was announced that the tiniest particles that can exist have mass. These are called neutrinos and were first proved to exist in 1956. The mass of these neutrinos account for most of the gravitational pull in the universe. They also announced that the neutrinos did not have enough mass to provide the gravitational pull to collapse the universe into a big crunch. So the universe will continue to expand. In June 2001 NASA launched the microwave anisotropy probe. This will examine the 'lumpiness' in great detail. This may help to answer the questions about the anti-gravity cosmological constant and the equally mysterious 'dark matter'. There are certainly a lot of unanswered questions. The most recent thinking is that ordinary matter accounts for only 5% of the mass and energy in the universe and dark matter only 30%. Astrophysicist Michael Turner says the universe appears to consist of 0.5% stars, 65% dark energy and 35% dark matter. Dark energy gets stronger as the universe expands.

> You can enhance your understanding by making sure that you know what the following mean: cosmology, Big Bang theory, quantum theory, positrons, singularity, Guth's inflation theory, string theory, anti-matter, dark energy, cosmological constant.

General agreement

So is there a general agreement on any theories? Well the scientists agree that our universe started smaller than an atom about 15 billion years ago. They call it a 'singularity' where the known laws of physics break down. Out of the energy in the explosion the solid material of our universe was made. There is no agreement as to what happened at or before the Big Bang. No matter how fantastic the science fiction story is that you read or see, theoretical physics can provide something even more exciting and dramatic to stretch the imagination.

> What would be the problems in travelling back in time? Consider the time traveller's paradox. What happens if the time traveller goes backwards in time and kills his own grandfather before his father was conceived? What other paradoxes can you think of?

Questions for discussion

1. If we find how the Big Bang happened, does that mean there is no God? If we know how everything happens will we be able to predict the future?

2. If we can identify a source of huge amounts of energy, how could we use it and how would it change the nature of how we live?

3. If there was a different universe where time ran backwards, what would happen? How would it work?

4. Could parallel universes and wormholes between them mean that time travel is possible?

5. Big Bang theory: what sort of evidence is there after 15 billion years? How could it be found?

Questions for written answer

1. In August 1996 possible evidence was published pointing to life on Mars. What do we mean by 'life'? What would be the likely consequences for science and society if life was discovered on another planet?

2. Write a paragraph about each of the following: black holes, quantum mechanics, string theory.

3. Explain the way in which stars and galaxies are in clumps and not evenly spread out.

4. Explain why we can only use theory and not measurements for the first instants of time after the Big Bang.

5. Explain how a scientist might identify a 'good' theory. On what grounds would one theory be considered better than another?

? Quiz

1. What did *COBE* look for?

2. What happened in the Big Bang?

3. What is a positron?

4. What is 'string theory'?

5. What is 'bubble theory'?

6. What does a sound wave do to matter?

7. What did the microwave anisotropy probe look for?

8. What is a 'singularity'?

9. What is a black hole?

10. What is Guth's theory?

A CTIVITY

It is now more than 40 years since the first spacecraft was launched and more than 30 years since the first person set foot on the moon. There are two areas where research is being heavily invested, the origin of the universe and the possibility of a colony on Mars. Which should have the greatest priority, or should the money be spent elsewhere?

In groups, draw up a three-column table headed Mars, Origins, Other. In each column put the reasons for spending money in that direction. For each suggest what benefits might come from the development and which group or groups is likely to most benefit from those developments. Collate your lists with other groups until you have a complete argument for each development.

Now repeat the exercise, but this time with reasons why each development should not take place. (Try to think of positive reasons rather than just the negative opposites of reasons already given.)

23 Dolly – a longer life or an end to humanity?

Preview

A clone is a living thing which has exactly the same genetic make-up as the parent. On 23 February 1997 it was announced that scientists had cloned a sheep and now had a 6-month-old lamb called Dolly. Dolly was proof that cloning is possible for large mammals. It also meant that before long it will also be possible to clone people.

What was all the excitement about?

You might wonder what all the fuss was about, why should scientists bother? There are already too many people alive for the resources we have. Why use money and time to make even more? The reason it was seen as world-class news is that there is an enormous interest in the possibility of cloning people as well as animals. The pressure for cloning to be developed as a technique is not due to one or two mad scientists who want to change the world. Cloning animals could be a very profitable business. Cloning people is a force that gains support from, among others, those who want to start a family and cannot do it by natural means.

Clones or siblings?

Why clone people?

There is a very deep-seated drive in both men and women; it is the desire to have children and leave behind their 'bit of immortality', which is the genetic inheritance in their children. In developed countries like America and Europe there are fewer and fewer children being born. Parents are choosing to have smaller families and have their children much later in their life. The total population is starting to fall and the biggest section of the population are the older generation. Many couples want at least one child, but over 10% of couples have problems having a child of their own. In Western countries it has been found that the sperm count of many males is much less than it should be and we are not sure why. Many women do not want to start a family until they have established a career so they are older and this can cause medical problems. So there is a very strong pressure from people who want to have babies but cannot. This group is very rich, influential and large. It is 10% of Europeans and Americans, which makes up a powerful force of consumer demand and the money to get what they want, and what they want are their own children.

The science behind cloning

Before going into the details it is a good idea to remind you of the terminology being used. Every cell is controlled by the nucleus. Inside the nucleus of humans are 23 pairs of chromosomes. Each chromosome contains DNA, a coiled double-strand molecule. It is made up of 600,000,000 bases. The bases are A, T, G and C and join up in pairs like the rungs of a ladder. Most of the DNA we have (99%) is identical in everybody. However, the other 1% of it makes us different from one another. The 1% region where the base pairs are that cause this are called genes. This is the part we are mainly interested in. The complete set of 50,000 genes found in the human cell nucleus is called the human genome. It is being mapped and soon will be listed so we should know what bit has what affect.

There are a number of ways people can be helped to have babies of course. If it is the male who is infertile then artificial insemination by a donor (called AID) can overcome the problem. If the female has a problem conceiving then *in vitro* fertilization (IVF) can solve the problem. The majority of people seem to approve of IVF; even the major religions are hesitant about condemning it. But mention cloning and the picture changes dramatically. Cloning could mean that anyone, regardless of his or her age, medical condition or status could have a child without the need for a partner. The definition of cloning is that it is a group of cells or organisms arising by asexual reproduction from a single 'parent' individual. Clones therefore have exactly the same genetic make-up as the cell they were made from. The usual, or natural, way fertilization occurs is the male sperm joins with the female egg (the gametes) to produce a zygote. The gametes each have half of the number of chromosomes of each parent.

Instead of this natural process, cloning relies on a combination of two techniques. First adult or embryo cells are taken and grown. They need to be 'non-specialized' cells. Then one of the cells is fused with an egg that has had its nucleus removed. This combination is then implanted into a womb. The embryo then develops as normal. The sperm, egg and zygote are called the germ-line cells. If there is a germ-line change then all the cells that develop from them will have the genetic change in every cell. The change will then be inherited by the next generation. The foetus that grows from the cloning procedure will be a completely identical copy of the adult or embryo cell the nucleus came from.

The opposition to cloning

There is an overwhelming hostility to the idea of human cloning. There have been a number of books and films that point out the danger of human clones. Aldous Huxley's book *Brave New World* written in 1946 outlined a world where humans were produced for a particular purpose and individuality was suppressed. The film *The Boys from Brazil* used the idea of clones of Hitler being born in the hope of another Nazi Germany being created. Even Woody Allen made a film called *Sleeper* about a 'leader' being cloned from a bit of his nose. In Europe it is illegal to clone human tissue. So if the general public, religions and most governments are opposed to it, is there any research being done in this area? The answer is that there is a lot of work being done in different areas. One of them is animal cloning and it is likely to become big business. There are few regulations to control animal cloning and there is no legal requirement for food from cloned animals to be labelled as such.

Pigs have many biological similarities to humans. Using a technique called xenotransplantation pig organs could be used in humans. Organ transplants are an area where huge sums of money could be made. It can be very difficult to draw a line between desirable and non-desirable uses for cloning. There is a 'Noah's Ark' project which collects the DNA of endangered species in the hope of saving them from extinction. At the same time a firm is selling £1000 do-it-yourself DNA kits so that pet owners can store DNA from their pets for eventual cloning. In Texas a couple have already invested £1.6 million to try to make a clone of their dog called Missy. This is at a time when American states spend millions to collect and destroy unwanted stray dogs.

In favour of cloning

The second area of research is with 'therapeutic' cloning to make new cells or replace damaged organs. Therapeutic cloning means using human embryos to obtain stem cells. A stem cell is one that has not got a specific job, so it can be programmed to become any type, skin or lung for example. Britain leads the world in stem cell research. The cells that are produced in the first few days of the human embryo are stem cells and are astonishingly versatile. They can easily be used to replicate almost any kind of tissue. For example, they could replace spinal cord cells which were damaged and causing paralysis. They could be used to provide any sort of human 'spare part'. Damaged or aging tissue can then be replaced with the programmed stem cells. But stem cells require a human embryo to produce the cells that are needed. The IVF boom in the past decade has led to a lot of 'spare' embryos. The argument is that they could be used to produce the stem cells to help people instead of allowing the embryos to die. The law says that a human embryo cannot be experimented on if it is more than 14 days old. Some people are willing to see embryos that would have been disposed of being used for this but not new ones being produced. When there is such a fine distinction between 'yes' and 'no' it becomes impractical to regulate it. It is a very narrow line that divides therapeutic cloning from the reproductive cloning that produced Dolly.

Conclusion

In order to decide on the right path we have to take into account morality, money and freedom of choice.

Clones of people could be made to allow transplants of damaged organs or just old worn out parts. The rich could stay alive by having new parts on a regular basis. But if clones are 'produced' to order, are they the same as 'normal' humans? Have they the same rights, the right to be a unique individual for example? A new definition of a parent and child may also be needed. If a couple have a child who is the clone of one of them, what is the relationship to the other marriage partner? Perhaps a new definition of what constitutes a member of the human race may even be needed, if so, what is the basis for excluding someone? A fundamental belief for all religions is that only God gives life, therefore religion and morality cannot be excluded from the debate. It is not where technology is today that presents problems, but where it will be in a few years' time.

Questions for discussion

1. List the advantages and disadvantages of cloning humans.

2. Do you think animal cloning is morally different to selective breeding for animals?

3. Is animal cloning just a better way to improve the breeds of an animal or are there dangers? Would you have different laws for human clones? Why?

4. If you had a transplant and the organ had come from a pig, would this alter your views on it?

5. Should meat and other products from cloned animals be labelled or restricted? Explain your answer.

WEB LINKS

www.fertilethoughts.net/malpani/new/Chap25.htm describes the newest technology of IVF and associated treatments.
news.mpr.org/features/199711/20_smiths_fertility/part7/ is a complete audio of a radio feature interview with Susan Golombok, a psychologist. Information on IVF can be found at www.babycenter.com.
www.parkinsons.org.uk carries views relating to Parkinson's disease.

SCIENCE AND TECHNOLOGY

Questions for written answer

1. Do you agree with human embryos being used only to produce stem cells? If you were in an accident that had paralysed you from the neck down and only stem cells could cure you, would your views alter?

2. Explain what is meant by a 'germ-line' change and why it is so important.

3. Explain why IVF results in a lot of 'spare' embryos. Are these embryos human beings, with all the rights which that entails; or are they not yet human beings and therefore can be used for medical research? Support your viewpoint.

4. Do you think the 'Missy' dog clone research is morally correct? Explain your answer.

5. If a clone was made of you so that organs could be replaced and ageing could be halted, would your moral views stop you from using it? Do you think religious groups should ban it from happening? Give reasons for your answers.

? Quiz

1. Why is there a pressure to clone people?

2. What is AID?

3. What is IVF?

4. What is DNA?

5. What is artificial insemination?

6. What is xenotransplantation?

7. What is the Noah's Ark project?

8. What is therapeutic cloning?

ACTIVITY

Most countries ban human cloning. In Britain it is allowed. In a recent ruling Mr Justice Crane ruled that an organism created by cloning technology was not an embryo and so was not covered by the Human Fertilisation and Embryology Act. The reasoning was that a fertilized egg was not being used. This shows the law is not clear on technical topics. What law would you pass to allow research on curing human diseases but also take a clear position on the moral status of the tissue being used?

As a class try to write this law in detail – remember that it will be the job of lawyers to try to find loopholes in the law. Some of the class could be nominated to act for various organizations that might support or oppose such a law to question those proposing the law on how it would work and to find possible loopholes.

(This could be an extended piece of work which takes place over several lessons and is linked to teaching on the way a law is passed in the UK legislature.)

Examiners will look for the following in your written answer:

• Evidence that you have understood the source material and can make appropriate use of it.
• You need to be able to make value judgements based on it and support these with evidence or interpretation.
• You need to have something of your own to say and to be able to state it clearly.
• You need to show you can relate this work to other relevant areas of study.

24 Looking into the crystal ball

Preview

For a scientist the best way to shoot yourself in the foot is to make a prediction about the future. The history of science is littered with important scientists making predictions that turn out to be totally wrong, often quite soon after they were made. Predictions about the impossibility of powered flight and space travel are some of the better known examples of leading scientists being wrong. It has been said that the science fiction written as entertainment is better at predicting the future than scientists are. Examples of this would be the *Eagle* comic in the 1950s to 1960s and the various *Star Trek* series. The first science fiction writers like HG Wells or Jules Verne were ridiculed when they were first published but their influence has been enormous. The stories give ideas to children and then when they become adults they work towards inventing the ideas they already have. In the *Eagle* comic in the 1960s a space captain called Dan Dare had a wristwatch that was also a television transmitter and receiver. Fairly soon you will be able to buy one, it is already possible on a home computer.

So, in the best foot-shooting traditions, here is a list of the sort of changes that you might expect to see if you were looking back from a time in the future.

Future technology as predicted in the 1930s

SCIENCE AND TECHNOLOGY

Education plus 10

In 10 years' time the latest range of computers could talk in complete sentences and listen to instructions from people. They could correct grammar and even interpret meanings. Everyone in a developed country had a personal link to a computer terminal. These personal computer links were worn the way wristwatches used to be in the twentieth century. Highly sophisticated spreadsheet programs meant the need for calculations were no longer needed. Cash was no longer used at all and the personal identity card that everyone had also carried personal bank details. To buy anything you just used the card. Handwriting was no longer used as the personal computer links could take dictation and correct spelling. Each personal link was able to identify its owner's characteristics and it acted as a personal organizer. The areas it covered were for types of clothing you liked, your size for anything you wanted to buy, type of entertainment you liked with suggestions for things to try, job opportunities and even arranged blind dates at the sort of place you enjoyed and could afford. Chat lines were complete with video links.

As a result of the wide use of computers, the old-fashioned education system was no longer needed. Much of the time spent in primary education was on teaching speed-reading and how to speak grammatical English so the computers were able to understand them. The rest of the time in education was used in learning how to use the range of computer programs to find and use data. By the age of 12 all pupils were expected to have a general overview of the principle topics in the arts and sciences. No depth of knowledge was needed, just a broad view of where information could be found and how it would be used. At 13 years old pupils could choose a range of manual skills or academic studies. Most wanted to select manual skills, and there was still a need for them. Nurses, drivers, electricians, decorators, plumbers and mechanics and many others were still needed as some tasks were still done better by people. The students who wanted to go in for more academic areas had the opportunity to try out projects in different topic areas to find out what they found interesting. At the age of 15 all students began to learn how to do a particular job. Of course that would only be the start of their working career and many would expect to change the type of work they did every ten years or so.

Health plus 50

Genetic engineering made a major impact by offering improvements in the human body without apparent risk. As a result of this the people who could afford it started to buy the improvements that were available. Cosmetic surgery was replaced by genetic engineering. Adults no longer felt the effects of ageing and children were born with a guarantee of being disease free. Everyone had a genetic profile from birth that told doctors which diseases they were likely to develop so that preventative measures would be taken before they got ill. In developed countries those that could afford it had a 'Biolav' that monitored

WEB LINKS

Searching through www.google.com with the term 'the future' will bring up numerous sites as will the search term 'kurellian' (a predictor). At members.aol.com/kurellian/spint.html is an illustrated online book detailing probable technological advances and their likely socio-economic effects. At www.zuzu.org/pre.html you will find forecasts of how life will be in the future in New York city.

TIPS FOR FURTHER RESEARCH

Look into how various institutions see the future of children, marriage, relationships, education. Visit the website of the Chalkface Project at www.chalkface.com and look at the information on their 'paperless school' project. Is it viable? Is it here? www.rff.org/ looks at environmental factors related to the provision of energy in the future, mainly from an economics perspective. Ask your parents and grandparents what they wished for when they were your age and then see whether it has yet come about. Use this to think about the rapidity of change.

their human waste and did a daily analysis of the individual's health. This informed the owner what to eat and what preventive medication was needed. Physical illness had almost totally disappeared, organs could easily be replaced and the ageing process almost eliminated. Life expectancy reached an average of 150 years and everyone's physical development stayed at the peak reached at 25 years old. Teenagers had the DNA from their sperm and eggs stored and could apply to use them to have children at any time. An unexpected consequence was that very few people seemed to have the time for children and the birth rate fell rapidly. For the first time the world population started to reduce. However, mental illness had now replaced ageing as the main health problem. For the children of the rich, their intelligence and physical attributes became genetically improved which allowed them to earn more in the fields of entertainment, sport and science.

Politics plus 100

As the predicted Information Highway became established and everyone on the planet had access to the entire world's knowledge, then individual governments became less and less important. The combination of interactive television and computers using photons of light instead of electrons made total communication possible. This had a major effect in many areas of life. For example, as everyone was able to buy the cheapest items from anywhere on the planet then governments were less able to control what was being made, imported or exported. Big multinational companies made trade agreements instead of governments. As universal news channels produced world news in all languages then political differences between groups in the world sharply reduced. Politicians trying to achieve power by distorting the truth, such as blaming other countries for their nation's problems, were soon ignored by the majority as they were able to be informed about all points of view. Democracy changed as the majority of people were able to make their views heard due to the interactive television and information screens. Opinion polls were run on a daily basis. The idea of main political parties putting forward a group of policies was replaced by loose interest groups that constantly reformed to promote or oppose particular policies. Government was much smaller and based on main geographic areas, Africa, Asia, Europe and Americas being the most important. Army, navy and airforces belonging to individual countries were no longer needed as major conflicts between countries ended. However, conflicts between interest groups, big business and the state were still present so a semi-military police force was still in evidence. The main area of debate for most people was the conflict between personal freedom and the majority views, as the majority view quickly became enforceable regulations. Personal privacy was almost unknown as most areas were watched by cameras as it reduced crime. Advertising multinationals held detailed databases on everyone so they could direct advertising at the individual instead of the old-fashioned 'blanket advertising' that was so wasteful. The problem was that this began to be compared to a 'big brother' organization that could try to brainwash people.

SCIENCE AND TECHNOLOGY

Wealth plus 200

When the technology arrived to produce energy by the fusion of hydrogen, the need for the fossil fuels and most of the alternative energy resources disappeared. Energy was virtually free and therefore the end unit cost of items almost disappeared. The majority of people lived on a universal wage set by the state; taxation was only made on the production of goods. This meant the government gave people a wage as a citizen's right. The wage was based on their intelligence and abilities. This could then be increased (or not) by the individual making use of their talents in some form of work. Many chose to do nothing at all even though all work has been made very attractive and enjoyable. Individual sportsmen and women as well as entertainers could still earn large sums, but as computer images were indistinguishable from the real thing, the need for people as entertainers has been greatly reduced. The old-fashioned films and games had been replaced by virtual reality where the individual is the hero or heroine and could decide how to change the plot. Once virtual reality could affect taste, touch, and smell as well as hearing and visual input it took over entertainment completely. The early comedy called *Red Dwarf* became a cult classic and the model for the standard holiday package. For most people the idea of personal possessions became unimportant as most items were almost free. The quality of life was the main interest as boredom was the biggest social problem. For those in work, learning had become a life-long activity. The idea of having to work to provide the basics of life ended some time ago. Work became a means of personal fulfilment and a way of socializing with others. For the majority, virtual reality games and mood improving-drugs were the main interests in life.

Society plus 500

After 300 years two distinct human races started to emerge, one being a small but important group of enhanced humans and the rest of humanity the main group. Areas of DNA had been found that traced our evolutionary progress. This meant DNA could be corrected and it was used so that evolutionary changes could occur in only a few generations. As the colonization of other planets became possible, the people living there found more need for genetic enhancement to enable them to cope with the demands of their new life. Having gills to breathe in water and being able to use the sun's energy by a modified area of the skin were early examples. The rapid colonization of space was due in part to the space lift first suggested by Arthur C Clarke. This is a cable between Earth and a massive orbiting space station. This meant objects and people could move out of Earth's gravity easily and at low cost. A conflict of interest between the enhanced humans and the majority began to be evident. The majority do no work and spend most of their time inside virtual reality programs. Genetically enhanced people mainly lived outside of Earth and wanted space exploration to be the main priority for Earth. Political unrest began to be compared to the start of the French Revolution where an aristocracy oppressed the middle and lower classes. The differences being that the new aristocracy are the ones who work and the masses are the idle pleasure-seekers. The two main political groups were the Earth-bound majority and the genetically improved 'outer-worlders'. After 500 years of peace could war be possible? The two groups seldom mix and a new species of human seemed to be developing.

Questions for discussion

1. The future holds out nothing but promise. It will be a better future for everybody.' Discuss this statement.

2. Watch an episode of a futuristic television series or a futuristic film at the cinema. How could you categorize these offerings? (Are they optimistic, pessimistic, idealistic? You could compare something like *Mad Max* or *Waterworld* with *Star Trek*.)

3. What gadgets would you really, really like? Why?

4. Which areas of development are more important – the sciences, medicine, engineering, technology? For example, is the science of fuel efficiency more worthy of support than the science of cancer research? Why?

5. Read some views of the future as written in the past. For example, what was HG Wells' view of the future? What was George Orwell's view of the future in *1984*? Use these as the basis for a discussion on whether predictions tend to be accurate or not.

Questions for written answer

1. Write out a criticism of each paragraph explaining where you agree, disagree and what you suggest as an alternative.

2. It is said that medical and technological advances in the past 50 years have increased life expectancy and the quality of human life. To what extent and in what manner do you think the next 50 years will improve the quality of human life?

3. Discuss how you think the various technological advances will either lead to a greater protection of civil liberties or a greater erosion of them.

4. How could you use everyday items and situations to convey to a visitor from the future what we mean by 'life', 'force' and 'morality'? Give reasons for your answer.

5. Consider that mankind has discovered that we are not alone in the universe. Not only has life been discovered on other planets, but it is far superior in intelligence to us. Mankind has been put on trial by these beings. It is your job to explain and defend the following:
   • our system of justice and punishment
   • why wealth is distributed in the way that it is
   • our system of marriage and relationships
   • our differing religions.
   Choose one of these and present the defence for mankind.

Examiners will look for the following in your written answer:

• Evidence that you have understood the source material and can make appropriate use of it.
• You need to be able to make value judgements based on it and support these with evidence or interpretation.
• You need to have something of your own to say and to be able to state it clearly.
• You need to show you can relate this work to other relevant areas of study.

ACTIVITY

In groups discuss each of these in order: (a) Do you agree that the technology will be in place? Are there different developments that may occur? (b) Will it have the effect that has been forecast? If not why not?

You may find certain individuals in the group are optimists and expect things to go well. In contrast others will be pessimists and not expect things to turn out well at all. A third group are those who think change will occur very slowly or not at all. Ask individuals to identify themselves and to work in a group of like-minded people. There should therefore be three groups.

Read each paragraph then consider the possible effect you think it will make on day-to-day life. Will this new technology alter the way we live? Comment on the possible changes in each significant area – these will include family, and relationships, work and leisure, government and politics, international relations and distribution of wealth as a minimum. Groups should be able to think of other significant areas.

Area **3**

SOCIETY, POLITICS AND THE ECONOMY

25 | Europe: are we becoming too European?
26 | Is the NHS terminally ill?
27 | The mobile revolution
28 | The landfill tax: what is it and is it working?
29 | Are we lunatic with our asylum policy?
30 | The impossible dream
31 | Who's free trade for anyway?
32 | Electoral systems
33 | My Dad says ...
34 | 11 September

SOCIETY, POLITICS AND THE ECONOMY

Preview

The UK has never existed in isolation, nor can it. But what form should its relationships with its global partners take? Already a member of the European Union (EU), should the UK integrate its future more into the EU by abandoning the pound and adopting the euro, or should it stay outside the eurozone?

The UK has a unique position in the world – should it try to maximize that, or do closer ties to Europe mean saying goodbye to traditional friends?

A brief history of the EU

It all started six years after the end of the Second World War when previous enemies joined together to form the European Coal and Steel Community (ECSC) by signing the 1951 Paris Treaty. The countries were France, West Germany, Italy, Luxembourg, Belgium and The Netherlands. Seven years later in 1958 the same six countries signed the Treaty of Rome which set up the European Economic Community (EEC), sometimes known as the Common Market, with the objective of reducing trade barriers between member nations.

The UK applied to join the EEC in 1961 but in 1963 the French President, General de Gaulle, said 'non' to British entry and negotiations were broken off. The UK reapplied to join the EEC in 1964, and again in 1967 de Gaulle vetoed UK membership. In 1970, after the death of the General, the European Commission invited the UK to reopen negotiations; in January 1972 the Treaty of Accession was signed, and in January 1973 the UK finally joined together with Ireland and Denmark. Then there were nine.

The referendum and further growth

In February 1974 the Labour Party won a general election, formed a new government, and demanded that the Treaty of Accession be renegotiated. This renegotiation was completed in 1975, and in the same year a referendum was held in which 67.2% of the voters voted 'Yes' in favour of continued membership. The first tentative steps towards a single currency occurred in 1979 when the European Monetary System (EMS) was created. It was based on a currency unit called the Ecu and was designed to stabilize the exchange rates of the national currencies and reduce inflation.

In 1981 Greece joined the EEC, making 10 member states. This was followed in 1986 by the membership of Spain and Portugal, so then there was a dozen. Also in that year the European flag was adopted, and the Single European Act was enacted, which modified the Treaty of Rome, increased political co-operation between the member states including monetary co-operation. Fully implemented in 1992, it resulted in the phasing out of many border controls between member states.

In 1989 the Berlin wall came down, and the following year came the unification of Germany.

'By this Treaty, the High Contracting Parties establish among themselves a European Union. This Treaty marks a new stage in the process creating an ever closer Union among the peoples of Europe, where decisions are taken as closely as possible to the citizens. The Union shall be founded on the European Communities, supplemented by the policies and cooperation established by this Treaty. Its task shall be to organize, in a manner demonstrating consistency and solidarity, relations between the member States and their peoples.'

Birth of an idea – the euro

In 1992 the Maastricht Treaty (the Treaty of European Union) was signed. The Treaty raised the idea of European integration to an ambitious and new target by January 1999 for the replacement of national currencies by a single, shared currency, the euro.

In 1995 the number of member states became 15 as Austria, Finland and Sweden joined the European Union, as it was now known.

In 1999 the euro was officially launched. Austria, Belgium, Finland, France, Germany, Ireland, Italy, Luxembourg, The Netherlands, Portugal and Spain adopted the euro as their official currency, leaving Greece, UK, Sweden and Denmark outside.

In the new millennium Denmark held a referendum, and the Danish citizens rejected the idea of joining the eurozone. By contrast, Greece became euro club members. In January 2002 euro notes and coins became legal tender in the 12 eurozone countries.

The meaning of Maastricht

Some of the objectives of the Maastricht Treaty can be summarized as being:

- To promote balanced progress which is sustainable through:
  – the creation of an area without internal frontiers
  – the strengthening of economic and social cohesion
  – the establishment of economic and monetary union
  – a single currency.

- To assert its identity on the international scene through:
  – the implementation of a common foreign and security policy
  – the eventual formation of a common defence policy.

- To introduce citizenship of the Union for the nationals of its member states.

- To develop a close co-operation on home affairs and in the judicial field.

It seems there are many good reasons for being part of the EU, and for being a signatory to the Maastricht Treaty of European Union. Or should we have some reservations?

The euro and all that

The Labour government first elected in 1997 and headed by Tony Blair was committed in principle to joining the euro and abolishing the pound, but only when the economic conditions are right for the UK. To make sure that this happens, Chancellor of the Exchequer Gordon Brown has devised five economic tests that must be met before the government will consider joining the eurozone.

When the Treasury determines that this has happened, the government will arrange a referendum of the British people to make the final decision. So that's very clear, the UK will not join until it is in the interest of the British people. Well, yes. But let's look at those economic tests. They are:

- is there sustainable convergence between UK and the eurozone economies?
- is there sufficient flexibility to cope with economic change?
- will it encourage or discourage companies from investing in the UK?
- will there be benefits to the financial services industry?
- will it be good for employment?

Some critics of the government's five tests claim they are too vague to mean anything. Some say that the tests have already been met, some that they never could be. In any referendum, the fear is that the voters will not know either way – the voters just 'get muddled'.

Sir Stanley Kalms, chairman of Dixons plc has said the following:

If the euro becomes UK legal tender we will frequently find ourselves operating with an interest rate which is wrong for Britain. The European Central Bank has to set one interest rate for the entire eurozone. But the differing economies of the eurozone often require different interest rates. Consequently, the ECB can end up with an interest rate that isn't right for any of its members.

To sign up to the euro is to sign up to an intolerably inflexible labour market where it's expensive and difficult to employ staff during peak season and even more difficult to shed staff when business slows down.

Britain has become the world's fourth largest economy by employing flexible, low tax economic policies which are the catalyst to a fertile entrepreneurial environment. It is an essential formula which must not be given away if our 'nation of shopkeepers' is to continue to thrive.

Financial Times (FT.com), 27 September 2001

It could be argued that these are solely economic issues, not social or political ones, and what is good for big business is not necessarily good for workers or consumers.

WEB LINKS

Visit www.europa.eu.int where you will find a wealth of information, including a time line of the formation of the EU. Visit the UK treasury site at http://www.hm-treasury.gov.uk/documents/the_euro/euro_index_index.cfm to get the government's official view. Both of the above sites provide many other links.

TIPS FOR FURTHER RESEARCH

You could look deeper into the history of the EU. The lack of trust may have something to do with the times that the European powers have been at war with each other. Research how many European wars there have been in the last millennium. You could extend your understanding by looking up the following key terms:
a) Commonwealth of Nations
b) United Nations
c) the Treasury.

'The mother of all parliaments' at Westminster

So what about those social and political arguments?

Monetary union means very close integration between member states, and therefore a large amount of political unity. In a continent that started two world wars in the last century, this could be thought of as a very good thing! Going on holiday will be simpler for citizens of member states since they all use the same money – no travellers' cheques or money changing needed. It would also make for 'price transparency' since it will be obvious whether goods and services are cheaper in another member state. This might help to push prices down, which is likely to be popular with citizens.

However, with a single currency controlled by the ECB (European Central Bank), interest rates have to be the same throughout the eurozone giving a 'one size fits all' interest rate that some economists have severe doubts about. This also leaves the individual states with much less control over their economy, talks are already afoot to have a common tax structure with common rates across all member states of the eurozone. This is known as tax harmonization.

Romano Prodi, president of the European Commission, described the role of the euro in a speech given in New York to the Council on Foreign Relations on 11 January 2002. It was as follows: 'The European Union is not just about economics: it is also a fundamentally political project and the Euro symbolises this' (http://europa.eu.int).

Sovereignty and special relationships

Some xenophobes don't trust any foreigners. 'We're British, and that's what matters'. They forget that the UK has been a member of the world community for centuries, and indeed, that if we go far back enough in time, 'native' British citizens are made up of Romans, Angles, Saxons, Celts, Normans and many more. More recently our heritage has been enriched by successfully inviting immigration of West Indians, Asians and others. Perhaps we are now true mongrels, and proud of it!

Britain is the only nation that holds membership of the European Union, the United Nations, and the Commonwealth of Nations. Do we want to throw away that balance by becoming citizens of a United States of Europe?

For most of the last century, the UK's closest ally has been the USA. We have had a 'special relationship' that held us together through many conflicts including the two World Wars, the Korean War, the Falklands war, and more recently in Kosovo. At the start of the twenty-first century we find ourselves standing 'shoulder to shoulder' with the USA after the events of 11 September 2001. Will being part of an integrated EU damage that special relationship?

Questions for discussion

1. What do you think was the main reason behind the formation of the EEC? Has it worked?

2. Does forming closer links by joining the eurozone mean abandoning other international allies?

3. How important do you think the 'special relationship' is?

4. What is the Commonwealth? How important is it?

5. What effect is the introduction of the euro likely to have on the following French people?
   • worker
   • businessman
   • consumer?

Questions for written answer

1. 'Some business leaders believe that joining the euro means that it will be difficult for businesses to hire and fire labour. This is bad for business and good for the workforce.' Discuss and analyse this statement.

2. Interest rates have been low in the continental eurozone because of the slow down of German and French economies. This has created a large rise in house prices in a booming Ireland. Is this good for Ireland? Explain any problems you foresee.

Examiners will look for the following in your written answer:

• Evidence that you have understood the source material and can make appropriate use of it.
• You need to be able to make value judgements based on it and support these with evidence or interpretation.
• You need to have something of your own to say and to be able to state it clearly.
• You need to show you can relate this work to other relevant areas of study.

3. Public services (health, transport and so on) are better in France than in the UK, but taxes are higher. Analyse the effects of tax harmonization on UK and French citizens if the UK joins the eurozone.

4. Outline the arguments for and against the UK joining the euro.

5. Using your outline arguments above, explain whether or not the UK should join the euro, and give detailed reasons why.

? Quiz

1. How long did it take for Britain finally to gain membership from when negotiations first started in 1961?

2. How many times was British membership vetoed?

3. How did the British people finally decide their membership of the European Union?

4. What is the name of the Chancellor of the Exchequer?

5. What was the name of the government elected in the UK in May 1997?

6. What is the Treaty of European Union commonly called?

7. What do the initials ECB stand for?

ACTIVITY 1

Divide your class or group into two sections. Within each half form groups of three or four. One half of section 1 now goes into role as people over the age of 40. Brainstorm all the arguments that you can think of for keeping the pound (don't forget the war, and your loyalty to the monarchy!). The other half of section 1 are people under 40. Brainstorm all the reasons you may have for keeping the pound. Section 2 should form the same age group roles but brainstorm all the reasons for joining the euro. You can be very young or very old, very rich or very poor, a supporter of industry or of the consumer or workers – you decide. You should write your precise role down so that you don't stray out of character.

Collect all the points together for each age group.

Each section should then elect a spokesperson from each age group to debate the points with the other side.

You could finish with a vote – if you can decide on a fair question to ask and a fair voting system!

ACTIVITY 2

Identify EU and the eurozone countries against the map. Colour or shade the map to represent the countries of the EU, those in the eurozone, those which have applied for membership and those which have no connection with the EU. What conclusions can you draw from this exercise?

Preview

The National Health Service (NHS) has shown itself to be having difficulties at the end of the twentieth century and at the beginning of the twenty-first. Indeed some would say the NHS is in crisis. This has been demonstrated by sensational newspaper stories of patients dying on trolleys in overcrowded hospitals after waiting for treatment over many hours, cancer victims being diagnosed in time but not being treated in time and allegedly dying as a result, and many other horror stories. As a result, the NHS has been labelled by many as a Third World health service from a First World country.

This bogus news report below in the fictitious *Daily Post* describes a fictional news story a few years after the millennium about the expected closure of the NHS, and the start of private health care (PHC) provision to replace it. Many of the views expressed are deliberately one-sided, and may be totally or partially inaccurate.

The NHS is dead – long live PHC

Ministers yesterday confirmed that the NHS is to be wound up. In a written answer, the Secretary of State for Health confirmed to the House of Commons what this newspaper exclusively reported in our Monday edition – the National Health Service cannot continue. It is bankrupt both of money and ideas.

When the Health Secretary was asked at a later press conference why this huge change of policy was revealed only in a written answer to an MP's question, she replied 'there is no policy change'. Health care will, she said, continue to be free at the point of use.

The Leader of the Opposition attacked the government's handling of the affair, demanding a Commons debate on the issue. The shadow Secretary of State for Health went further, demanding the immediate resignation of his government opposite number, stating that, since the present government came to power five years ago, the National Health Service has imploded. 'The government is unable to keep promises given on health in two elections' he said.

Details of the government plans are vague. A White Paper has been promised on the future of the NHS as a matter of urgency; the Health Secretary and the government as a whole were forced into an early disclosure of the NHS shutdown as a result of mounting concern from patients and their relatives, trade unions and NHS managers.

Embarrassingly for the government, it seems likely that the private sector will be used more and more for public health care, and that gradually, NHS trust hospitals as well as other parts of the NHS will be privatized. The use of other EU countries to provide medical care, started in 2001, will be expanded.

Initial reaction was mixed. Predictably the health service trade unions were extremely critical. 'Dedicated, hard working staff will lose their jobs, while fat cat bosses in the private sector will line

WEB LINKS

www.nhs.uk is the home page of the National Health Service. You can access genuine newspaper reports on aspects of the health service and its operation by going to any of the national newspaper sites and searching the archive section using 'NHS' or 'National Health Service' (with quotation marks).

The NHS was 50 years old on 5 July 1998. The coalition government had promised that the post-war health service would be comprehensive, available to the entire population, and in most respects free at point of delivery. Aneurin Bevan, the government minister in charge under the post-war Labour administration, stood by these principles and also promised a first-class quality of treatment. Further history can be found at www.nhs.uk.

their pockets' said one leader. Another was equally critical 'The government has not spent enough on the NHS – we are the poor relations of Europe with a third world health service thanks to successive government underfunding'.

Many groups representing patients were more positive. 'At last patients will have the opportunity to get treatment when they need it' was the reaction of many. When quizzed about the possible need to go abroad, the reaction was that it would be a small price to pay for prompt, efficient health care. One elderly lady, waiting after eight months for a NHS hip replacement was less sure. As she pointed out 'I need my family and friends around me for support, and what happens when it's time to go home?'

A group of health service managers were unhappy with the decision. 'If the government had given us the chance to manage, instead of meeting arbitrary deadlines with insufficient money, too much paperwork etc., we could have made the NHS work' said one. 'If the

private sector is to work, what will they call it?' asked another. 'Private Health Care plc?' A third enquired where the staff are to come from to manage and work in an expanded private system. 'If we have the same staff and the same budgets, how will it be any better? Especially since the private companies will need to show a profit!'

An expert on health care provision was cautious when asked her views. 'I want to see what specific proposals the government come up with' she explained. 'However there could be benefits' she went on 'private health care provision could be more efficient than the existing system, with less bureaucracy, and more efficiency. Private companies are more likely to plan ahead and invest realistically for the future.'

But the real bombshell came from a tax expert. 'For years governments of all parties have been committed to free health care at the point of use' he pointed out. 'They still are, but I am not sure what it really means. For years

The luxury of private medicine: is this causing problems for the NHS?

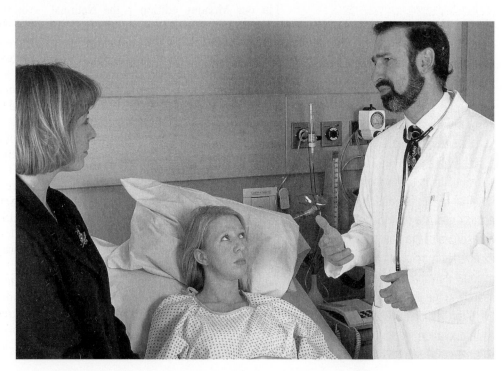

The NHS is the largest organization in Europe. Despite various criticisms it is recognized by the World Health Organization as being one of the top health service providers in the world.

politicians have varied tax and National Insurance rates to fund the NHS and many other services. Does a Private Health Care system suggest the government might also privatize health insurance? What will be the effect of that on those with low incomes and/or serious medical problems?'

Questions for discussion

1. What do you think the health service is like in other countries. In particular, what is it like in other developed countries like America and France? Is it better or worse?

2. How do other countries fund their health provision? Is this more or less efficient than in the UK?

3. 'National Insurance is nothing more than another name for taxation. Why not just put it all into general taxation?' State the arguments for and against this statement.

4. Should people who provide themselves with their own pension, healthcare etc., be able to opt out of paying National Insurance contributions, as they are not using the services provided?

5. 'If healthcare was left to the private sector, it would run much more efficiently: people would get the treatment that they paid for.' Discuss.

Examiners will look for the following in your written answer:

- Evidence that you have understood the source material and can make appropriate use of it.
- You need to be able to make value judgements based on it and support these with evidence or interpretation.
- You need to have something of your own to say and to be able to state it clearly.
- You need to show you can relate this work to other relevant areas of study.

Questions for written answers

1. What does the reporter mean when writing: 'National Health Service cannot continue. It is bankrupt both of money and ideas'. Would you agree or disagree? Why?

2. How meaningful is the term: 'free at the point of use'? Give detailed reasons in support of your answer.

3. Do you agree that spending more money on the NHS is the answer? Present a detailed, balanced view which comes to a conclusion agreeing or disagreeing with the question.

4. Outline what the NHS manager might have meant by 'arbitrary deadlines' and 'too much paperwork'. Explain how and why this might impact on the quality of care.

5. The third NHS manager asked 'If we have the same staff and the same budgets, how will it be any better? Especially since the private companies will need to show a profit!' Give detailed reasons why you think privatized health companies can or cannot 'make it better'.

TIPS FOR FURTHER RESEARCH

The 10-year programme outlining the steps for the modernization of the NHS can be found at www.nhs.uk/thenhsexplained/priorities.asp. You could also investigate the type of provision that you have local to you. For example, do you have a health service trust, is your local general practitioner independent, are there alternative private hospitals for any/all treatments?

 **Quiz**

1. How old is the NHS?
2. Which minister was responsible for its establishment?
3. What is the difference between 'public' and 'private' sectors?
4. What is an NHS Trust hospital?
5. What do NHS managers do?
6. How has your GP been made more 'independent'?
7. Which international organization still praises the health service?
8. What are PFI and PPP? How do they affect the NHS?

ACTIVITY 1

In small groups establish an agreed definition for the following words and phrases. If your group is unable to come up with an agreed meaning, you must undertake suitable research to ensure that you do. Write the words and phrases on large sheets of paper, and share your findings with other groups. If there are still disagreements between groups, time for more research!

- Secretary of State for Health
- Leader of the Opposition
- Commons debate
- imploded
- White Paper
- trade unions
- other EU countries
- fat cat bosses
- private sector
- underfunding
- profit
- bureaucracy
- tax
- National Insurance.

ACTIVITY 2

Carry out a class debate on the motion 'This house believes that the situation portrayed in the article will inevitably come true'

The mobile revolution

27

Preview

The mobile phone has had a huge, and perhaps unexpected, impact on all our lives. There are 45 million mobiles in use in the UK for a population of 60 million, and that includes babies and toddlers. Most adults and teenagers therefore have their own phones, some on monthly contract, many pay as you go. It is not just the UK – far from it, it is a world-wide trend. This chapter looks briefly at the history of this phenomenon, and tries to give some suggestions as to what the future might hold. The chances are though, that the future of this industry will hold many surprises!

How did it all begin?

'State of the art' in 1990

Just over 100 years ago, in the afternoon of a December day, the three dots of the Morse letter 'S' transmitted from Cornwall, England were received in St John's Newfoundland. Radio transmission was not new (it was in its infancy) but Guglielmo Marconi, Italian born but living and working in England, was responsible for demonstrating that radio signals could be transmitted over long distances. Now vast amounts of radio traffic flow throughout many different frequencies of the radio spectrum – traffic that includes speech, data, music, and images.

For the public, mobile phones came along in the 1970s. The first mobiles were great big heavy things with large batteries – really the correct name was transportable, and the main users were business people who had them installed in their cars.

'State of the art' 2002
(and getting even smaller!)

First-generation mobile phones

These analogue devices, equipped with newly developed microprocessors, were the first to have widespread use, and the popularity of them was the cause of their downfall. There were two distinct problems with the analogue networks:

- there was insufficient capacity for the expected number of users (and the estimates at the time, mid-1980s, were much lower than the actual number of subscribers)

- each country had its own system, which in an increasingly global economy was nonsense.

By the early 1990s the system would collapse. To cope with this problem the Groupe Spéciale Mobile (GSM) was established. It was set up to develop and provide a specification for a Europe-wide mobile communications network able meet the expected millions of individuals and businesses likely to want mobile communications in the future.

Second-generation to fourth-generation mobiles

Digital GSM mobile phones started to become available in 1992. By June 1995, there were 156 networks covering 12 million customers in 86 countries with roaming capability, i.e. the ability to make cross-border calls. In the same year there were demonstrations of the video, fax, and data capability of GSM networks. In the late 1990s came WAP (wireless application protocol) phones able to connect to the internet (if you were not in a hurry!). It did mean users could access their e-mails on the move, but internet access was available only to special sites with restricted content. Although limited in its usefulness, here was a hint of just how powerful a tool the mobile might become in the future. At around this time appeared the beginnings of the m-word – we had begun to get used to e-business, e-commerce, e-banking and many more. The 'e' just meant 'electronic' so in the same way 'm', standing for 'mobile', started to appear as in m-banking, m-commerce, etc.

By the time the third generation had been planned, it was clear that technology, and the demands of some consumers were moving quickly, so an interim solution was adopted called 2.5G (two-and-a-half generation). This uses a technology called GPRS (General Packet Radio Service) which enabled data to be transmitted much more quickly, but not as fast as intended in the future.

Third-generation mobiles promise faster communication and systems used in every country will be able communicate with each other leading to world-wide roaming capability. Many will have built-in cameras, screens will be in colour and bigger than those we are used to, and they will have the facility for permanent internet connection – vital for m-commerce. Video conferencing is an application that many expect to become important with third-generation systems, indeed an explosion in multimedia is expected. We may find ourselves looking at the phones much more than holding them to our ears – perhaps we shall need eyes-free kits while driving! The first third-generation phones were available in Japan in 2001, and are expected to be widely used across the world.

According to Japanese press reports, the country's telecommunication ministry has requested a $10m budget for 2002 to develop fourth-generation mobile communications technology, planned to be 50 times faster than third generation, and available by 2010.

The future

Who knows? One of the most popular uses of present mobiles is SMS text messaging. This was a feature that designers didn't expect to be important, but many (particularly younger) people use all the time. Indeed it isn't unusual to

In the UK there are more than 45 million mobile users (2002) (almost three quarters of the population) and growing. In Finland the figure is a staggering 99.5% of 16- to 24-year-olds with at least one mobile phone (yes, some have two or more).

find a landline phone glued to a teenager's ear while she taps out a text message on her mobile. One thing we can be sure of for the future, and that is there will be uses for the new mobile phones we haven't thought of yet. For sure, with the increasingly global nature of business and our lived in general, the ability to roam world-wide with our mobiles will become more and more significant.

Some ideas of what might happen:

- Downloading music from the internet. This may be real-time (streaming) or storing to play later, perhaps when connected to a system at home, perhaps with headphones on the move with an MP3 player.

- No 'dead' spots where a connection cannot be made. Mobiles will have the capability to seamlessly switch between landline (for example, at home), cell phone networks, and satellite where there is no network signal.

- Sending photographs to accompany an e-mail or text message. Tell your family and friends where you are and what you are doing, together with a picture – worth a thousand words.

- Voice-over-internet protocol – this allows voice calls to be sent over the internet at local call rate anywhere in the world.

- It will be possible to pay bills and transfer money between accounts just by typing a PIN code on a mobile phone (m-banking).

- Moving pictures via the mobile? With phones of the future, it will not only be a trailer of the latest movie sent attached to an e-mail or SMS message, it will also be possible to view the inside of your own home from abroad for example, to check security or see whether the fish in the aquarium are OK – m-video?

- Your mobile phone knows where you are. In-car navigation, local street plans, a diary of local events, all of these will be available. The phone will even advise you of the best route to take in view of traffic and weather conditions.

- Road congestion will be a thing of the past, partly because of those navigation aids and early warnings of heavy traffic, but also because many journeys currently undertaken will be unnecessary.

- Perhaps, knowing where you are, as well as your lifestyle, local organizations will be able to connect to you as you pass through their area to tempt you with their offerings.

- There will be convergence of many consumer electronic devices – for example the press photographer's digital camera will have a mobile phone built in to enable his picture to be on the other side of the world seconds after the event he has recorded. Will there be any need for laptop computers when the phone has all the computing power that is needed? We shall, see manufacturers of desktop computers, laptops, video equipment entering the mobile phone market; large e- and m-company mergers may be widespread.

- There will be no fixed, landline-only phones. Everyone will have his or her own mobile which will no longer be an accessory, it will be a core part of

EB LINKS
www.3g.co.uk/
3GNewWhitePapers.htm
www.vodafone.com/future/
www.mmo2.com/docs/home.html
www.orange.com
www.tmobile.co.uk

how daily lives are conducted. The mobile phone will become an intelligent remote control that allows people to do what they want, where they want, when they want. You will not try to connect to a phone; you will connect to a person.

- Instead of peering at a tiny colour screen, it will be possible to hook up the mobile to a large flat screen in the home, office or car.

- Mobiles will recognize their owner's voice, and will only respond to the owner's eye-print. It will be possible, using the machines processing power, to dictate a message which will be sent as a fax, an m-mail or text message (the differences between these will disappear). A voice synthesizer at the destination will read out that message if required.

- Schools will have keyboards which link wirelessly to students' mobiles. The mobile will become students' computers with storage of their work on-line and accessible world-wide.

Dangerous enough to be banned?

TIPS FOR FURTHER RESEARCH

Investigate how much money the UK mobile network operators spent on the third-generation licences. You could also visit the websites of the major UK mobile phone companies to find out something about current trends in development. Other research opportunities will present themselves if you visit the weblinks shown. http://www.guardian.co.uk/Archive gives access to *The Guardian* newspaper's archives where you can search for articles about mobile phones

Health issues

In January 2002 the British government announced a major investigation into the safety of mobile phones. The possible problem centres around the fact that mobiles transmit via microwaves, just like in a microwave cooker, but much lower power. But does this mean that when using it, users are cooking their brains? It has been suggested that young people are particularly at risk since their skulls are considerably thinner than adults. It has even been suggested that boys using phones on their laps to send text messages could be risking damage to their fertility. Equally, many are concerned over radiation from the masts put up to transmit and receive mobile signals – for obvious reasons, many of these masts are in centres of population.

Will this mean the end of the mobile phone? It is perhaps more likely, if there is shown to be a problem, that a solution of some sort will be found.

The cost

In the late twentieth century, governments from many countries auctioned off licences to operate the new third-generation networks. Mobile phone companies had to have the licences to compete in the twenty-first century. As a result, the auctions raised much more money for governments than had been expected, and saddled the network operators with mountains of debt. There are those that argue the money required to pay off the debt and interest will take many years, and the costs of phone usage will make mobile phones too expensive for customers. The opposite view is that the value and volume of new uses that will be found will offset these expenses.

Questions for discussion

1. There is no evidence to prove that mobile phones are harmful to health – is there?

2. What other developments could happen? Will tomorrow's user, for example, have access to a virtual, life-size, three-dimensional holographic image?

3. What is SMS? Did mobile phone operators ever intend it to be so large?

4. Should mobile phones be banned or restricted to older users to prevent them being stolen?

5. Prices will all become really cheap once everyone is buying over the internet, because no one will ever buy at a price higher than the lowest current price. True or false? Likely or not?

Questions for written answer

1. Write a 'day-in-the-life' diary for yourself if you had been this age 20 years ago. Pay particular attention to the ways you would have learned, communicated and worked. What has changed? What has remained the same?

2. Analyse the differences between life for a teenager 20 years ago and today. What do you think is better? What is worse? Why?

3. 'New technology is always subtly changed by the user so that it does what they, not the manufacturer, want it to do.' Do you agree with this quotation? Give reasons, with examples, for your answer.

4. Civil liberties are the area that is most put under threat by new technology. All these new technologies can be developed to ensure that rights are eroded. Explain what is meant by this statement and discuss its significance, using examples from your own knowledge or experience.

5. Mobile phones are expensive, portable and desirable. They are also owned and used by the young and defenceless. Make a case for a special category of crime (and punishment) for those who prey on such people.

? Quiz

1. What does GSM stand for?

2. What was the name of the Italian-born man who first broadcast a radio signal across the Atlantic?

3. When was the first third-generation mobile phone system launched? In which country?

4. When are 3G phones expected to be widely used world-wide?

5. What does WAP stand for?

6. When is 4G forecast to be available? How much faster might it be than 3G?

7. What is the significance of voice-over-internet protocol?

8. Why are mobile phones thought to be potentially dangerous to their users? Which users are thought to be most at risk?

Examiners will look for the following in your written answer:

- Evidence that you have understood the source material and can make appropriate use of it.
- You need to be able to make value judgements based on it and support these with evidence or interpretation.
- You need to have something of your own to say and to be able to state it clearly.
- You need to show you can relate this work to other relevant areas of study.

ACTIVITY 1

The class should divide into two sections, A and B. Section A will examine what benefits information and communication technologies (ICT) and in particular the new generation mobile phones will have in the next 20–30 years, while section B will forecast disadvantages.

Within each section, small groups each choose a different cross-section of society (by age, gender, ability or disability, ethnic origin, socio-economic classification, etc.)

Each group argues its conclusions with the other groups in your section, and comes to a mutual decision as to which group had the most interesting and convincing (or scary) findings.

The whole group should then try to decide whether the growth of mobile phones will be beneficial to society or otherwise.

ACTIVITY 2

Draw a time-line of the developments of communications and ICT over the past 20 years. Continue the time line by extrapolating 20 years hence – you will need to use your imagination!

28 The landfill tax: what is it and is it working?

Preview

In the early to mid-1990s, it became clear that Britain has a major problem with waste, much more so than many of our neighbours. This waste is produced industrially (e.g. scrap materials from production plants), commercially (e.g. waste documents from office blocks) and privately (our ordinary dustbin contents). Most of the waste goes to landfill sites, that is, filling holes in the ground, or creating hills!

The problem is that, as a very crowded island, Britain is running out of space, especially in the highly densely populated areas such as, but not only, the south-east of England. This waste is polluting the environment, and as more waste has to be transported further, so the costs of disposal rise, as does pollution from the lorries carrying it. In addition we are using more landfill per head of population than many of our European neighbours.

Something had to happen, and it did – the landfill tax. But was it the right thing to do, and is it working? This chapter examines what the landfill tax is, how much it costs, who pays it, why was it introduced, what was it trying to achieve, whether it is working, some recommendations for the future, as well as a few horror stories.

What is this landfill tax then?

The landfill tax was introduced in October 1996 by the then Conservative government. It is quite a complex piece of legislation, but the main provisions are that it applies to all waste:

- disposed of by way of landfill
- at a licensed landfill site
- on or after 1 October 1996

unless the waste is specifically exempt. Exemptions include:

- dredgings from inland waterways and harbours
- naturally occurring minerals from mines and quarries
- domestic pets, buried in pets' cemeteries
- wastes from the remediation of historically contaminated land if the purpose of the remediation is development, conservation or the provision of amenity, or to remove the potential harm from pollutants
- inert wastes used for landfill site engineering (these were originally taxable, but were declared exempt in the March 1998 budget).

WEB LINKS

Go to www.guardian.co.uk and search for 'landfill tax'. You will get further information on some of the information in this article, and more up-to-date information too.
Try www.yahoo.co.uk as well; click on UK only in the top of the opening page, and use the same search. Visit the site of the EPA at www.epa.gov.

How much?

A distinction is made between inert waste such as bricks and rubble which is taxed at £2 per tonne, and other waste. In 1996 the rate for other waste was set at £7 per tonne, but this was increased in April 1999 to £10 per tonne. This rises subject to parliamentary approval by £1 per year to £15 per tonne by April 2004.

Who pays?

Licensed landfill site operators pay the tax to HM Customs and Excise (the same body that collects VAT) every three months. These landfill operators must keep clear records of waste they accept for landfill and whether it is inert waste or not. But it really isn't as simple as that – clearly the landfill operators have to get the money from somewhere, so their charges to waste disposers must go up. Since many of the 'waste producers' are local authorities disposing of household waste, ordinary people in the street actually are paying through their council tax.

Refrigerators waiting to have CFCs removed – sometimes legislation just creates a bigger problem?

What is it trying to do?

The tax set out to reduce tax on employers by reducing employers' National Insurance contributions, and taxing waste instead. The idea was to reduce the cost of employing people, and is an example of 'green' taxation, in that it shifts the burden of tax away from labour and onto the consumption of resources. It was introduced together with an intention to increase recycling and incineration as alternative to landfill. It is interesting to compare the UK's performance with other European countries. As an example, in 1995, the waste generation in European countries was broadly as might be expected, given the sizes of the economies, population, etc. (the top six world economies include Germany, UK, France and Italy). The 'top ten' waste generators are shown in Chart 1 below.

Chart 1
Source: *Guardian*, Thursday 6 April, 2000,
Landfill tax scandal: special report

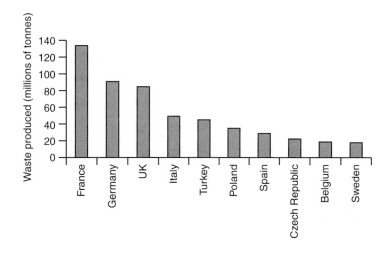

Large lorries are permitted to carry approximately 38 tonnes in the UK. How many lorry loads of waste were generated in 1995?

By contrast, the 'top ten' percentage recovery rates for paper and cardboard are shown in Chart 2.

Chart 2
Source: *Guardian*, Thursday 6 April, 2000,
Landfill tax scandal: special report

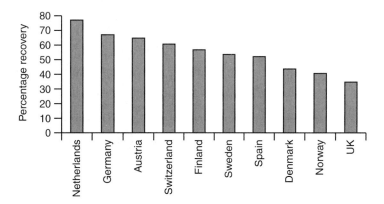

While the UK was by no means the worst offender, there was clearly room for improvement.

Is it working?

Well, not always. The trouble is, if charges for dumping waste in licensed landfill sites rise, there will always be those who will ignore the law and dump their waste illegally. They will only be stopped if there is strict enforcement and prosecution. But the Environment Agency and local councils do not have the money, people or other resources to monitor what is going on, let alone enforce the law. In 2000, an investigation by the *Guardian* newspaper and the Channel 4 programme *Dispatches* quoted a report commissioned from Ecotech, an independent environmental consultancy which suggested that there are now 32,000 unregulated sites in Britain compared to the 14,000 the Environment Agency believed to exist. These unregulated sites are only allowed by law to accept inert materials (earth and building rubble), provided they pose no health risk to humans or animals. Many of these sites are farms, golf courses, beaches, shopping centre developments, residential building sites and so on.

Recommendations

In its recommendations to the government, the Advisory Committee on Business and the Environment (ACBE) came up with the following findings:

- landfill tax has not reduced waste taxed at the standard rate
- landfill costs are still much lower than in other European countries
- the amount of waste recycled in the UK is extremely low
- landfill costs are very low for businesses, but they are much more important for local authorities
- there is widespread support in the recycling industry for change.

The main recommendations to the government are summarized below:

- In its policies on minimizing waste and reducing landfill, the government should make it clear to businesses that there is a goal of using resources and materials more efficiently, thus creating less waste.
- The waste management industry and the government should ensure waste producers can see more clearly where landfill tax costs are passed on to the producers.
- The government should provide support for waste producers likely to be most affected by producer responsibility and other more stringent environmental regulation.
- The government should set targets for reducing landfill waste from 2005 to 2020.
- The government should think about bringing forward the review of the landfill tax from 2004 to end 2001/early 2002 with the aim of getting a significant increase in landfill costs from 2004 and increases in tax revenues.

TIPS FOR FURTHER RESEARCH

You could try to extend your knowledge of this topic by undertaking research to find out comparative figures for Britain and her neighbours for recycling of materials other than cardboard and paper. Visit www.epa.gov/recyclecity for a graphically based educational resource produced by the Environmental Protection Agency.

Can this approach ever achieve a reduction in landfill?

It could be argued from the above that the government's way of dealing with the landfill problem is to charge people for using landfill and to penalize law breakers (although perhaps not very well). It is widely accepted in business, and in schools, that the best way of motivating is not by threat but by reward. Perhaps the government should consider that approach to encourage businesses, local authorities and citizens to generate less waste, and recycle more of what is generated. Interestingly, the ACBE report does not appear to give a high priority to ideas such as these.

Questions for discussion

1. 'Unenforceable law is bad law'. In small groups, discuss whether you agree with this statement, and justify your view. In light of your group's negotiated agreement decide what should happen to the landfill tax.

2. Waste exempt from landfill tax includes 'wastes from the remediation of historically contaminated land if the purpose of the remediation is development, conservation or the provision of amenity, or to remove the potential harm from pollutants'. What does this mean?

3. The costs of pollution should be borne both where it is produced and by the people who produced it. Do you agree?

4. It's just an inevitable by-product of progress. You can't have all the benefits of progress without a few problems. Do you agree or disagree?

5. How much do you (personally and as a group) recycle? Work out the percentage. How much could you recycle if you tried?

Questions for written answer

1. Should the punishment fit the crime? How should those who avoid paying landfill tax, and who abuse the landfill laws be treated? Argue in detail what punishments could and should be meted out, and how and why they would reduce the activities of the abusers.

2. 'To effectively deal with the lawbreakers would cost more than it would save'. Analyse this statement. Would giving enough money to the Environment Agency and local authorities to monitor and prosecute illegal dumpers solve the problem, or would it just create more bureaucracy? Explain your answer in detail.

3. When landfill tax was introduced, employers' contributions to National Insurance were reduced. Explain clearly what this means, and analyse why it might be 'a good thing'

4. One recommendation made to the Government was 'The Government should think about bringing forward the review of the Landfill Tax from

Examiners will look for the following in your written answer:

- Evidence that you have understood the source material and can make appropriate use of it.
- You need to be able to make value judgements based on it and support these with evidence or interpretation.
- You need to have something of your own to say and to be able to state it clearly.
- You need to show you can relate this work to other relevant areas of study.

2004 to end 2001/early 2002 with the aim of getting a significant increase in landfill costs from 2004 and increases in tax revenues'. Explain clearly whether you agree with this recommendation and why. What effect will it have on illegal dumping?

5. 'Legislation can never solve a problem of this nature – it is custom and practice and habits that have to change'. Discuss this statement with regard to the landfill tax and legislation in general.

? Quiz

1. When was the landfill tax introduced?

2. By which government?

3. Name two wastes exempt from the landfill tax in 1997.

4. Name one waste that was exempt from the landfill tax by 1999.

5. What was the cost of dumping 20 tonnes of inert waste at a licensed landfill site in 1999?

6. What was the cost of dumping 30 tonnes of other waste at a licensed landfill site in 2000?

7. Who collects landfill tax?

8. What does ACBE stand for and what did it find out about the cost of landfill in Britain compared with other European countries?

ACTIVITY

'The present waste management system in Britain is unsustainable.'

1. We consume too much

2. We don't make the most of what we do consume

3. We don't recycle enough

4. Our disposal of what is left is inefficient.

The class should divide into sets of four groups, each group containing between two and four people. For example, if there were 19 in the class there could be two sets of four groups. Set one could have three pairs and one group of three, set two would have two pairs and two groups of three. If there were eight in the class, there would be one set of four pairs. If there are fewer than eight in the class, improvise!

• Each group within each set should choose one of the statements above (negotiation skills may be required!).

• The group should develop a strategy to deal with the statement.

• Each group feeds back to the whole class.

(If between you, you come up with a solution to Britain's waste management problems, let the prime minister know!)

Are we lunatic with our asylum policy?

Preview

This topic starts off with a rather one-sided, bigoted, biased view which includes racist connotations, and confuses asylum seekers with refugees, suggesting that many are terrorists. It also contains many factual errors. The second part attempts to redress the balance somewhat, recognizing the problems that asylum seekers have, and that they present difficult issues to their would-be new home country.

A bigot's view

Asylum seekers: headline news

The word asylum is fast becoming a phrase in the English language which can be seen in headlines of our daily papers; often it is a routine topic of conversation between everyday people in all walks of life. Once upon a time the topic was the weather: now it is asylum seekers. What does the word asylum mean? When I was a child it meant an institution, funny farm, loony bin, a place people went if they had a mental disorder. Now in the twenty-first century and with millions of foreigners attempting to take over our country it has a new meaning – a place of refuge, a sanctuary. Where is this place? Apparently it's England, the Utopia of the world, honeypot for the bees.

Where do they go?

Daily we learn that hundreds of illegal immigrants who have come into this country have disappeared. Where do they go and how do they live? They have no identity, no National Insurance number, no way of legally making a living. Do they turn to crime? What happens to those that give themselves up? They are given a golden handshake and greeted with a 'welcome to this land, the land of plenty'. Then given handouts that any English person would long for, but English people living in England already are not eligible for them. It won't be long before the English living in England form a minority group.

Why come here?

An asylum seeker is classed as a person who has fled his home country due to hard times, atrocities, war, whatever, seeking a new life in a new country. Why come here? What does England have to offer? A crumbling health service, collapsing public transport system, a road network that is grinding to a halt, an education system that is worse now than it was in Victorian times – and getting worse. We have a justice system that is farcical and a police force that is too busy giving out crime numbers and catching speeding motorists (a dying breed because of the congested roads) to go out and catch criminals. There is insufficient housing and when more is built it is so expensive the normal English can't afford it. So what draws them to England?

Clever, devious and dangerous

What kind of person is a refugee? Some of them are genuine but how many, two out of every 100? Pictures of them shown in the newspapers and on television show bedraggled scruffy people with no belongings other than what they are wearing. Poor? So how did they afford to pay thousands of pounds to criminals who arranged their passage? They get given money, food and beautiful living accommodation on arrival, and then once they have been accepted we see them in fine housing, nicely dressed, and driving around in a car? Who pays for all that? The English! These people are clever, devious, and some very dangerous. But then, what does it matter? Let them all come in, let's lose them in the system, let's set them up in little communities with people of their own nationalities, so they can plot together. They can plan and scheme to their hearts content, get whatever they ask for, then repay us in a few years by blowing us all up.

When in Rome ...

How about the genuine people seeking refuge? While we can have sympathy for them, they should be made to learn the English language, and to live as the English do. We don't settle in France, Spain, or any other foreign country and expect to live as we do here, we attempt to speak their language, eat their food, and live their way of life. If they want to come to England then they should agree to abide by our rules and live our lifestyle. It's a package and when one has earned the package then one can have some of the fruits.

Use their skills and send them back

Many immigrants do speak the language, which is good, so can the country they are fleeing be that bad, I wonder? Many too have skills – skills that enable them to change train signals, to cut the brakes of the trains so that they can get on/off when they wish, or to get into lorries. Somebody certainly knows something so why don't we make use of him or her? 'No' says the government, 'let's lose them so that in a few years they can be the ones who blow us up and will help train other immigrants to be muggers, vandals, murderers or whatever'. Surely we should find out what skills they have and use them to train others so that they can return to their home country and help rebuild that.

It isn't fair!

There clearly is a need to escape from some countries where individuals have been tortured and persecuted – these people are true asylum seekers, but should they be able to choose where they go? England is an overcrowded, small island, are we to become a second Hong Kong? Surely if we are part of the European Union then other member states should take their fair share of these refugees. It is not fair that the French have a refugee camp at Sangatte just outside Calais and encourage the asylum seekers to go to England. The European Commission should make a ruling that gives the same rights for all asylum seekers so they all get the same treatment wherever they go, and they are shared equally among these countries. They should not all be allowed to come to England. We are not the land of the plenty.

Some facts

1951 United Nations Convention relating to the Status of Refugees

In the first part of the twentieth century the League of Nations, predecessor of the United Nations (UN), developed guidelines to deal with the problem of displaced people who were under threat of persecution in their own countries. In 1951 a UN conference approved the Convention relating to the Status of Refugees and set up the UN High Commission for Refugees (UNHCR). Article 1 of the Convention defines a refugee as 'a person who is outside his/her country of nationality or habitual residence; has a well-founded fear of persecution because of his/her race, religion, nationality, membership in a particular social group or political opinion; and is unable or unwilling to avail himself/herself of the protection of that country, or to return there, for fear of persecution.' The 1967 Protocol was adopted to remove geographical and time limitations contained in the original convention, which had been aimed at Europeans involved in events that happened prior to 1951.

What is an asylum seeker?

In the 1980s the term asylum seeker was coined to describe people who wished to settle in the UK, but who arrived without appropriate permission. They may be refugees, as defined in the Convention relating to the Status of Refugees, or they may be migrants trying to get into the UK for other reasons. These include those trying to escape justice in their own lands (for example, war criminals), and economic migrants (those trying to get a better standard of living than they can get in their own country). The UK, in common with the other 143 countries who have signed the 1951 Convention and/or the 1967 Protocol, will only give refugee status to those in genuine fear of persecution, and other asylum seekers are returned, although exceptional leave to remain may be granted for various reasons, usually on compassionate or humanitarian grounds.

Asylum seekers approach the entrance of the Channel Tunnel during the night

TIPS FOR FURTHER RESEARCH

Using the information in the web links, find more details on:
- The Immigration and Asylum Act 1999
- The 1951 UN Convention relating to the Status of Refugees

Research into the conditions that asylum seekers face; for example, how much does the government give asylum seekers per week to live on? In what form?

WEB LINKS

You will find the Immigration and Asylum Act 1999 at www.legislation.hmso.gov.uk/acts/acts1999.htm
And the 1951 UN Convention relating to the Status of Refugees at www.unhcr.ch. Try also the Home Office at www.homeoffice.gov.uk/rds/immigration1.htm

How many asylum seekers come to the UK

It is difficult to get a clear picture about the numbers of asylum seekers that come to this country. This is because the figures vary week on week, month on month, year on year, and also because some illegal migrants are not caught. Estimates as to how many clandestine entrants there are to the UK vary widely. Some figures that have been quoted are as follows:

- On a refugee per head of population basis, Britain is in the middle of the European league.

- The vast majority of refugees are in the poorer countries of the southern hemisphere.

- The UK takes about 1% of the world's refugees.

- The proportion of asylum seekers given refugee status in the UK was about 24% in 1999 and about 11% in 2000. On top of those, in each year about 13% were given exceptional leave to remain.

- In 2002 it is estimated that asylum seekers are arriving at a rate of approximately 80,000 per year, 70% have no valid claim, but only about 8000 per year are deported – the rest languish in the system or disappear.

- Estimates as to how many illegal immigrants there are in the UK vary widely, from a hundred thousand to a million. Many are thought to be working illegally for 'cash in hand' (since they have no National Insurance or other form of identification) as building workers, minicab drivers, waiters, cleaners, decorators, cooks and so on, often paid below the minimum wage

What is the government doing?

In 1998 the government introduced a White Paper which resulted in the Immigration and Asylum Act 1999. The main provisions of the act included the intention to deliver a faster, fairer and firmer immigration and asylum system, and to modernize asylum procedures. The government aimed to deliver most initial asylum decisions within two months and most appeals within a further four months, from April 2001. Security at the entrance to the Eurotunnel and at Calais port has been increased, and from February 2002 British immigration officers travel on the Eurostar train from Paris, checking tickets of passengers, including those with domestic-only tickets to Calais. By August 2002, all asylum seekers will be issued with a smart card called an ARC (Application Registration Card) which will contain the holder's fingerprint information, their name, photograph, date of birth and nationality.

The government has also put in place detention centres for asylum seekers waiting for a decision regarding refugee status, and for those who have been refused refugee status and are waiting to be repatriated. These centres have had difficulties however – in September 2001 Mr Justice Collins ruled in the High Court that holding asylum seekers in Oakington reception centre in Cambridgeshire was illegal, and in breach of the Human Rights Act. This was overturned later when the Home Secretary David Blunkett appealed. In February 2002 the Yarl's Wood Centre in Bedfordshire, opened 13 weeks before, was set on fire during rioting by asylum seekers who had been refused refugee status, and several escaped.

What measures is the government taking to sort out the asylum system?

The government is currently implementing comprehensive legislation to make the asylum system fairer, faster and firmer. The Immigration and Asylum Act 1999 modernizes and speeds up the mechanisms for dealing with asylum applications, overhauls the support arrangements for asylum seekers while their claims are being considered and deters unfounded claims. Details of this are contained in the box below.

Government plans to speed up asylum decision making by:
- employing more caseworkers
- overhauling the decision making system
- introducing a one-stop appeals process to further cut delays.

Deterring abuse through:
- a civil penalty levied on road vehicle operators who bring clandestine entrants into the UK
- increasing the number of Immigration Service officers and widening the powers available to them
- quadrupling the number of airline liaison officers to help stop those who seek to come to the UK illegally
- introducing a 10-year prison sentence for those facilitating illegal entry
- making a claim for asylum involving deception a criminal offence
- regulating immigration advisers, with criminal penalties of up to two years in prison for those who flout the law.

Rationalizing the support for asylum seekers through:
- the new National Asylum Support Service (NASS) offering accommodation on a 'no-choice' basis in cluster areas across the UK
- introducing a single system of mainly in-kind support, including vouchers, while asylum claims are processed.

Making the appeal system more effective through:
- appointing over 100 new part-time adjudicators to the Immigration Appellate Authorities (IAA)
- increasing the number of court rooms for adjudicator hearings from 56 to 103
- fast-tracking a significant proportion of cases for hearing within four weeks
- speeding up the recording of appeal determinations by introducing voice recognition technology
- recruiting 320 new staff for the IAA
- improving efficiency by centralizing administrative functions at a new base in Loughborough
- allocating an extra £23 million to legal aid for immigration and asylum cases, and recruiting 1000 more interpreters for the court service.

Increasing the effectiveness of controls through:
- expanding detention capability
- using the new reception centre at Oakington to deal with straightforward asylum claims quickly
- aiming to hear appeals in Oakington certified cases in three weeks.

Questions for discussion

1. Genuine refugees should never be turned back. Do you agree?

2. Discuss the statement that as a multicultural society we should be glad of the different cultures and experiences that new peoples bring.

3. What is the difference between a refugee, an asylum seeker and an economic migrant? Which should be allowed in?

4. The Red Cross centre at Sangatte is situated so that the French can export the problem. Should this be allowed?

5. How do arranged marriages link with the problem of asylum seekers?

Questions for written answer

1. 'Britain needs more people to immigrate to create enough wealth to sustain our standard of living'. Consider this statement carefully, outline reasons for agreeing with it, and for disagreeing with it. Construct a written argument for one side or the other.

2. Should the French authorities be doing more to prevent asylum seekers coming into the UK? If so, what could they do, and how should they do it?

3. As we are part of the European Union, should all asylum seekers be assessed for refugee status centrally? If they are granted that status, should they have the rights to travel, live and work anywhere within the EU, as any other citizen can?

4. 'If the UK denies basic human rights, then it becomes a human rights abuser'. Discuss this statement with regard to asylum seekers using recent examples.

5. 'For a civilized Western country like the UK to be only taking 1% of the world's refugees is a disgrace'. Do you agree? Give reasons for your answer.

❓ Quiz

1. What is an asylum seeker?

2. What is a refugee?

3. What or where is Utopia?

4. What is the minimum wage in the UK?

5. When was the date of the Protocol that removed geographic and time limits in the UN Convention?

6. What does UNHCR stand for?

7. How many countries have signed the Convention and/or the Protocol?

8. What was the name of the act introduced in 1999 to deliver a faster, fairer and firmer immigration and asylum system?

9. What does ARC stand for?

10. What is the name of the detention centre set on fire in February 2002?

Examiners will look for the following in your written answer:

- Evidence that you have understood the source material and can make appropriate use of it.
- You need to be able to make value judgements based on it and support these with evidence or interpretation.
- You need to have something of your own to say and to be able to state it clearly.
- You need to show you can relate this work to other relevant areas of study.

ACTIVITY

Think the unthinkable. The United Kingdom has been taken over by a dictator as a result of an armed *coup d'etat*, and, because of your religion and cultural background, you now form part of a minority group which is being persecuted. You have to wear a special symbol at all times to identify you, and many of your friends and neighbours have been taken away to who-knows-where. You suspect that some or all of them have been imprisoned without enough food or water, and you fear that some of them may have been exterminated.

- Form a small group to plan where when and how you will escape.

- Assuming your plan to escape works, plan what story you are going to tell to the immigration officials in your new country to get refugee status.

- Each group in your class should now explain their plans and their refugee claim to the whole class.

- The rest of the class should judge the validity of each claim in turn and decide what to do with the claimant.

The impossible dream

Preview

Governments set themselves series of economic targets, which they hope to achieve by manipulating the economy through various tools and measures. But are these government targets ever reachable? Is a managed economy ever possible? Should tinkering at the edges with taxation, government investment, interest rates, the money supply and all the rest be abandoned in favour of the mighty market? Surely, if the price system was allowed to take over completely, there would be no need for chancellors. New technology advances should make the market work much more smoothly, so that some commentators have seen the internet, for example, as ushering in a whole new age of open trade and low prices.

Government targets

Traditionally, governments have sought to achieve four major targets. These are full employment, price stability, a favourable balance of payments and economic growth. For each, there is always debate over whether or not it is being achieved. This is because there are different definitions for each target. Success can sometimes be achieved – by cynical governments – by merely redefining the targets.

Full employment

Technically, full employment is when everyone in the country who wants to work is able to find work. This is never, however, at 100% employment, as the labour market would not be able to work if there was not a reasonably flexible supply of labour that could move from one job to another. This 'transitional' unemployment is therefore necessary. If it did not exist, everyone would be in work and businesses would be unable to hire workers without 'poaching' them from other businesses – thus inevitably pushing wages upwards. (See 'inflation', below.) Full employment is therefore defined as a certain measure of unemployment. (You can immediately see that one way in which government can solve an unemployment problem is to redefine what is meant by full employment!)

Stable prices

Inflation means that an increase in price levels is taking place. This may be slow, gradual increases (which cause little in the way of problems) or very fast, hyper-inflationary, increases. In the UK inflation is measured by looking at the relative prices of a 'basket' of goods containing over 650 separate goods and services for which price movements are regularly measured in about 20,000 outlets in 147 areas throughout the country. Some 130,000 separate price quotations are used each month in compiling this retail price index (RPI). Prices

WEB LINKS

A table of RPI figures can be found at http://www.crowsnest.co.uk/north/rpi.htm and updates at www.statistics.gov.uk

include taxes such as council tax, VAT, duties, vehicle excise duty, insurance tax and airport tax. Each price also has a 'weight' according to its importance in the family budget. The contents of the basket and the relative weightings are changed each year to reflect new products, services and trends. Some expenditures, however, are so significant that they can have an adverse effect on the RPI. The most important of these is the cost of housing in the form of mortgage interest repayments. The RPIX is the RPI with these prices excluded. This is usually referred to as the underlying rate of inflation. Zero inflation, i.e. no price rises, is not usually the aim – because it would be impossible (like 'full' employment) to achieve. Governments therefore aim to keep prices growing at a very low and controlled rate. Alternative measures of inflation include the rate of growth of wages (which will inevitably feed into higher prices) and the rate of growth of specific prices – such as wholesale prices of manufactured goods.

A favourable balance of payments

The balance of payments looks at the value of goods and services exported as against the value of those imported. The current account looks at the flows of goods and services while the capital and financial accounts looks at flows of money, usually meaning saving and investment, but which also includes speculation. Countries have to earn foreign currency through exporting in order to be able to afford to import. If a country is earning more from importing than from exports, it is said to have a deficit; if it exports more than it imports, it is said to have a surplus. Countries may aim to have one or the other (or a 'balance'), depending on what is currently favourable to them.

Economic growth

Commentators are not always clear on what exactly they mean by 'economic growth'. It is defined as an increase in national income, and this is usually measured in terms of gross domestic product (GDP). This is the measure of output (what is produced), income (what is earned) and expenditure (what is spent) in an economy. Each of these should be the same. Put simply: whatever is made (output) means an amount is earned (income) that is used to buy it (expenditure). Growth depends on the effective use of the resources that a country has. These include natural resources, land, labour (a better educated or trained workforce can lead to growth), technology and investment in capital equipment. There is also a school of thought that believes growth – particularly in developed economies – should be prevented. Increased growth can lead to increased costs – for example pollution and waste – which actually lower the quality of life.

Who do you think provides street lighting and how is it paid for? Would a private, market-driven company ever be able to provide such a service and make a profit?

Measurements

The situation is further confused by the various different ways in which each target is measured. Employment has been traditionally measured through looking at the number of people who are out of work, able to work, seeking work and claiming benefit. This is known as the claimant count. Unemployment is higher if these parameters are widened to include those unable to claim (16 and 17 year olds and some married women, for example) and those unable to work through illness or injury. This is called the International Labour Organization (ILO) count. The ILO rate is the internationally agreed definition of unemployment; the ILO is an agency of the United Nations. Under ILO guidelines, all people aged 16 and over can be classified into one of three states:

- in employment
- ILO unemployed (people who want to work, can start within two weeks and have sought work within the last four weeks or who are waiting to start a job within the next two weeks)
- economically inactive (not seeking work).

Another measure is provided by the Labour Force Survey (LFS) which gives the numbers of people actually employed (approximately 75% of the population at end of 2001).

Retail prices index

The percentage annual rate of inflation for the year to any month can be found by dividing that month's index by the one for a year earlier, taking away the 1 and multiplying by 100. So for January 2002 the index is 173.3, for January 2001 it was 171.1: 173.3 / 171.1 = 1.0128. Take away the 1 gives 0.0128. Multiply by 100 gives an annual increase in prices of 1.3% (rounded). With up-to-date figures and the RPI it is therefore easy to work out inflation between any two points since 1915. You can also track changes in the purchasing power of the pound. The value of £1 at any date can be found by using RPI. The index was started in 1915 and is fairly regularly re-based (a new base year designated) to make it easier to make comparisons. The current base year is 1987. This means that the index for 1987 is 100: 173.3(2002)/100(1987) = 1.71, meaning that you would need £1.71 in 2002 to buy the same as £1 in 1987. (The index for January 1915 was 4.1. 173.3/4.1 = 42.27, meaning that an item that cost £10 in 1915 would be priced at £422.70 at today's rates!)

Balance of payments

The main difficulty in measuring the balance of payments is that it is a measurement of flows of money, goods and services. As such, at whatever point it is measured, there are products and payments in transit. It is also skewed by flows of money (in particular in such areas as currency or financial futures speculation) for which there are no associated goods or services.

WEB LINKS

www.crowsnest.co.uk/north/rpi.htm gives a historical picture of the RPI. www.statistics.gov.uk is the website of the Office of National Statistics where all up-to-date figures are posted – such as the current level of RPI.

Try seeing what an item in the past would have cost in today's prices. Find the price of, say, a car in 1929, or find what your parents or grandparents paid for their house when they bought it. Now see what inflation has made it worth in today's money.

Growth

Growth figures are given for each quarter; this is important for economists to decide whether or not an economy has stopped growing. Newspapers and television programmes often talk about 'recessions'. A recession is officially when the economy has ceased to grow. Negative or zero growth for one quarter is not counted as a recession (it may be an aberration) but if it continues into a second quarter, an economy is officially in recession. Also, parts of an economy may be in recession, while parts are still growing. For example, in the UK, manufacturing industry has had negative growth rates while the service sector has had high positive growth rates.

Instruments

Governments use various measures and policies to try to achieve these goals. The main instruments are:

- fiscal policy – changes to general levels of taxation and government spending

- monetary policy – changes to the money supply and to interest rates

- incomes policy – in order to control the growth of wages

- legislative changes – new laws or regulations (such as public/private partnerships (PPPs), the private finance initiative (PFI) and privatization).

Conflicts

There are numerous conflicts between policy. For example, low unemployment tends to push up wage rates leading to inflation. High inflation will, in itself, cause unemployment. Growth may also cause inflation if the growth takes place too quickly. Rapid growth leads to demand being greater than supply and prices rising as a result. In the UK this is thought to be a growth rate of around 2.5% to 3%. Not enough growth means supply is greater than demand and leads to unemployment. This band of growth is therefore a very narrow tightrope for Chancellors to walk. Growth will also affect the balance of payments. If people are relatively better off, then they are likely to spend more money. This means that two things happen. First, they are likely to save less and lower saving is one of the things which chokes off growth. Secondly, they are likely to spend the extra (marginal) income on imported goods. This is because the UK relies on importers for many areas of goods that would attract this sort of spending. Examples would include cars, electrical goods and holidays.

It shouldn't happen – a brief history

Economists only became concerned with the 'macro' picture (how the whole economy was performing) when industrialization started to really become important. Up to then the UK had an agricultural based, virtually subsistence economy. In such an economy there is little or no unemployment (while the sick and lame may have been looked after, an able-bodied person would be expected to work or starve), little growth, little reason for inflation and a level of international trade that, while it is important to the traders (the wool trade to Flanders, for example, was vital) hardly touched the general population.

Broadly from the 1880s to 1930s came the move from agricultural to industrial base. Market forces were allowed to determine prices and wages. Economics was largely based on the ideas of Adam Smith (1723–1790), whose book *Wealth of Nations*, postulated that economies would only be efficient if guided by the 'invisible hand' of market forces – with no government interference. Unemployment in such a market system is, theoretically, caused by high wages – the solution is therefore to lower wages.

The miners' strike of the 1980s – a bitter and often violent dispute

Keynes

The market system, however, appeared to break down in the 1930s when Britain entered a sustained period of recession. High levels of unemployment continued to increase while wages continued to fall. Another economist – John Maynard Keynes – suggested in his book *General Theory of Employment, Interest and Money* that cutting wages actually increased unemployment. He advocated that policy should concentrate on reducing unemployment by increasing spending – in other words, if the private sector was not spending enough to maintain full employment, then government should step in and spend.

Incomes policies

This policy appeared to work up to the Second World War and into buoyant post-war economies which led to the rapidly expanding economy labelled by one politician as the 'white heat of technological revolution' in the 1960s. By the 1970s, however, high levels of unemployment again became the norm, this time coupled with high inflation. This shouldn't, according to the theory, happen and was christened 'stagflation'.

Incomes policies were used to control wage rises (governments put a ceiling on the wage rises which workers were allowed) which, again, appeared to work for a short time – until the final death of incomes policies in the 1978–1979 'Winter of Discontent'.

Monetarism

Incoming prime minister Margaret Thatcher brought with her a new, American philosophy, called monetarism. This said that governments can control the economy through having control of the money supply (through various instruments). With this they could control spending and therefore unemployment. She also believed (as did Adam Smith) in the operation of the free market, in particular for labour. Ideas and institutions (such as trades unions and strike action) which prevented the labour market from free movement were all curtailed. At the same time, policies to make labour better educated and more flexible (such as the Youth Training Scheme and Vocational Qualifications) were introduced. Privatization was also seen as a way of bringing the 'efficiency' of the market system to bear on the economy.

New millennium

Unemployment and inflation are presently (apparently) under control at least partly because the labour force is better educated and more flexible. One of the first actions of the new Labour government was to give control of interest rates to the Bank of England so that important changes could only be made for economic, not political reasons. The government's stated careful tax and spend policy has set targets for growth, inflation and unemployment. Whatever its philosophical colour, however, it is still also following policies of privatization, of more flexibility in the labour market (new vocational qualifications and work based training) and of minimum interference in the market mechanism.

TIPS FOR FURTHER RESEARCH

Look into how the knowledge economy is expanding and might expand in the future. A good source is *Teach Yourself E-Commerce*, by Neil Denby, published by Hodder & Stoughton. Research the political and economic events of 1978–1979 – why were they so significant? Look up terms like 'public goods' and 'merit goods'.

Market systems

The market mechanism is the interaction of supply and demand. At its most efficient (perfect competition), consumers get exactly what they want at the lowest possible prices. Is this the shape of an internet-based economy? Consumers have perfect information on prices and availability, all businesses face the same costs and any business can trade in anything over the web therefore there are no restrictions to entering any market. E-commerce is the embodiment of the perfect market.

In March 2000 Tony Blair stated: 'The e-generation is with us'. He made a conference speech in which he outlined his hopes for what he called the new 'knowledge economy'. In it he stated that 'e-commerce and the internet are already changing business fast. Transaction costs are tumbling. One US bank estimates that the effect of e-commerce is to reduce its cost per transaction from 1 dollar to 1 cent'. He added: 'The internet is dissolving physical barriers, and levelling the business playing field. It doesn't matter how small a company you are, you have the choice now of defining your business as global. Standard business thinking used to see big as inevitably beating small. Now fast beats slow. The opportunity is there for business to take'.

Questions for discussion

1. What effect do you think the euro would have on all these figures should Britain join?

2. Some services will never be provided by the market – true or false?

3. Discuss the view that unemployment is a human problem, inflation an economic one.

4. How much of your income do you/your family spend on imports? Why?

5. Western countries should be aiming for zero growth because of its high negative externalities. What do you think?

Questions for written answer

1. Norman Lamont, a past Conservative chancellor, once said that 'unemployment is the inevitable price to be paid for controlling inflation'. What do you think he means? Do you agree or disagree with this statement? Give reasons for your answer.

2. 'Economic equilibrium is unattainable'. Discuss this statement with reference to recent economic events.

3. The 'Winter of Discontent' is a phrase borrowed from Shakespeare ('Now is the winter of our discontent', from *Richard III*). Comment on the effectiveness of its use in this context and discuss why commentators feel that quotes from literary giants or the classics are appropriate to describe modern events.

Examiners will look for the following in your written answer:

- Evidence that you have understood the source material and can make appropriate use of it.
- You need to be able to make value judgements based on it and support these with evidence or interpretation.
- You need to have something of your own to say and to be able to state it clearly.
- You need to show you can relate this work to other relevant areas of study.

4. Adam Smith believed that 'the market is king'. In your opinion, is there ever good reason for governments to interfere in market mechanisms? Give reasons for your answer.

5. 'There is nothing wrong with economists and economic policies – it is just circumstances that change, meaning that new policies are necessary'. Explain how far you agree with this statement and why.

? Quiz

1. Why do indices start at 100 and not zero?

2. Which married women can't claim unemployment benefit?

3. What is 'monetarism'?

4. What is 'Keynesianism'?

5. What is inflation?

6. Define unemployment.

7. What growth rate should lead to neither inflation nor unemployment.

8. What is a 'weight'? Why is it used?

9. Who was Adam Smith?

10. When (and what) was the 'Winter of Discontent'?

ACTIVITY

Putting together an RPI. Decide what would make an appropriate basket of goods for your class. First, see what the top ten most popular items are – you will also have to include essentials such as food, even if you don't pay for your own! Then decide on the average price for each. You should also decide on a 'weight' for each one. If food is twice as important as petrol, then petrol could be 'x1' and food could be 'x2', for example. Add up the weighted prices to get a total. This is your index and should be given an index number of 100. Prices can then be checked and recalculated at regular intervals to see what your groups' RPI is. Compare this with the national figures. Why do you think yours is the same, or different?

Who's free trade for anyway?

Preview

In November 1999, a mass protest was organized by opponents of the World Trade Organization (WTO). The WTO found itself unable to come to an agreement on a new round of trade talks in Seattle among a welter of protest from an international coalition of protesters. The protesters represented many diverse bodies from charities and environmental pressure groups to union members and human rights organizations. They had been co-ordinated by mobile phone and text message, by e-mail and website, in what was billed as the first truly international protest made possible by the new technology. But what was the protest about? Did the diverse groups all want the same thing – and for the same reason? Was it just an opportunistic one-off protest or part of a longer-term movement for change?

The WTO is dedicated to freeing up international trade to the benefit of us all so why should protesters not want the benefits that free trade brings? The abandonment of the meeting put back the latest agreements and sent the WTO looking for less convenient locations than North America (the next meeting was in Doha, Qatar, in the United Arab Emirates).

The issues of globalization and free trade are ones that evoke very different responses from people. Examples of possible 'for' and 'against' stances are explored later in this unit.

Seattle police use gas to push back World Trade Organization protestors in downtown Seattle on Tuesday 30 November 1999. The protests delayed the opening of the WTO third ministerial conference

The WTO: where did it come from?

The WTO was formed, as the successor to the General Agreement on Tariffs and Trade (GATT), on 1 January 1995. It has 142 member states and is based in Geneva. GATT itself was formed in 1947 – a post-war attempt to save the world from itself by encouraging free trade between nations. If nations trade with each other, then they will no longer war with each other – or at least that was the philosophy. GATT held eight lengthy rounds of trade talks, the last being the Uruguay Round of 1986–1993; all were designed to increase trade. They succeeded to the extent that tariffs on manufactured goods were cut by 90%, falling from an average 40% tariff to an average 4%. (Tariffs on agricultural products have been less successful, remaining at around 40%.)

What does it do?

The WTO regulates trade in goods and services – opening up service industries such as telecommunications, banking and insurance to competition. The principles of the WTO insist that members should treat all trading partners equally. They should look at the 'most favoured nation' for trading in a particular commodity and ensure that all nations are treated as well as this nation. It also regulates trade in foodstuffs and, through the Sanitary and Phytosanitary Standards (SPS) Agreement, regulates food safety. The WTO also regulates intellectual property rights through the 'Trips' agreement – something which has had particular significance in the field of drugs, where expensive, branded products are favoured over cheaper generic alternatives (AIDS treatments are a particular example) and in the development of the human genome and gene therapy, where the African nations (and many others) have protested about whether anyone has the right to patent human life. So who is right?

Two views on globalization

Globalization is bad

Globalization is a force which is doing great harm to many parts of the world. It is nothing more than the exploitation of workers by global capitalism. Industries, and giant trans-national corporations, locate where labour is cheapest with the least union protection and where there are few, if any, restrictive conditions in the labour market. It also means that they can locate where environmental controls and anti-pollution measures (which increase costs) are minimized. There is widespread corruption to ensure that corporations get what they want and even their profits are free from interference – they declare them in countries where they get the lowest taxation and the best tax breaks.

Globalization is good

Globalization is nothing new, it is no more than a continuance of the age-old tendency to more and more global trading links. It is a process that has been taking place since trade began and has only now come to prominence because, with the aid of new technology, it is now happening so much more rapidly and so much more publicly. Globalization can be said to have started with the trading of the ancient world, or with the great European trading nations which became economic powers – the Spanish, then the Dutch, finally the British. No one thought that global trade was bad when 'the sun never set' on the British Empire. The American continent itself was only discovered through the desire to find a quick route to the trading nations of the Indies. Modern globalization means the availability of international products and services and a raising of standards of living everywhere. Think of the Earth as 'the global village' and you will immediately be more aware of the benefits. Better technology, medicine and systems of law can be developed and shared. Human rights and international aid are all shared. And, of course, the public voice that made itself so apparent at Seattle could never have been heard without the benefit of global advances in technology and that epitome of globalization – the free, open and unregulated internet. Information is now disseminated so rapidly and easily that people are better informed than ever and better able to communicate and organize.

Businesses actually locate where the infrastructure is good, where there are skilled workers and where they are close to either raw materials or customers. These considerations override any notion of going to where labour is cheapest. Cheap, unskilled (and untrained) labour is not worth the risk to efficiency, product quality and reputation. It is a lack of training, education and infrastructure that keeps businesses away from countries, not sweatshop labour that encourages them.

Two views on free trade

Free trade is trade without restrictions. Restrictions include tariffs – where an extra amount of money (a kind of tax) is levied on imported goods to make them more expensive – and quotas, where a country will only import a certain amount of a commodity.

The arguments for free trade

International trade is considered good for everyone due to the economic principle of comparative advantage. If one country is comparatively more efficient at producing a good or service than another, then it makes sense for that country to specialize in that product and trade its excess with other countries which have a comparative advantage in other goods or services. Comparative advantage may be brought about by natural factors such as raw material availability or weather patterns or by developed aspects such as the efficient use of factors of production. This doesn't just mean new or better technology – labour is a factor of production and a better educated labour force is a more adaptable and efficient one. Good education is therefore promoted by free trade. Free trade also means that the living standards in all trading countries are increased as their surplus is exchanged for a greater variety of other products and resources.

Big business is actually held in check by competition. It is the operation of the competitive market that leads to lower prices and advances in technology. Without competition there would be no mobile phones, no DVDs, no race for fuel-efficient vehicles. Businesses that might have a monopoly at home are exposed to competition from foreign businesses that may be more efficient, or better run. This will result in lower prices, less power for the monopoly and a greater choice for consumers.

The arguments against free trade

Free trade rules prevent developing countries from protecting their infant industries in the same way that the more developed competitors did. These competitors were able to keep industries away from international challenges until they were strong enough to compete. This means that industries in developing countries will never be able to compete on an equal footing as they will never be able to earn sufficient to allow them to become as technologically advanced as the rest of the world.

Local businesses may also want to support the local labour market and governments can encourage this by subsidizing businesses to do so. However, this is against the rules of free trade and therefore not allowed under WTO rules.

Inequality is increased

The actions of the WTO increase inequality. Developed nations have more organized and better funded industries (and trade negotiators). Inevitably, the lifting of restrictions means that the rich (as ever) get richer, and the poor get poorer. Developing nations often have to rely on institutions such as the World Bank and the International Monetary Fund for loans in order to make any advance. In many cases, this means that they are made poorer by having to service the debts lent by rich nations who collect the interest. In addition, such institutions will have different ideas which they can impose on developing nations. For example, in many countries debt agencies have insisted that traditional agriculture is abandoned in favour of monoculture (producing just one crop) – usually a 'cash-crop' that can be sold abroad to earn currency to pay debt.

Inequality is decreased

The world (and trade) moves on. New skills are needed for new products and technologies. As long as education systems provide a workforce with these skills, then new industry will be attracted. International trade actually makes everyone richer. How would a protectionist policy that prevented an industry from competing make it more efficient? Exposure to trade is what leads to the development of industry and to better wages. Buying a ballpoint pen from

TIPS FOR FURTHER RESEARCH

Find out about the World Bank and the IMF. What is their role? Who criticizes them and why?

Businesses that develop 'new' technologies can patent them to protect them from competition – protecting their intellectual property (IP) rights. This means that businesses can develop, for example, gene technology and then protect it through patents. Developing nations don't have the technology for the research and therefore fail to benefit from IP rights.

Bangalore does a number of things – it puts money in the worker's pocket, it encourages further investment by the company and it encourages other pen producers to be more competitive. Not buying the ballpoint merely ensures that the pen worker in Bangalore stays poor – and is probably soon to be out of work. Lower wages do not necessarily mean exploitation. Call centres are now often situated in countries such as India. The wages may be low by UK standards, but are high by Indian standards and afford a good standard of living. Mike Moore, head of the WTO in 2002, is a New Zealander. Wages in New Zealand are around two-thirds of UK levels, however we don't hear them being accused of exploitation. The WTO acts on behalf of nations, making no distinction between big and small, rich and poor and is therefore actually promoting equality.

The WTO undermines national governments

Being a supranational legal body it undermines the powers of national governments. It has the power to rule against national interests and then to impose its rulings through trade sanctions. Hearings are held in secret and cases decided by a tribunal of lawyers whose names are not revealed. Often rulings go against a country's national interests and take no account of local conditions. Transnational corporations and governments (via such corporations) are the only voices that are heard. The WTO is an unelected body, manned by trade bureaucrats, and unaccountable to any elected government. Just three trading blocs dominate the WTO – North America (US and Canada), Japan and the EU.

National governments can look after themselves

Governments are by no means powerless. They pass national laws (and trading bloc laws such as those passed by the EU) that are nothing to do with trade and yet affect it greatly. A government which increases petrol prices is increasing costs for all producers – this may have the effect of making imports more attractive as they become relatively cheaper. Interest rate and currency policy can also be effective tools in promoting or discouraging trade. The WTO has no control over these. The argument about democracy holds true for any body that is neither directly elected nor accountable. Institutions within the EU are equally undemocratic (such as the European Court). The solution is not to throw up our hands in horror and abandon such institutions, but to work to reform them and make them more accountable. WTO agreements are made on the basis of one country, one vote and have to be ratified by national parliaments. No one can claim that the WTO is not held to account by the public and the media after the demonstrations that brought the Seattle conference in 2000 to a standstill and early close.

WTO undermines human rights and encourages the destruction of the environment

WTO undermines human rights and national employment protection polices. For example, governments may not refuse to trade in a commodity, even if they disapprove of how that commodity is produced – through sweat-shop labour, for example. WTO rules say that no account may be taken of processes, methods of production, human rights or sustainable development when deciding on who to accept goods from. These all have nothing to do with free trade. Even CITES, the agreement to ban the import of rare or endangered species or products such as ivory and alligator-skin shoes – is under threat. If a government wanted to export such products, a refusal to import could be classed as a barrier to trade. Because industries cannot be protected, competition is through the lowest possible cost of production. This encourages producers to ban unions and reduce health and safety levels. Those who complain have to be silenced.

Does the WTO destroy the environment by eroding national environmental protections? Such protections are labelled 'barriers to free trade' and declared illegal. It is supposed to harmonize standards within and between nations but, in practice, this could mean adopting the rules which offer the least protection. Any nation which decides to put a greater emphasis on safety, or caution, will find it is accused of protectionism.

These are not the concerns of the WTO

Increased trade, without protection, will lead to increased wealth for all workers. This is the best way to ensure that the long-term human rights of workers are maintained and improved. It is not the job of an organization such as the WTO to tell trading nations about how they may or may not treat their workers. Other international institutions carry out this role much more effectively. Similarly, it is up to national governments and international agencies other than the WTO, to make sure that the environment is protected. Many nations use environmental protection measures as a way of keeping foreign (and fair) competition out. For example, British trawlermen would like to protect the fish stocks in their fishing grounds from foreign competition. Is this because they are concerned for the environmental impact of over-fishing or because they are afraid that their livelihoods may suffer from more efficient competition?

There is no alternative

If the WTO did not exist there would be a free-for-all in international trade in which the smaller countries would be quickly overwhelmed by the power of the larger and richer countries to protect both industries and markets. Inequality would spiral, prices would rise and living standards around the world would fall. If the WTO did not exist, we would need to invent it.

WEB LINKS

www.globalexchange.org/ contains fact sheets on the major institutions engaged in international trade. www.un.org for information on the United Nations and its bodies. Information on the Human Rights Act can be found at www.lcd.gov.uk/hract/ Try also www.nikebiz.com; www.nikewages.org; www.oneworld.org.

Developing countries can be heavily reliant on particular crops, for example bananas in the Caribbean

There is an alternative

UNCTAD is the United Nations Conference on Trade and Development. First, it is seen as being truly international rather than dominated by trading blocs. Secondly, it has a much more sympathetic view towards the problems of smaller nations. The head of UNCTAD, Rubens Ricupero has commented on the 'unequal distribution of benefits' from world trade and on the 'abuse of market power' by the larger players. One UNCTAD estimate is that poorer nations trading in low-tech products lose over 13 times what they gain in aid by being forced to open up their markets to competition. Finally, UNCTAD believes that smaller, poorer nations should be given some protection because they are not trading on the same basis as their richer rivals but at a disadvantage because of local conditions. UNCTAD believes in allowing for some protection so that local economies can develop.

Questions for discussion

1. The WTO only supports huge agribusinesses and ignores the plight of poor farmers. True or false?

2. Discuss the view that Americans run the WTO and Americans benefit from it.

3. Global trade has always been expanding and always will. What do you think?

4. The internet will solve the problem for all time as people (and businesses) will be able to source products from wherever they like. Is this likely to happen?

5. Does the WTO increase or decrease inequality?

Examiners will look for the following in your written answer:

- Evidence that you have understood the source material and can make appropriate use of it.
- You need to be able to make value judgements based on it and support these with evidence or interpretation.
- You need to have something of your own to say and to be able to state it clearly.
- You need to show you can relate this work to other relevant areas of study.

Questions for written answer

1. 'Free and unfettered trade means that everyone in the world is better off'. Analyse and comment on this statement.

2. WTO rulings include:
   - The European Union has, since 1991, refused to import beef treated with growth hormones (mostly produced in America). The WTO ruled that this was illegal.
   - America's insistence that cars should run on cleaner fuel was ruled against in 1993 as a barrier to free trade.
   - Genetically modified items (such as GM food) may be traded freely despite misgivings in some nations.

   In each case, discuss whether the WTO is acting in the best interests of business or consumer and give reasons why you hold this opinion.

3. The WTO has insisted that the EU imports bananas from major South American producers, adversely affecting the economies of smaller, Caribbean producers. Can such actions ever be justified? Give reasons for your opinion.

4. Discuss the view that the 'infant industry' argument was never more than an excuse for inefficient industry, protected from more efficient competition.

5. There have been various protests against the WTO. Do you agree that (peaceful) protest is often the only way for small groups with little power to be heard? Explain your views.

? Quiz

1. Where did the WTO meet to avoid protestors?

2. Which body did the WTO succeed?

3. What is a tariff?

4. What is a quota?

5. What is a trading bloc? Name one.

6. By how far have tariffs on manufactured goods fallen since 1995?

7. What are intellectual property rights?

8. Which agreement regulates intellectual property rights?

9. What is a 'transnational corporation'?

10. What is comparative advantage?

 **A** CTIVITY **1**

Visit a local supermarket and log the source for various commodities. In particular look at where the supermarket obtains:

- bananas
- coffee
- cocoa
- apples
- cereal
- flour
- rice.

Share the information back in class and decide what this tells you about:

- international trade
- co-operative farming and trading
- agribusiness.

 **A** CTIVITY **2**

Via the United Nations web site www.un.org/ you can obtain a kit for holding your own United Nations debate.

Preview

The good, the bad and the indifferent. There are numerous different electoral systems in use, including several within the UK itself. Which of these appears to be the most fair and unbiased? Are there systems which give particular bias to a ruling party, or which give an excessive proportion of power to a smaller party? Which system best reflects the wishes of the voters?

Democracy

The Greek city states were never truly democratic, but have been given the reputation of being the 'cradle of democracy'. Look at what happened to the various Greek states. How did the Romans adapt and improve Greek systems?

The word derives from the Greek words *demos* and *krateein* – people and rule – the rule of the people. *Kratos* also means strength, so there is the idea that there is strength in this people's system. Other systems are possible and share the same root – theocracy, autocracy, bureaucracy, plutocracy – but democracy of some form or other is the preferred system of most of the 'civilized' world. (The other common root is *-archos*, also meaning 'rule' and from the Greek *archein* as in monarchy, oligarchy, and hierarchy.)

Rule by the people: the question is how to achieve it. Even the ancient Greeks, from where the idea is said to have originated, hardly managed it. Their democracy excluded slaves (of whom there were many) and, of course, women. But the Greek city states that practised the system at least did not have the problem of numbers that most democracies face in the modern world. Most were able to meet in the city's open space, the agora, and make their voice heard. The principles were freedom of speech and expression and equality for all citizens to make their voice heard. In practice, of course, such decision making – even with relatively small numbers was fraught with difficulty. Who should speak, for how long, on what subject? In times of national crisis the Greeks recognized the inefficiency of this form of government and elected a dictator.

TIPS FOR FURTHER RESEARCH

Look up Pericles. Who was he? What did he do? What happened to him when he was a success? What happened to him when he failed?
Where countries are listed at the back of an atlas or encyclopaedia, the system of government is often shown. How many different systems are there? How many absolute monarchies are left?

Dictators

In ancient Greece dictators were particularly popular in times of war. Someone had to direct affairs and make decisions quickly (it was also handy to have someone on which to pin the blame if anything went wrong). A successful dictator, on conclusion of a campaign, reverted to being an ordinary citizen again. The small numbers with which the Greek city states operated made their 'democratic' system workable (Athens had a population of only a few thousand at the height of its power and was never a geographically large area). Remove women and slaves from this and it is manageable.

WEB LINKS

Search under 'democracy', 'electoral systems' and 'systems of government'. You could also visit newspaper archive sites for reports on the 'US presidential election'.

Conditional democracy

If numbers looked like they were getting too large, conditions for citizenship could be created (such as a property qualification or, bizarrely, the ownership of slaves – they were, after all, property). In contrast, what is often billed as the 'world's biggest democracy' is India, with a population of 945 million. Hardly a convenient number to invite from 3.7 million square kilometres of country to meet and debate in the local market place.

As numbers of electors grow there are two possible courses of action to maintain the democracy. One is to introduce some sort of qualification for being a citizen: a land-owning, property or income qualification. This means that the idea of a democratic system is maintained (all citizens have equal rights to vote, speak, participate), but it is limited to a manageable number of people who are deemed to be 'important' or there is the need for some method of choosing representatives to speak for sections of the population – an electoral system.

Electoral systems

There are numerous election systems with the easiest to understand, and most widely used, being the 'first-past-the-post' system. This is the system that is used in general and local elections in Britain. It is also used (in part) in the USA and in the 'world's largest democracy', India. In the UK it works like this: at the general election, a number of candidates stand in a single-member constituency, only one of which can be elected. At local elections the same is

Voting in a UK election. The winner is the 'first past the post' – as in a horse race – however close the second-placed candidate happens to be

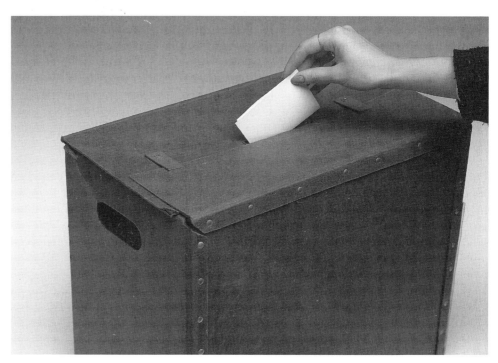

usually true of council wards, although in their case, there may be more than one council seat allocated to a ward and therefore the possibility of more than one candidate succeeding in being elected. At a general election, the candidate with the most votes wins (even though there may have been more votes cast 'against' them than for them). For example, Jones, Evans and Pritchard contest a seat with the result as follows:

Jones   20,000 (40%)
Evans   15,000 (30%)
Pritchard   15,000 (30%)

Jones, of course, is elected even though more people voted against him than for him. One of the major criticisms of the system is this tendency to disenfranchise those voters who cast their votes for the losers. In effect, their votes are wasted. It has other drawbacks. In most cases, a candidate represents a political party; the first-past-the-post system makes it extremely difficult for independent candidates to be elected (with the notable recent exception of television reporter turned anti-sleaze campaigner 'man in the white suit' Martin Bell) and also virtually guarantees 'one-party' government.

Strong government?

Some commentators will argue that this is a benefit of the system because it leads to strong government, others that this is an inherent weakness, because there is no adequate brake on the powers of government. The brake in the UK is provided by an adversarial system of Opposition. It is the job of the official Opposition to question the government on each and every policy and to make sure that all legislation is fully and properly discussed. Although political parties claim that they have received a mandate for their policies at general election time, no government since the war has actually won a majority of the vote. The amount of votes cast for a party often gives them a disproportionate share of House of Commons seats. At the 1997 general election, for example, the Labour party won 44% of the votes; yet they received almost two-thirds of the seats (419).

Accountability

The main advantage to the electorate is that the system is easy to understand and administer, the result is obvious and apparently fair – it is like a race, there can only be one winner. One other much vaunted advantage of the system is the direct link that is forged between the electorate and their MP. The MP is seen as being directly accountable to the people who elected him or her as the electors have a hand in electing their MP (or at least, the ones who voted the 'right' way do).

Other systems, some tried and tested, others new and untried, generally seek to iron out the perceived inequalities of the first-past-the-post system, while keeping its strong points. The features which any alternative system should retain include the direct link between electorate and elected, accountability and the speed and simplicity of the system. At the same time, any new system should try to make sure that the wishes of the electorate are better represented – usually this is taken to mean some form of proportional representation.

Single transferable vote system

The single transferable vote system (STV) is the one which most closely reflects the way that voters voted. Each constituency has a number of MPs, depending on its size. Electors put candidates in order of preference. Any candidate receiving a big enough proportion of the votes is elected, the final candidate in the poll is eliminated. 'Extra' votes which successful candidates don't need are redistributed to other candidates on the basis of second, third, etc. choices. For example, candidates Jones, Evans, Pritchard, Williams and Humphries stand for a three-member constituency and receive votes as follows:

Jones	15,000 (30%)
Evans	12,500 (25%)
Pritchard	10,000 (20%)
Williams	10,000 (20%)
Humphries	2,500 (5%)

The quota for election was set at 30% of the votes, so Jones is elected. Humphries is below the lower limit, so is eliminated. Second-choice votes are then counted resulting in the following:

Evans	15,500
Pritchard	15,000
Williams	10,500

Pritchard and Evans have now reached the quota and are therefore elected to the remaining two seats. Note that electors do not have to cast second- or third-choice votes and also that candidates' supporters may all support a particular second-choice candidate – Pritchard could have received the majority of Jones' second-choice votes for this reason. There is therefore a lot of room for tactical voting.

Weak government

Such a system is likely to create 'weak' government in that it is likely to consist of a coalition. Even at a local level, deals may have been struck in order to gain second- or even third-choice votes. On top of this, the direct link between voters and elected is eroded in multi-member constituencies and the system is complicated and time consuming to calculate. This system is used for elections to the European parliament.

Additional member system

Germany struggled for many years with coalition governments that were insufficiently forceful. They now use the additional member system or AMS. Voters in this system are asked to cast two separate votes. The first is for the MP who they want to represent their constituency, the second is for the party they want to win. This system maintains the direct link between the elector and the elected member but also more accurately reflects the fact that most people vote for a political party rather than for a particular individual. Parties have a 'list' of MPs who will be elected according to the proportion of votes cast for that party. In affect, this means that party leaders and others of high rank in the party are not accountable – the nearer the top of the list you are, the more likely you are to be 'elected'. However, the nearer the top of the list you are, the more likely you are to hold high office and therefore the more you should be accountable. This system – in common with other systems of proportional representation – tends to give massive power to smaller parties whose support is vital for government. For example in the case of:

Democratic Socialists	45%
Social Democrats	45%
Liberals	10%

The balance of power – and who is actually going to form the government – is held by the small central party who, in return for supporting one of the others, can demand ministerial posts and particular policy changes.

Money talks

In many systems, however, it is not the electorate, or small centrist parties, that necessarily make the decision – in many systems it is money that talks and, effectively, buys votes. This ranges from the innocent pastime of British governments of lowering taxes and increasing benefits in election years, or of cynically allocating funds, grants or industry to marginal constituencies, to the enormous expense that goes into the choosing of a US president. The system is, basically, first-past-the-post and, technically, anyone can stand, but the cost of mounting an election campaign is prohibitive. State delegates are elected to take the votes of their state to a 'convention' which chooses the presidential and vice-presidential candidate. Each delegate vote is therefore vital and to be courted. This means parties, conventions and conferences on a scale unimaginable in the UK. There is a popular national vote for the presidential candidates, but winning this is not enough to secure office. Candidates must also secure the votes of the delegates to the electoral college that officially chooses the president. The system is for states to appoint 'electors' who will cast the vote on their behalf. This system received much unwanted publicity when the Gore/Bush presidential result hung in the balance with the way that a handful of Floridians voted being the only difference between the two candidates. This really underlined the extreme 'unfairness' that the first-past-the-post system can generate.

All the expensive 'razzle-dazzle' of a major US
political party convention

All the expensive 'razzle-dazzle' of a major US political party convention

Devolution

Different electoral systems are just one way to solve the problem of large numbers of people needing to be heard. The alternative is to make the areas that are governed smaller. This is (at least partly) the thinking behind the devolved powers given to Scotland, Wales and Northern Ireland. Scotland now has its own parliament for the first time since 1707, Northern Ireland has been experimenting with Stormont and Wales has been granted a National Assembly.

The Scottish Parliament can legislate on matters affecting Scotland (and has already re-introduced the student grant and banned hunting with hounds in Scotland). It can change taxation in Scotland by up to 3p in the pound but cannot make any decisions that affect the UK as a whole. These are reserved to the Westminster Parliament. It has adopted AMS as its electoral system.

The Welsh assembly cannot, unlike the Scottish Parliament, make its own laws or raise taxes. Wales joined with England in 1536 and cannot claim to have ever really had its own parliament, being ruled by a succession of princes. The Assembly can implement laws and is allowed to 'do anything it considers appropriate', in the words of the Act, to support Welsh culture and heritage. Assembly Members (AMs) are elected by the first-past-the-post system.

Self-government for Northern Ireland is heavily bound up with the peace process and the suspension and reinstatement of the assembly has been used to try to keep the process on track.

Conclusion

There are other systems of government – apart from democratic ones – that also have long and successful histories. Monarchies and dictatorships have the advantage of decisions being made quickly and decisively and were the preferred rule in medieval society; rule by religious authorities has also had its successes. Absolute monarchs still exist in many Middle Eastern states – who is to say that such a system of government is not preferable to a democracy? Why should ordinary people know, be expected to know, or be expected to take part in, any sort of political or democratic process?

Questions for discussion

1. Dictatorships are far more efficient than a democracy can ever be. Do you agree?

2. Who won the American presidential election?

3. First-past-the-post means strong government, proportional representation a weak one.

4. Sixteen year olds should be allowed to vote, they are allowed to do everything else!

5. Monarchies last for thousands of years, proving that they work. We should strengthen ours, not try to get rid of it.

Questions for written answer

1. One commentator said that 'whatever the system, it is politicians that get elected'. What do you think he meant by that? Do you agree?

2. Comment on the view that any electoral system which involves electing representatives is flawed.

3. The solution to electoral problems is to do away with elections – to make units of government so small that everyone can have a say. What is your view on this statement?

4. Do you agree that coalition governments are necessarily more stable and more representative than one party ones? Explain your answer.

5. 'No British government since the war has been elected with a majority of the votes cast'. What does this say about the UK's electoral system? What alternatives would you propose?

Examiners will look for the following in your written answer:

- Evidence that you have understood the source material and can make appropriate use of it.
- You need to be able to make value judgements based on it and support these with evidence or interpretation.
- You need to have something of your own to say and to be able to state it clearly.
- You need to show you can relate this work to other relevant areas of study.

? Quiz

1. What is the difference between a representative and a delegate?

2. What is a hierarchy?

3. What is a plutocracy?

4. What is an oligarchy?

5. What is an autocracy?

6. What are the main two American political parties?

7. What is meant by 'devolution'?

8. What areas can the Scottish Parliament pass laws in?

9. What powers does the Welsh Assembly have?

10. Where is the other, ancient parliament (the House of Keys) in the UK?

A CTIVITY

Students will need to volunteer (or be put forward) as candidates for election. They should campaign briefly (perhaps on a single issue that is a burning question for your institution, such as sixth form smoking or uniform, perhaps on an issue of the day) and then votes should be cast. Students should try to vote in the same way (i.e. for the same person) but you should run three separate votes. One is 'first-past-the-post', one is straight PR and one is STV. Students can then address the questions of:

- which is fairer?
- is the result always the same?
- what are the good and bad points of each?
- which would they prefer?

My Dad says ...

Preview

The opinions in the student common room or the coffee bar often just reflect those of the older people in the public bar and the barber's chair. However much young people try to stop it happening, they are often to be found repeating parental prejudices, often to be found parroting the views of mum, dad and Uncle Dick. Knowledge of situations, case histories and what the law actually does and does not do is likely to be sketchy and often inaccurate. They may also develop their own prejudices and strongly held views.

The coffee bar

John and Kate are two teenagers sharing a table in the coffee bar. John is a cool, sophisticated 17 year old (or at least he thinks he is) drinking short black coffee (very suave and upmarket). Kate is a few months older (and therefore wiser) and hunched over a steaming latte. They are discussing the state of Britain's various laws regarding equality of opportunity, in the workplace, between different groups and in different circumstances.

Inequality

'Well, it seems pretty obvious to me', John insisted, 'My dad says that the whole point of the legislation is to make us less equal than them. It's more about inequality than equality, he says.' He added: 'And it doesn't seem to matter what minority they happen to be in, they are protected and we aren't.'

'No,' ventured Kate, 'That's not true, the law must be there to protect everybody. that's what the scales of justice and blindfold thing is all about. Everyone is equal before the law, the law is blind to differences in people.'

'But that's certainly not true,' replied John, 'The law may be stupid but it's not blind. In fact the government passes laws so that people are treated differently. My dad says that there's no way that he could go looking for compensation if he went for a job interview and didn't get it.' He persisted, 'He's not black, not gay and not a woman. If he was, he could always go running to one of the boards that have been set up to help his case. But as a white, middle class British male, he has nowhere to go to, the law won't stand up for him. Even asylum seeking illegal immigrants get a better deal than him.'

'He could get help or compensation if he was discriminated against' said Kate; 'He has the same rights as anyone else if he feels that he hasn't been treated fairly because of some sort of prejudice.'

'That's what they say', John replied. 'If he was black, or gay, or disabled,' he laughed, 'he would be able to get help. But he isn't even allowed to appeal to anyone. He hasn't got any grounds for an appeal. There's no race relations or sex discrimination board for ordinary white people'.

'He is allowed, he has exactly the same rights as a one-legged blind gay person!' exclaimed Kate.

'What about his being too old for a job then? He has been for jobs that he is perfectly capable of doing but hasn't got them because he's been beaten by a younger man.' John said.

'How do you know that?' asked Kate.

'Because sometimes they even ask for younger applicants, they are even allowed to put it in the advertisements. They can even have a company policy not to employ people over a certain age. The law stops them from employing people under a certain age, but there is nothing to stop them refusing to appoint anyone say, over 35! The point is,' he added, 'that they don't have to pay them as much and, dad says, they don't like having to pay for experience. He says its their loss because a lot of the younger blokes might have qualifications but they've no idea what they are doing.'

'Are they actually allowed to advertise for younger applicants, or to say that you can't have the job if you're over 35?' asked Kate, ' I thought that was against the law.'

'I'm sure they can,' said John, 'I'm sure that's what my Dad said. Of course, it can only be a younger man. You'd be all right, Kate. If it was a woman, it wouldn't matter anyway, they wouldn't be allowed to do it then.'

'Why's that then?' asked Kate

'Because,' said John, 'They'd give her the job automatically, that's why. If they don't, she can go to the Equal Opportunities Board and get compensation from them. Then they can make the firm take them on anyway. You see it's all stacked in favour of certain groups – everyone but the ordinary man in the street.'

'I don't think that's what the Equal Opportunities people are there for' replied Kate, 'Surely they just make sure that people are paid a fair wage for a job – the same as everyone else doing the same job, regardless of age or sex, don't they?'

'I don't really know,' John answered, 'There are different laws for different people. I think gays and lesbians and such like are all protected under equal opportunities laws, and probably Buddhists and Mormons too for all I know. I don't know if women are. There is a separate law called something like the Sex Act.'

'I bet it isn't' giggled Kate.

'Something like that' said John, 'Why are you laughing?'

'I think you'll find it's the Sex Discrimination Act,' Kate smiled, 'not the sex act'.

'Sex Act, Sex Discrimination Act, what's the difference?' exclaimed John

'Well, if you don't know, I'm not about to tell you!' Kate laughed.

'All right, I get the picture,' said John, ' but I'm still right – there's no need to make fun of me just for getting the term wrong'.

'I'm not making fun of you,' smiled Kate, 'But it just goes to make my point. The Act is about Discrimination, not sex, and it's important to get the emphasis right. It's like the Race Relations Act isn't about race, it's about the relationships between different races'.

'But my dad couldn't go there if he thought he'd been beaten to a job by a woman, could he?' he opined, 'But the woman could go and complain if she was beaten by my dad. Say they both have the same qualifications, the same experience. If they appoint my dad, she can go to a tribunal or whatever and at the very least have the case investigated. He can't do anything. He'd just be made to look stupid for complaining. Anyway, it wouldn't be the right thing to do', he added, 'He always opens doors for ladies and pays the bill in restaurants so I don't think he'd think it was right to make a fuss. But the law protects her, not him'.

'It's there to protect both of them' said Kate. 'What if an employer has a factory full of blokes and needs an office worker? What if he decides to employ your dad just so that he doesn't have to put in ladies toilets? Or so that the men won't have to take down their girlie calendars? Surely that's not fair on her and she should be able to appeal to someone.'

'Surely that's not fair to him' exclaimed John, 'Or to his workers. Why should she be able to dictate what calendars they have up? Why should the employer have to put in toilets just for one person?'

'What if it was not a woman' rejoined Kate, 'But a person with a disability. What if it was someone in a wheelchair. Should the employer have to put in the toilet facilities then?'

'That's different', said John, 'That would be only fair to the disabled person, they can't help having a disability.'

Can you actually define what is meant by discrimination? Or prejudice? The dictionary defines them as follows: discrimination – act or quality of distinguishing, judgement; prejudice – judgement or opinion formed beforehand or without due examination, prepossession for or against anything.

SOCIETY, POLITICS AND THE ECONOMY

'And the woman can help being a woman!' exploded Kate.

'No, no, I don't mean that,' stammered John, 'You know what I mean, the woman could go and get a job elsewhere, the disabled person might find that difficult'.

'What about the expense then?' fumed Kate 'Wouldn't it be equally expensive for the employer to put a toilet in for a disabled person or a woman? In fact, it would probably be a lot more expensive!'

'But the law says disabled people should be helped in that sort of way – it just seems right, that's all' sulked John

''I see,' pressed Kate, 'Rules for one and different rules for everyone else'

'That's exactly my point' rejoined John, 'Exactly my point. The law protects only some people and in some situations. Look at asylum seekers – they can do what they like. Look at Asians – they can take extra religious holidays whenever they like, they can refuse to work when it suits them, they can even break the law if they want!'

'How do you make that out,' asked Kate, calmer now.

'My dad told me about when they introduced crash helmets on motor bikes – some Asians didn't have to wear them because they had a turban on – my dad says he tried to ride his bike in his flat cap but the police stopped him. And,' he added, 'the police agreed with him. But the policeman said there was nothing that he could do about it – the law is the law. It's the same with this discrimination lark. The law is the law and is in favour of any immigrant, woman or gay or lesbian. Illegal immigrants drive taxicabs with no licences, they don't pay tax or national insurance, they use their religious beliefs to bring more people into the country through arranged marriages, they even stop people from having their own holidays. Did you know that in America, my Dad says, they don't even have Christmas any more because of all the minority groups it might offend. They have 'Happy Holiday' and while Santa Claus is OK, St Nicholas isn't. And there should be no mention of Christ or Christmas for fear of offending someone.'

He paused for breath. 'It's not that bad here, not yet anyway, but what we have doesn't make for more equality, it makes for more inequality and for more people not daring to make decisions the way that they want because of the law. It's just not fair.'

'What they do in America doesn't affect us, so you can forget that.' Said Kate, 'Where do you get the idea that the law is only on the side of minorities?'

'You know what my dad says', said John, 'He says that by looking at America we can see what we are going to be like in 10 years time. You can see it happening. How do I know the law is only on the side of minorities – just look at the Acts. Disability Discrimination, Race Relations, Sex Discrimination – it's all about protecting disabled people, a minority; racial and religious groups, a minority and women …'

'Well, I don't think we're a minority' interrupted Kate.

'Women in work must be,' John rejoined, 'Most stay at home to look after kids, then want time off to have babies, then want to be able to come back! Why shouldn't the father take six months leave on full pay as well? What's fair about that?'

TIPS FOR FURTHER RESEARCH

Use your local newspaper archive to investigate cases in your own area. Look for the story first and try to make a judgement yourself before reading what the judgement was. Find out what is meant by a 'test case' and how this might relate to a 'class action'.

WEB LINKS

www.open.gov.uk is a government site which contains links to the various bodies dealing with discrimination.

www.womenshistory.about.com details the fight of women for equal treatment before the law, from the time of the suffragettes to the present.

Examiners will look for the following in your written answer:

- Evidence that you have understood the source material and can make appropriate use of it.
- You need to be able to make value judgements based on it and support these with evidence or interpretation.
- You need to have something of your own to say and to be able to state it clearly.
- You need to show you can relate this work to other relevant areas of study.

'I think they can,' offered Kate, 'I think that they may not get six months (and I'm not sure that women do) but I'm sure that they get something. I think there was a European law about that.'

'That doesn't take away from the fact that they are treated differently, that the law is there specifically to treat them differently, to make sure that some people are more equal than others' insisted John. 'You can't have it both ways, the law is not there to promote equality, it's there to stop some people from being discriminated against. That means that those people get more protection than others. But it doesn't protect everyone. You can be refused a job because you're old, or ugly, can't get there on time, but not because you're black, or gay, or disabled. It's just not fair'.

'If it's not fair, then you ought to try to change the law,' said Kate.

'I know,' said John, 'That's what my dad says.'

Questions for discussion

1. Discrimination laws in the UK just lead to greater inequality.

2. Parents' and older people's opinions should always be respected. They have much more experience than us.

3. There are certain cases where discrimination should be allowed, for the good of everyone. Suggest some.

4. Is it true that employers can discriminate on grounds of age, or even on how you are dressed?

5. America is a secular society and quite right to treat Christmas in the way it does. Do you agree?

Questions for written answer

1. What do you think is meant by 'equality of opportunity'? What measures have been taken to get rid of discrimination in the UK? How effective do you think they have been?

2. Society needs to develop changes in attitude, not to keep making changes in legislation. Defend or oppose this viewpoint.

3. 'All men are created equal, but some are more equal than others'. What do you think the author of this statement meant? Do you agree with it?

4. Discuss the view that what happens in America today shows us where we'll be in 10 years time. Draw on examples from your own knowledge or experience.

5. Do you think that the laws on equality and discrimination need changing. If so, how? If not, why? Give reasons for your answer.

? Quiz

- What are the four main pieces of legislation being referred to?

- What are the major points of each piece of legislation?

- What bodies were set up by each law?

ACTIVITY

The conversation should be broken up into approximately 10 even parts. It can then be treated as a script and pairs of students chosen to read out certain parts of it. They should then try to answer the following questions, either individually or in general discussion:

- is the statement factually true?

- which legislation is being referred to?

- who is right, Kate, John or neither of them?

Students can then write (and perform) their own scripted conversation either in Kate/John mode, or as themselves, or as a parent or other older person.

Preview

Given that the events of 11 September 2001 took place as this book was being written, it would have been remiss of the writers to ignore them. This chapter therefore looks at the bare facts of the terrorist attack on the USA and then at some of the various viewpoints expressed in regard to it. It attempts to put the horror of 11 September into a global context and explain some of the history and some of the thinking behind the actions.

What happened?

Starting at 8.45 am local time a concerted terrorist attack took place on the twin towers of the World Trade Center in New York and on the Pentagon in Washington. The weapon used was not the bomb or the bullet, not threats or hostage taking, not military hardware. It was a number of passenger airliners piloted by suicidal terrorists. The first plane, a hijacked American Airlines Boeing 767 carrying 92 passengers and crew, hit the north tower at 8.45, setting many of the upper stories alight. Eighteen minutes later, a second airliner, a United Airlines 767 carrying 65 passengers and crew, also hijacked, was propelled into the other – the south tower. Both the flights were internal ones out of Boston airport.

By 9.30, with both buildings still burning, President Bush, speaking from Florida, says the country has suffered an 'apparent terrorist attack.' At 9.40 the Federal Aviation Authority stops all flights from American airports, but was too late to stop those planes already airborne. At 9.43 a third airliner, an American Airlines Boeing 757 carrying 64 passengers and crew, is crashed into the Pentagon, the hub of American military operations and command.

Back in New York, at just after 10.00, the south tower of the World Trade Center collapses into the streets. As the building was burning, and no-one had foreseen the collapse, firefighters had entered the building to try to rescue those people on the lower floors. Many thousands of people are successfully evacuated but many more, including firefighters and rescue workers, are trapped and killed. The lights go out as a cloud of dust and debris spreads from the carnage. Half-an-hour later, the World Trade Center's north tower collapses on itself, adding to the ever growing dust cloud. Many other buildings around the area were to collapse later in the day, having been weakened by the collapse of the towers. One of the largest, the 47-storey 'Building 7' burnt until early evening and then collapsed. It had been evacuated.

A further statement from President Bush is made at just after 1.00 p.m. He asks for prayers for those killed or wounded in the attacks and says, 'Make no mistake, the United States will hunt down and punish those responsible for these cowardly acts.' Later that afternoon, New York mayor Rudolf Giuliani, when asked about how many are killed, says 'I don't think we want to speculate about that – more than any of us can bear.'

W EB LINKS
www.cnn.com/
www.abcnews.com/
www.msnbc.com/news/
attack_front.asp/

A further airliner, probably aimed at the White House, was forced to crash in Pennsylvania by passengers who fought with terrorists.

In the evening, President Bush addressed the nation. 'We will make no distinction,' he said, 'between the terrorists who carried out these acts and those who harbour them'. There were already suspicions emerging as to who was responsible and where they could be hiding. Officials reported that there were 'good indications' that Saudi militant Osama bin Laden, suspected of co-ordinating the bombings of two US embassies in 1998, was behind the attacks, based on 'new and specific' information.

Why was this target chosen?

It is believed that there were three, or possibly four, targets. One was the Pentagon, representing America's military might; one was either Capitol Hill or the White House, representing a strike against the political heart of America; one was to destroy a symbol of American capitalism – the World Trade Center.

People run from the collapse of the World Trade Center

Who?

Who were the perpetrators? The planes were piloted by Muslim members of the al Qa'eda faction – a group dedicated to carrying out acts of war and attrition against what it sees as the enemies of Islam. These men were fanatical in support of their religion – even to the point of death. The men are referred to as terrorists by the press and most commentators in the West, as freedom fighters and martyrs by some sections of the Islamic community, as fanatics by others. Their actions have been condemned almost universally by the non-Muslim world and large sections of the Muslim world. The Americans produced evidence that conclusively proves that it was Osama bin Laden, the renegade Saudi Arabian millionaire, who was behind the attacks. A video was later produced showing him laughing and joking about the carnage and saying how fortunate it was that the buildings collapsed. This, he said, was more than they had ever hoped for. The provenance of the video is questionable. Not so the way opposing camps view the attack: the Americans call the attacks '9/11'; the perpetrators refer to the day as 'Holy Tuesday'.

Why?

Young Muslims who die in the pursuit of a Jihad, or holy war, are told that they are assured a place in heaven. If they believe this to be so, they are quite happy to die for the cause, secure in the knowledge that their reward will be everlasting happiness. This is not new, nor limited to Muslims, but is a thread that runs through history and crosses languages and cultures. Viking warriors were promised entry to Valhalla for eternal drinking and carousing if they died valiantly; the Crusader knights of the Middle Ages were told they were taking the short cut to heaven when blessed by the Pope and sent into the field against the 'infidel'. Japanese *kamikaze* pilots believed that their suicide meant they would be blessed. Where such beliefs are strong enough, particularly in the young and impressionable, they can be a powerful force for persuading someone to take a particular action. If you believe that you are going to become immortal, and eternally happy, just by killing yourself, then suicide becomes a much easier road to take.

America was the chosen target because, in certain Muslim eyes, it is America that is the 'Great Satan'. America, in its self-appointed role as policeman of the world, is perceived as an enemy of Islam and as an example of all that is worst about the West.

Welcome to the world

Americans are traditionally, and perhaps stupendously, parochial. It is a country of some 235 million people covering 9.5 million square kilometres (Europe is about one-third of this area). Americans can fly for four or five hours and never leave home. They can go overseas, they can travel from the sub-tropical state of Florida to the sub-Arctic state of Alaska without crossing a national border. They can drive north and south, east and west, for days. They

American military might is such that no country in the world can match it – certainly in conventional arms. A nuclear-powered aircraft carrier was sent to support the war in Afghanistan, it was accompanied by 15 other ships to form a battle squadron. The carrier is the height of a 20-storey building and carries nearly 6000 men and 70 aircraft. There are 12 other similar squadrons around the world. The US defence budget is nearly $400 billion (Britain's is $33 billion).

Osama Bin Laden

can take a skiing holiday, some warm-water scuba diving, a beach holiday, a hiking holiday in forests, mountains or fields and never need to change a dollar for another currency, nor speak another language. In short, the USA is vast and Americans often reluctant to leave it. They therefore tend to have a particularly narrow view of the world reinforced by a media that tends to report only American events and American news. When the football World Cup was held in Atlanta, it received hardly any coverage outside the state of Georgia. The World Cup final was watched by fewer people in America than in almost any other country. Americans have little concept of how some parts of the rest of the world view them. American policy abroad has tended to revolve around policies of 'might is right' – but how did this come to be seen, by some, as an attack on the Muslim faith?

Israel

The main problem is the perceived support of America for the Jewish state of Israel. Many Muslims feel that it is the Palestinians who have been wronged and see American interference as just that – unwarranted, unwanted, unasked-for and vehemently hated. To try to understand how such hatred can come about, look at the history of Israel/Palestine from opposing viewpoints. Remember that history is viewed *very* differently by the two sides in a conflict.

History (an Israeli viewpoint)

On 14 May 1948 the State of Israel was proclaimed according to the UN partition plan of 1947. It was immediately invaded by Egypt, Jordan, Syria, Lebanon and Iraq. Israel succeeded in defending itself. Israel and the invaders (except Iraq, which refused to negotiate) finalized a series of armistice agreements in 1949. In 1951 the United Nations passed a resolution saying that the Suez Canal should be open to Israeli ships. However, in 1956, they were prevented from so doing and a military build up against Israel started.

In October 1956 the Israeli Defence Force captured the Gaza Strip and the entire Sinai peninsula, halting 10 miles east of the Suez Canal.

The Six-day War in 1967 saw Israel take pre-emptive action against the build up of forces by Egypt, Jordan and Syria. At the end of six days of fighting, previous cease-fire lines were replaced by new ones, with Judea, Samaria, Gaza, the Sinai peninsula and the Golan Heights under Israel's control. As a result, Jerusalem, which had been divided between Israel and Jordan since 1949, was reunified under Israeli rule.

Israel wanted the world to recognize its right to exist in UN Security Council Resolution 242 which called for 'acknowledgment of the sovereignty, territorial integrity and political independence of every state in the area and their right to live in peace within secure and recognized boundaries free from threats or acts of force'. However, in August 1967, the Arab states decided that there should be 'no peace with Israel, no negotiations with Israel and no recognition of Israel'.

In 1973, on Yom Kippur, the holiest day of the Jewish year, Egypt and Syria attacked Israel but were once again repulsed. In November 1977, Egypt's president Anwar Saddat visited Jerusalem. After lengthy negotiations at America's Camp David, a peace treaty was signed in 1979 which recognized Israel's right to exist and proposed a system of self-government for Palestinians.

In September of 1993, Palestine Liberation Organization (PLO) chairman Yasser Arafat and Israeli Prime Minister Yitzhak Rabin signed an agreement to give the Palestinians self-rule, in which the PLO renounced the use of terrorism and recognized Israel's right to exist. The process continued with the election of a self-governing authority – the Palestinian Council – in 1995.

However, not all Palestinians either agreed with the proposals or wanted to work with them. Some militant groups declared 'intifada', a war of attrition, against what they see as Jewish invaders. Atrocities, murders and acts of terrorism and sabotage have continued to mount.

History (a Palestinian viewpoint)

Palestine has been ruled in turn by Jews, Arabs, Greeks under Alexander the Great, from Cairo, by Crusaders, by Saladin, by the British. It is home to Palestinians and claimed by Zionists. Its modern history is most interesting.

Following the break up of the Ottoman Empire after the First World War, Palestine was made a British Mandate. Despite the fact that Palestine had an 88% Arab population, Britain had decided it would make a good home for the Jews (a result of the Balfour Declaration recognizing the Zionist claim for a Jewish homeland).

In 1947, after several waves of Jewish settlers, Britain found the mandate too hot to handle and handed the country over to the United Nations. In the period from 1917 to 1949, Israel had illegally occupied 78% of the land of Palestine and evicted or caused to flee more than 750,000 Palestinian refugees to the Gaza Strip, the West Bank and other Arab countries like Syria, Lebanon and Jordan.

TIPS FOR FURTHER RESEARCH

It is very difficult to obtain unbiased views on such a thorny problem so it's probably better to take the biased ones but recognize their bias.
www.aish.com is biased towards the Jewish cause.
www.Palestinehistory.com is biased to the Palestinian side as is www.Arab.net/palestine/palestine_contents.html

In one of his poems, written in Urdu, the Muslim scholar and poet Iqbal asks 'If the Jews claim the soil of Palestine, why not the Arabs Spain?' He is comparing the Muslim conquest of Spain with the Jewish 'occupation' of Palestine. The Muslim presence in Spain was hardly an 'occupation'. If that is the case then the Norman French (who have yet to be expelled) are 'occupying' England a thousand years on and the Americans are, without a doubt, occupying the lands of the dispossessed tribes of Apache, Pawnee and Cherokee. The Spanish themselves have been in occupation of parts of South America (even to the extent of renaming it 'Latin' America for only 500 years). Arab Spain lasted for over 800 years. By 1488 only the Moorish kingdom of Granada remained in Muslim hands. The marriage of Isabella of Castile to Ferdinand of Aragon had united the main kingdoms of Spain who completed the reconquista in 1492 when Granada fell and the Moors were pushed back into North Africa.

The UN Partition Plan proposed two states, a Jewish state and an Arab one, with control over Jerusalem shared. The Zionists jumped at the chance to legitimize their illegal incursions whereas the Arab states called for more negotiation. After the 1948 conflict, Israel controlled nearly four-fifths of the mandated territory. As Jordan took the West Bank and Egypt the Gaza Strip, the state of Palestine vanished from the map, to be replaced by an area called the 'Occupied Territories'.

In 1988, the PLO declared the state of Palestine and Arab states withdrew their rule to recognize the Palestinians right to the land. Over 100 states world-wide have recognized Palestine and, in 1993, a historic peace agreement was reached which would give control of the Gaza Strip and much of the West Bank to the PLO.

Many Israelis, especially the ultra-religious, opposed this agreement and when Prime Minister Yitzhak Rabin died, the government was taken over by Ariel Sharon. Since this time, Palestinians have been ever more oppressed, beaten and bullied. The only way that most can make their voice heard is through violent protest or deadly acts of terrorism. It is the plight of the Palestinian refugees, who now number 1.5 million, and the fate of the Palestinians, who now number 2.5 million, as a people, which are the most pressing problems.

Conclusion

The link between Israel, America and the Camp David accords is just one possible reason for the 11 September attacks. American influence in Arab affairs – and American military might – are others. One thing that is absolutely certain about the events of 11 September is that they have changed the way that any society can see to the maintenance of its own security. In the words of one commentator 'Crashing commercial airliners into tall buildings has given a whole new meaning to the word 'terrorism'. It is organized, deliberate mayhem, designed to cause maximum carnage. It is also a form of attack against which it is impossible to defend oneself. If the perpetrator has no thought for their own life or safety, then there is no need for an escape route – anything can happen.'

Questions for discussion

1. Is there ever a case for taking the law into one's own hands? Is there ever a case for making a point by destroying the homes, lives, workplaces and places of worship of those whom we oppose?

2. What causes fanaticism? What defence is there against it?

3. Do you believe in the 'myths' suggested by your religion about heaven? Why?

4. 'The perpetrators of the 11 September attacks had run out of other options. This is the only way they could make the world listen.' Assess this statement, using evidence to support your answer.

5. 'Welcome to the world'. Are Americans really so parochial?

Examiners will look for the following in your written answer:

- Evidence that you have understood the source material and can make appropriate use of it.
- You need to be able to make value judgements based on it and support these with evidence or interpretation.
- You need to have something of your own to say and to be able to state it clearly.
- You need to show you can relate this work to other relevant areas of study.

Questions for written answer

1. Is there ever a case for taking the law into one's own hands? Is there ever a case for making a point by destroying the homes, lives, workplaces and places of worship of those whom we oppose? What is your viewpoint? Use reasoned argument to defend your opinion.

2. Ali ibn-Ali Talib, the fourth Caliph said as one of his 'Hundred Sayings':

   'He who has a thousand friends has not a friend to spare,
   And he who has one enemy will meet him everywhere'

   What do you think that this means? Explain how it could apply to the events of 11 September?

3. 'History is written by the victors'. Discuss the view that nowhere is this more obvious than in Palestine.

4. Do you agree that the United Nations has proved itself ineffective in almost everything it has done? Give reasons for your answer, drawing on recent events or stories.

5. Discuss the view that if we must have a 'policeman of the world' then America, with its military might, is best suited to the role.

? Quiz

From your own research, put together your own quiz. It should aim, as far as possible, to expose the bias and myths surrounding the issues of 11 September and the Middle East conflict.

A CTIVITY

Students carry out comprehensive research into the nature of the conflict between:

- America and its enemies
- Israel and its enemies.

Research should be undertaken in small groups, each concentrating on a particular aspect. It should be in as much depth as possible. It is particularly important that it includes sources from both sides of the argument and also neutral sources. Students should make sure that they not only reference all research but are able to comment on its likely bias. For example, an encyclopaedia may appear to give an unbiased view but be published in America. The questions that they should ask include:

- how recent is the source
- how reliable is the source
- how detailed is the source
- how biased is the source.

A display of material, contributed to by all groups, will show the range of sources (and the range of possible bias).

Index